Scandinavian Crime Fiction

Jakob Stougaard-Nielsen

Bloomsbury Academic
An imprint of Bloomsbury Publishing Plc

B L O O M S B U R Y
LONDON • OXFORD • NEW YORK • NEW DELHI • SYDNEY

Bloomsbury Academic

An imprint of Bloomsbury Publishing Plc

50 Bedford Square   1385 Broadway
London   New York
WC1B 3DP   NY 10018
UK   USA

www.bloomsbury.com

**BLOOMSBURY and the Diana logo are trademarks of Bloomsbury
Publishing Plc**

First published 2017

British Library Cataloguing-in-Publication Data
A catalogue record for this book is available from the British Library.

ISBN: HB: 978-1-4725-2275-7
PB: 978-1-4725-2774-5
ePDF: 978-1-4725-2213-9
ePub: 978-1-4725-2908-4

Library of Congress Cataloging-in-Publication Data
A catalog record for this book is available from the Library of Congress.

Series: 21st Century Genre Fiction

Cover design: Alice Marwick

Typeset by Newgen Knowledge Works (P) Ltd., Chennai, India
Printed and bound in India

Scandinavian Crime Fiction

21ST CENTURY GENRE FICTION SERIES

The *21st Century Genre Fiction* series provides exciting and accessible introductions to new genres in twenty-first-century fiction from Crunch Lit to Steampunk to Nordic Noir. Exploring the history and uses of each genre to date, each title in the series will analyse key examples of innovations and developments in the field since the year 2000. The series will consider the function of genre in both reflecting and shaping sociopolitical and economic developments of the twenty-first century.

Also available in the series:

Apocalyptic Fiction by Andrew Tate
Crunch Lit by Katy Shaw

For Federica, Lukas and Emma

CONTENTS

ACKNOWLEDGEMENTS

This book grew out of a series of meetings and conversations in London's Nordic Noir Book Club. The book club was conceived in 2010 as a way for scholars and students in the Department of Scandinavian Studies, University College London, to engage with fans and readers of Scandinavian crime fiction in an exploration of what the success of 'Nordic Noir' could tell us about how Nordic cultures and societies are presented and understood in the United Kingdom through the popular forms of translated and subtitled crime fiction. I am particularly grateful to the many members of the Nordic Noir Book Club, who have generously shared their insights and enthusiasm for crime fiction and the Nordic countries. I would like to extend my gratitude to colleagues and students for their collaboration and dedication to advancing our understanding and appreciation of contemporary Nordic languages, cultures and societies through the book club. Special thanks to Karin Charles, Claire Thomson, Mary Hilson, Elettra Carbone, Helga Lúthersdóttir, Jesper Hansen, John Mitchinson, Annika Lindskog, Agnes Broomé, Nicky Smalley, Pei-Sze Chow and Henriette Steiner.

It has been a special treat of the book club to meet and listen to crime writers from the Nordic countries including Haakan Nesser, Yrsa Sigurðardóttir, Gunnar Staalesen, Thomas Enger, Jussi Adler-Olsen, Sissel-Jo Gazan, Lene Kaaberbøl and Agnete Friis; the translators Victoria Cribb and Mark Mussari; the producer Francis Hopkinson; the director Annette K. Olesen; and the critics Hans Skei, Gunhild Agger and Bo Tao Michaëlis. A special thanks to Barry Forshaw, who has been an invaluable presence in the book club, a force in the promotion and appreciation of Nordic crime fiction in the United Kingdom and an insightful and enthusiastic 'partner in Nordic crime' over the recent years. I am also grateful for the support provided by the Nordic Embassies in London, in particular Lone Britt Christensen and Kirsten Syppli Hansen at the embassy of Denmark. Throughout my work on this book, I have had the opportunity to present my ideas and share my interest in Scandinavian crime fiction with a wide audience, and I am grateful to Jonathan Sadler at Arrow Films for inviting me to speak at the Nordicana festival in London and to Vibeke Johansen for invitations to speak at the Horsens Crime Fair in Denmark.

I have benefitted immensely from presenting and discussing my work-in-progress in research networks with excellent and most generous colleagues. Particular thanks to Peter Simonsen and Anne-Marie Mai at the University of Southern Denmark, whose innovative research into Danish literature and the welfare state has influenced the central perspective presented in this book. My work in the area of literature and society has benefitted greatly from continuing conversations and collaborations with Svend Erik Larsen, Leverhulme Visiting Professor at UCL Scandinavian Studies in 2013, and David Napier, director of the UCL Science, Medicine and Society Network.

Earlier versions of sections in Chapters 1 and 7 have previously appeared in a *Post45 Contemporaries* special series ('Nordic Noir') edited by Bruce Robbins and in a special issue of *Aktuel Forskning* ('Velværelsen: Ny humanistisk velfærdsforskning') edited by Peter Simonsen. I am particularly indebted to Bruce Robbins's advice for my work on Anne Holt and post-Utøya crime fiction.

This book might never have materialized if it wasn't for the series editor Katy Shaw's initial proposal and continuous encouragements. I am deeply grateful to her for this opportunity and for her editorial acumen, which has greatly improved the final book. My gratitude also to my publisher and editors at Bloomsbury, whose professionalism and patience nurtured the project at every stage. Special thanks to David Avital and Mark Richardson.

Final thanks to my parents, Benny and Eva, who brought me up a Danish welfare citizen and an all-consuming reader; and to Federica, Lukas and Emma who make it all possible and worthwhile. This book is for you.

Introduction

Stockholm syndrome

On 23 August 1973, a masked Janne Olsson entered Kreditbanken on Stockholm's Norrmalmstorget (Norrmalms Square). He drew a sub-machine gun from under his coat, fired at the ceiling and shouted in English to disguise his identity: 'Get down to the floor! The party starts.' What could have been the beginning of just another bank robbery soon evolved into a nail-biting six-day hostage crisis. Olsson demanded three million kronor, a fast getaway car, safe conduct out of the country accompanied by the hostages and, curiously, the release of his friend, the notorious criminal Clark Olofsson, who was serving time in Norrköping prison for armed robbery and as an accessory to the murder of a policeman in 1966. The police agreed to the requests. Notes were counted, a blue Ford Mustang was parked in the square, and Olofsson was escorted to the bank where he joined Olsson and the four hostages. However, the Minister of Justice Lennart Geijer, in agreement with Prime Minister Olof Palme, refused to let Olsson leave the bank with the hostages.

The following stand-off between the hostage taker and the police was followed intensely by the national and international media and broadcast live on television. Phone interviews with the hostages from the bank were broadcast on public radio. One of the hostages even called Prime Minister Palme and pleaded with him to let her and the other hostages leave the bank with Olsson – she was, she explained, more afraid of the police attacking and killing them than she was of her captor, who 'had been very nice' (Graham et al. 1994: 5; Cronqvist et al. 2008: 46). In the end the police decided to force Olsson to give in by pumping tear gas through a hole drilled in the ceiling of the vault, and the situation was resolved with no physical harm to the hostages and their captor.

What made this attempted bank robbery and hostage-taking the most infamous in Swedish history was not, however, the ultimate success of an otherwise ill-prepared police force. The reason why we still recall this incident today is mainly due to the fact that it became synonymous with the psychological syndrome to which the Swedish capital lent its name: the Stockholm Syndrome. Over the six days of the hostage drama, it became oddly apparent to the police and the general public that the hostages seemed to have developed deep sympathies with their captor.

Viewed from the vantage point of a twenty-first-century media culture, saturated with reality-TV game shows and a 24-hour news cycle thriving on sensationalism and the breakdown of traditional notions of what constitutes 'public interest', the mass-mediated drama in and around Kreditbanken appeared well ahead of its time. Per Svensson has called the Norrmalms Square drama the first live-transmitted docudrama in Sweden (2003). The bank robbery could have been just another abstract figure in the crime statistics of the well-managed Swedish welfare state or a classic narrative about incurable career criminals, terrified hostages and a successful police force that in the end reinstates trust in the judicial system and a belief in the persistence of the 'good state'. However, the 'actors' did not conform to their expected roles. The hostages did not seek to escape when given the opportunity, Olofsson's role as part notorious criminal and part mediator between Olsson and the police was confusing and Olsson, as described by the hostages, did not conform to the image of a ruthless criminal. Instead, the drama that played out on the nation's TV screens conformed to already ongoing revisions of crime and its psychological as well as social conditions in the increasingly more popular home-grown crime fiction that gradually took over the bestseller lists in Sweden as well as in Denmark and Norway in the same period.

This book is an investigation into the murky contact zone between the dramatic and still ongoing changes in perceptions of Scandinavian social realities, attached to the 'rise and fall' or the 'crisis' of the welfare state since the early 1970s, and the equally

dramatic history of the national, regional and international obsession with a more or less distinct, localized Scandinavian take on
the most globalized of popular genres: crime fiction. I consider the
Norrmalms Square drama a suggestive way into this story for several reasons, which I hope will become apparent as this book progresses: it dramatized a growing distrust in the inevitable 'goodness'
of the Scandinavian welfare state, it displayed ambiguities in traditional perceptions of good and evil and, perhaps more than any
other 'true crime' story, it initiated an age where crime and crime
investigation became the dominant mass-spectacle across media as
the new 'normal' genre. The Norrmalms Square drama unfolded
at the beginning of an era which would witness the unprecedented
commercial success of Scandinavian crime fiction in print and on
screens across the Nordic countries, culminating in nothing less
than a global literary and media phenomenon in the first decade
of the twenty-first century (Berglund 2012; Handesten 2014: 433;
Nestingen and Arvas 2011: 1).

Crime fiction for comfort junkies

Leonard Cassuto has said of genre fiction that it should be read as a
'cultural symptom, not a cultural cure' (Cassuto 2009: 16). Perhaps
some genres and some stories more than others 'scratch a collective
itch that appeared at a specific time' and as all 'complicated cultural
symptoms, that itch has a lot of causes' (261).

It has been suggested that 1973 was the year in which, in many
ways, the still-content, affluent and progressive ideal of the Swedish
welfare state started to crack – a year that also witnessed the exposure of the IB affair, the possible high-level political involvement in
the Swedish intelligence agency's illegal monitoring of the political
left: 'It was a time initiating a change of roles between inside and
outside, centre and periphery, good and evil, honest and dishonest,
criminal and police, victim and culprit' (Cronqvist et al. 2008: 38).
In his book about the Norrmalms Square drama, Per Svensson suggests that it initiated a new epoch in Sweden; it symbolized, in the
words of Yrsa Stenius, 'the shattered illusion of the Swedish comfort junkies about the ability of the welfare state to expunge evil
from society' (Stenius 2004; Svensson 2003).

Proceeding from this diagnosis of a shattered self-perpetuated collective image of the harmonious welfare state, where perceived notions of what constitutes the 'good society' were turned on their head, Slavoj Žižek's dialectical analysis of violence may throw further light on the significance of this wider social Stockholm syndrome, which in various forms would come to inform contemporary Scandinavian crime fiction. Olsson's 'subjective violence' ('violence performed by a clearly identifiable agent') against the hostages, police and the bank can be seen as symptomatic of a deeper 'systemic violence' made invisible, so to speak, by illusions created by the welfare state itself. 'Systemic violence', as Žižek notes, pertains to the 'catastrophic consequences of the smooth functioning of our economic and political systems' – an illusion of comfort underwritten by the very forces that the 'smooth' system actively seeks to dispel (Žižek 2008: 1–2).

The potential of crime fiction as a privileged genre through which to detect the symptoms of the 'shattered illusion of comfort' in order to reveal the 'systemic violence' inherent to the Social Democratic welfare state was central to the final instalments of Sjöwall and Wahlöö's trendsetting crime serial *Novel of a Crime* (1965–75). From a clear ideological standpoint on the radical new left, they went behind the facades of an idyllic Stockholm to depict a dystopian and totalitarian Swedish welfare state where innocent individuals were pushed into criminal activities by a corrupt, alienating and consumerist welfare state that had sold out to capitalist interests.

Scandinavian crime writers have since then continued to use a great variety of crime fiction's subgenres to 'scratch the collective itch'. As Scandinavian crime fiction became increasingly preoccupied with the social conditions of crime, readers were asked to sympathize with vigilante lawbreakers and to question the morals of the welfare state and its promise of social justice. In Swedish police procedurals from Sjöwall and Wahlöö to Henning Mankell's Wallander series (1991–2009) and the global phenomenon of Stieg Larsson's genre-hybrid *Millennium* trilogy (2005–7), eccentric and victimized women are abandoned, if not outright assaulted, by the justice system and the welfare state. Some like Larsson's Lisbeth Salander became unlikely Scandinavian heroines bestowed with the detectives' and readers' sympathies even if, or perhaps because, she was ready to take the law into her own hands when abandoned by the state and its representatives.

In psychological crime thrillers by the Dane Anders Bodelsen (1968–), in Gunnar Staalesen's Norwegian hardboiled Varg Veum series (1977–) and in later procedurals by the Swede Arne Dahl, a persistent genre trait in Scandinavian crime-writing is taking shape as the familial conflicts and alienation of detectives, victims and criminals in an inauthentic, urban consumer society is presented as intricately connected to the welfare state's rational and amnesic obsession with progress and social engineering. Here crimes are viewed as symptoms of deeper or wider mostly invisible social processes, before which detectives such as Mankell's Kurt Wallander are left utterly helpless and desperately anxious. This book will propose that the crimes recorded in Scandinavian crime fiction are symptoms of an age of uncertainty where the comforts of the welfare state have ceased to provide the ointment that may relieve the collective itch.

Svensson's diagnosis of the collective itch that began to irritate the social body of the 'comfort junkies' in the early 1970s is illustrative of the socio-critical preoccupations of much of the crime writing that began to appear in the same period across Scandinavia. It is also symptomatic of a notable shift in the foreign gaze on Sweden, which in turn became internalized in the local gaze of home-grown crime-writing. In 1936, the American journalist Marquis Childs published the international bestseller, *Sweden: The Middle Way*. Written in the time of the Great Depression, Childs viewed the Swedish Social Democratic compromise between liberal capitalism and state communism as a pragmatic model that could guarantee full employment, social security and equality without jeopardizing economic development and democratic institutions. Even to this day, the utopian image persists abroad in various shapes and forms when, for instance, the popular Democratic US presidential candidate Bernie Sanders in 2015 talked about his version of democratic socialism as inspired by the successes of the Scandinavian welfare states, or when the news media report on international surveys such as the World Happiness Report or the OECD Better Life Index that rank the Scandinavian countries amongst the happiest in the world.

However, in the 1970s, this utopian view on Sweden and the Social Democratic welfare state changed radically with the British journalist Roland Huntford's controversial book *The New Totalitarians* (1971). To Huntford, Swedes, dominated by the Social Democratic Party for forty years, had come closer to living in Aldous

Huxley's dystopian Brave New World than the Soviets – a totalitarian state where individual freedoms had been sacrificed willingly for state-guaranteed comforts and material wealth. Even Sweden's otherwise much admired sexual liberalism became an expression of totalitarian state control in Huntford's opinion. High suicide rates and heavy taxation were other less-than-perfect trends he sought to highlight. Huntford's acerbic portrayal of Sweden in the early 1970s has certainly dated but has also found a more contemporary voice in the British journalist Michael Booth's tongue-in-cheek travelogue *The Almost Nearly Perfect People: The Truth About the Nordic Miracle* (2014) in its portrayal of conformist Swedes, jingoistic Danes on antidepressants, lethargic Norwegians drunk on oil wealth, and gun-toting, binge-drinking Finns. However, it is not only British journalists who have looked behind the idyllic facade of the Swedish and Scandinavian welfare states. In Jan Troell's 1988 documentary *Sagolandet (The Land of Dreams)*, for instance, a decaying, alienating welfare state is portrayed with contrasting images of the modern consumer society and its destruction of nature, creativity and an idyllic childhood.

As Michael Tapper has pointed out in his work on the Swedish police procedural, it is curious how similar in perspective Huntford's liberal-conservative critique of the Swedish welfare state was to the contemporary dystopian sentiments held by many on the political and ideological new left in Sweden – sentiments which found a popular form in the rise of the socio-critical Swedish police novel and, according to Tapper, may account for the wide appeal of Sjöwall and Wahlöö and later Mankell's novels (Tapper 2014: 87, 163). However, as I shall argue throughout this book, while Swedish and Scandinavian crime novels are sensitive to the systemic violence of the welfare state and are preoccupied with showing the dark sides of the once 'idyllic' welfare states, novels from Sjöwall and Wahlöö's most dystopian portrayals of a criminal Swedish welfare state to Stieg Larsson's indictment against a violent, patriarchal society more than three decades later, from Gunnar Staalesen's portrayal of a morally corrupt, petroleum-infused Norway to Anne Holt's investigation into a violent and broken nation-family in a post-Utøya Oslo and from Anders Bodelsen's hyper-realistic depiction of a claustrophobic Danish, consumerist welfare society to Peter Høeg's critique of the systemic violence of Danish colonialism in Greenland, Scandinavian crime fiction is centrally preoccupied with how to restore the health of the social body in an age where the state and its representatives have lost their former self-evident moral authority.

A socio-critical genre

Given the central place of Sjöwall and Wahlöö's *Novel of a Crime* in modern Scandinavian crime fiction, it is no surprise that subsequent crime writers and critics alike have used and explored the crime genre for its socio-critical reflections of life in the welfare state. Indeed, over the past decades crime fiction has been re-evaluated and invigorated as particular modes of writing well suited for capturing societies undergoing dramatic change, for representing and responding directly to an age of social conflicts, risks and inequalities.

The present book participates in this broad international discussion of crime fiction as a genre made for the crises, conflicts and indeterminacies belonging to the last decades of the twentieth and the first decades of the twenty-first century. This is the age of intensified globalization, an age of perpetual transience marked by the restlessness of a rampant global consumer society, the uprooting of identities, communities and nation states, a period characterized by Zygmunt Bauman as our 'liquid modernity' (Bauman 2012). Crime fiction is modern genre writing with a dense undergrowth of subgenres and local expressions, borne out by the nineteenth century's obscure urban environments and labyrinthine modern state bureaucracy, which today has become a dominant literary form readymade for a thoroughly globalized, mediated and fluid age.

This book is certainly not the first to explore the ways in which Scandinavian crime fiction reflects and responds to the late-modern welfare state and the changing social reality of the Scandinavian countries from the optimism of its 'solid' golden age through decades of uncertainties, angst and fluidity. Sara Kärrholm's study of the post-War 'golden age' of Swedish crime fiction is particularly interesting as it finds in the puzzle-crime novels by authors such as Stieg Trenter and Maria Lang contemporary moral sagas about good conquering evil, where the idyllic welfare state, as the country-houses of their British predecessors, is under constant threat from outside forces (Kärrholm 2005). The crime novels of this period shore up values and communal responsibilities against the threats of an uncertain and encroaching Cold War world. While the cultural work of the post-War whodunits, in Kärrholm's view, upheld and helped construct the idyll of the welfare state's modern familial and national collectives, Daniel Brodén's study of Swedish crime films from the Second World War and post-War years relates a complementary narrative where these early filmic experiments with the genre show an alternative interest in 'the shadows of the people's home' (*Folkhemmets skuggbilder*), the dark side of the welfare state (Brodén 2008). Swedish noir films, as the later police procedurals, according to Brodén, begin to shed a critical light on the uncanny or 'un-homely' ('hemsk') everyday life in the rapidly industrializing Swedish welfare state, or seemingly idyllic 'people's home' (12). In different ways, Kärrholm and Brodén employ crime fiction as cultural historical sources for exploring the increasingly more pressing uncomfortable ambivalences that disturb the idea of the idyllic Swedish welfare state – a society either constantly under siege or threatened by its own accelerated modernization. The present study brings these ambivalences related to the welfare state and their negotiation in crime fiction into the late-modern period and broadens the view to include parallel developments in the three Scandinavian countries, Denmark, Norway and Sweden.

As the golden age of the welfare state faded, a new golden age of Scandinavian crime fiction ensued, and critics have over the most recent decade begun to explore and question why crime fiction, which of course does have a long and popular history also in the Scandinavian countries, has become so ubiquitous in the first decades of the twenty-first century. The obvious question to ask is how is it that these seemingly peaceful, affluent, healthy and happy welfare states in Scandinavia, nations that are constantly being lauded for leading the world in European and global surveys, whose image abroad is mostly of safe if not rather boring orderly societies, are punching well above their weight in terms of the production and export of violent and often dystopian crime novels and TV series. In Ian Macdougall's review of Stieg Larsson's *Millennium* trilogy, 'The man who blew up the welfare state', 'the country's well-polished façade' and 'welfare-state comforts', which is, he claims, what American readers would expect to find in depictions of Sweden, 'belies a broken apparatus of government' run by ubiquitous crooks.

In Larsson's crime novels 'the state itself is the greatest villain', and, Macdougall suggests, the novels' 'reliance on hard facts' (e.g. the statistics of violence against women, which Larsson reproduced as epigraphs) 'suggest that the crime novel we're reading is not a work of pure imagination' (Macdougall 2010). Barry Forshaw is another critic who has found that 'to some degree, the picture of Scandinavian society conveyed through its crime literature is an accurate one, though inevitably tendentious' (Forshaw 2012: 11).

Scandinavian crime writing since the 1970s has insisted on painting rather grim pictures of societies in which the welfare state has failed to protect the most vulnerable, where the welfare system is overburdened and unable to care and where, even after half a century of social engineering, crime appears as present and wide-spread as ever. This apparent paradox does seem to suggest that all is not well in Scandinavia, assuming that the crime narratives provide a realistic view into the dark side of these Nordic utopias. While crime fiction does employ realistic descriptions of everyday lives, urban and natural locations in Scandinavia, and while crime writers, who in many cases are trained journalists (e.g. Per Wahlöö, Anders Bodelsen, Jan Guillou, Stieg Larsson, Liza Marklund, Sara Blædel and Mari Jungstedt) may present statistics or provide, as many of them do, postscripts in which they thank their well-placed sources and informers for their help in the authors' research for the novels, crime fiction does not, of course, represent Scandinavian societies realistically, least of all when it comes to their inflated levels of crime – if it did, the small town of Ystad, the setting of Mankell's Wallander novels, would have seen more murders than the rest of Scandinavia combined.

Why is it, then, that such dark, dystopian and excessively violent narratives have taken root in Scandinavia and been such a success abroad in the twenty-first century? Mary Evans posed the same question in a slightly different way in her book *The Imagination of Evil: Detective Fiction and the Modern World* (2009): 'So, why, we might ask, since most of us live generally safe, relatively prosperous and "crime free" lives, are we so fascinated by the pathology of crime, by the process of identification of the murderer or the unmasking of the criminal?' (15). Part of her answer is that 'just as we might, arguably, have reached a point at which the social world becomes both relatively safe and relatively reliable, we have also imposed upon ourselves a myriad of new anxieties, in particular, the question of how to live up to the expectations of an (apparently) highly qualified world' (16). This is the world of the post-welfare state, the neoliberal competitive state, which, according to the Danish economist Ove K. Pedersen, has roots in the crises of the early 1970s, eventually replacing the Social Democratic welfare state in the 1990s (Pedersen 2011). The present book proceeds from Evans's suggestion that the ubiquity of crime fiction in Scandinavia, apart from being part of a wider global cultural phenomenon, uses generic crime narratives, the spectacle of the dead body and cordoned-off crime scenes in idyllic Scandinavian landscapes teeming with puzzled investigators, as proxies for investigations into wider and more complex 'new anxieties' produced by an increasingly competitive world marked by 'fluid' individualism, the denigration of the social state and the erosion of social trust between individuals, communities and institutions. Also in this sense, Scandinavian crime fiction can be seen to voice a social critique or perform cultural work relevant to particular national or regional conditions, using a global genre that has proven particularly well suited for exploring the symptoms, the itch, the anxieties arising from the less-visible societal changes and systemic violence. According to Evans, 'of all fiction in the past 200 years, it is detective and crime fiction that has most vividly and often persuasively engaged with social reality' and 'reading fiction about crime is the most vivid account that we have of western societies' various fears and preoccupations' (2, 7).

A nostalgic genre

Several of the crime novels discussed in this book investigate how individual desires and social responsibilities may be adjusted through collaboration and trust in order to produce and, at times in a sentimental or nostalgic mode, to reintroduce social justice, communal belonging, even comfort, in an age of widespread anxieties, where the Scandinavian countries have come to be seen as less the exceptional states they appeared to be in a polarized Cold War world and more like everywhere else in a world of rapid globalization.

For this reason, while I agree with the widely shared perception that Scandinavian crime fiction, as crime fiction from many other regions of the world, should be viewed as a genre preoccupied with changing social realities and conflicts between more or less corrupted states and victimized individuals, I believe that the local as well as the international success of Scandinavian crime narratives in print and on the screen is centrally tied to their at times nostalgic, sentimental and melodramatic insistence on values associated with fundamental, perhaps long-forgotten, aspirations of the Scandinavian welfare societies. Such common values may have been expressed most programmatically in the Swedish Social Democrat Per Albin Hansson's famous 'people's-home' speech in 1928. His vision for a future welfare society based on social citizenship was modelled on the synecdoche of the 'good home' with its foundation in equality and mutual understanding: a home which would not be divided by social classes, but based on consideration, cooperation and helpfulness.

Scandinavian crime fiction, in my view, is as diverse as its various locations, languages, cultural and historical contexts may suggest, but also united in worrying about and nostalgically longing for the good home and the comforts of a just, egalitarian welfare society in a turbulent and increasingly globalized world. It is a genre preoccupied with individuals and families, police officers, private investigators, forensic psychologists, journalists, victims of crime and criminals, who in various ways and by different means struggle to keep their homes together through cooperation, the cultivation of empathy, and by reclaiming individual freedoms through the cultivation of social trust.

Therefore, this book's exploration of what I call the Scandinavian welfare-crime novel does not merely find in the last four decades of Scandinavian crime-writing a dystopian portrayal of the welfare state, but a widely shared nostalgic longing for an imagined past of social and cultural justice and belonging, a longing for better times, which in some cases turns out to be a 'paradise lost' and in some a partial realization of, or hope for, a better future. In this, my wider perspective on present discourses about the state of Scandinavian welfare, as exemplified in the dominant genres belonging to crime fiction, concurs with Jenny Andersson's study of a prevailing 'people's-home nostalgia' (*folkhemsnostalgin*) in Sweden, where the promises of a better society lie not, as in the golden age of the welfare state in the 1950s and 1960s, in the near future, but in the missed opportunities of the past (Andersson 2009b). As in Svetlana Boym's study of nostalgia in post-1989 Eastern Europe, I do not consider nostalgic sentiments, as they are expressed in Scandinavian crime fiction, necessarily a bad thing (Boym 2001). Nostalgia can of course lead to anxieties about an unknown future, to xenophobia and ring-fencing of perceived ethnic values, to isolationism, but it can also help us face an uncertain future with shared values that may have suffered under the transformative pressures of modernization, neoliberalism and globalization. In this sense, I propose to view Scandinavian crime fiction as a genre made for the twenty-first century, a nostalgic age as well as an age of social and financial crises, a late-modern, post-national age of widespread anxieties about formerly perceived stable identities, families, communities and welfare states, which have become, to many, dissipated, unrecognizable and uncanny 'homes' in the new millennium.

Crime fiction has at least since its nineteenth-century origins functioned as a seismograph for emerging conflicts and anxieties between individuals, the social order and the state, the state's (in) ability to police and discipline the alienating physical and social spaces of the growing cities or the breakdown of social structures in the national peripheries where mysterious and violent crimes became symptomatic of the uprooting and alienating effects of rapid modernization (Mandel 1984: 29–30, 135; Scaggs 2005: 98–9; Symons 1974: 16). The social form of crime fiction is dependent upon and reflects local and national circumstances at particular moments in time where individuals' sense of belonging and identity 'thicken' around specific social insecurities and anxieties. A central argument and leitmotiv of this book is that the rise of Scandinavian crime fiction from the late 1960s to the first decades of the twenty-first century is intimately tied to the local disruptions associated with the late-modern or post-welfare society, which Shane McCorristine, with reference to the crime novels of Henning Mankell, has described as 'a sense of critical transition, a community that is envious of the past and uncertain about the future' (McCorristine 2011: 81). Such nostalgic sentiments inherent to the post-welfare state saturate post-1968 Scandinavian crime fiction; partly, I shall argue, because writers have been centrally concerned with giving a narrative shape to the shared experiences of unsettling social transformations.

Here, this book is indebted to Andrew Nestingen's seminal study *Crime and Fantasy in Scandinavia* (2008), wherein he demonstrates how popular and transnational genres have recently played a central role in 'reshaping Scandinavian national cultures' (257). Particularly the Scandinavian penchant for the police procedural, Nestingen suggests, must be seen in the light of its generic form ready-made (due to its focus on the collective of a police team representing the state) for exploring 'the social dynamics and ethical crisis of the Scandinavian nations' (217). Complementing the collective realism of the police novel, the increasingly more melodramatic mode of the crime novel in Scandinavia, Nestingen argues, is similarly well suited for 'contesting the morality of the welfare state's transformation under neoliberalism' (Nestingen 2011:172). The present study adds to this view of the social function of genre fiction, apart from its more holistic sample from the recent tradition of Scandinavian crime fiction, a discussion of a variety of nostalgic modes through which novels from the late 1960s to the 2000s construct a persistent view of not only what has gone wrong in the welfare state, what has been lost over the past four decades, but also what a 'good' state of the present and future might be.

This argument not only confirms the persistent realist and socio-critical ambitions of Scandinavian crime fiction, a central generic 'Nordic' trait noticed by most readers, reviewers and critics, but also points to a much wider historical and generic trait of crime fiction across subgenres and cultural origins: In Ernest Mandel's Marxist-inspired critique of the classical detective story of the interwar years, its inherent nostalgia is viewed as fulfilling the subjective needs of the 'upset, bored and anxious individual member of the middle class', and, more recently, Erik Dussere has argued that the gritty realism or 'authenticity effects' employed in the American noir tradition can be viewed as attempts to recapture, at times nostalgically, a lost 'elsewhere' in an American post-War era marked by the artificiality of an omnipresent consumer culture (Mandel 1984: 29; Dussere 2014: 8–9). Scandinavian detectives, faced with an inscrutable, complex and violent world, knee-deep in personal and familial conflicts, wonder what has happened to the welfare state's promise of a better, more just, equal and trusting society – and they do so in their various Scandinavian languages and accents, yet in a (nostalgic) mode that conforms to the expected generic 'language' of crime fiction.

A global genre

Scandinavian crime fiction is, on the one hand, thoroughly located within specific national concerns about the fate of the Nordic universal welfare state under the increasingly globalized pressures of consumerism, transnational crime, neoliberalism, Europeanization and migration. On the other, however, these local, generic and societal concerns are perhaps also what have made these fictions travel beyond their local origins. Societal concerns about the erosion of communities, families, individual freedoms and welfare institutions are widely shared across the world having spawned international movements and national political upheavals in the wake of the global financial crisis in the first decade of the twenty-first century. Stieg Larsson's *Män som hatar kvinnor* (2005, *The Girl with the Dragon Tattoo*, 2008), 'the all-flattening juggernaut' of Scandinavian crime fiction, according to Barry Forshaw and, in Kerstin Bergman's assessment, *the* novel that turned Swedish crime fiction into a 'worldwide phenomenon', is a good example of the global resonance of crime fiction's local responsiveness (Forshaw 2012: 5; Bergman 2014: 11). As I argue in Chapter 4, an often overlooked point in this novel, behind its more dramatic theme of violence against women and terrifying Nazi serial killers, is the social backdrop of financial crisis and loss of interpersonal trust, referring to the crisis in Sweden in the early 1990s. While most global readers probably know very little about Sweden and the wider sociopolitical consequences of this event, the novel might have resonated so widely as translations began to spread simultaneously with the unravelling of the global financial crisis of 2008; it is, after all, essentially a contemporary cautionary tale of financial corruption, its social consequences and an impotent welfare state.

In the twenty-first century, Scandinavian crime fiction, or 'Nordic Noir' as it has become labelled in the UK, became a local as well as a near-global obsession described as forming a recognizable international brand, which has spread like a wave from the Scandinavian epicentres to the mainstream European markets and beyond: Several crime series have been translated into more than thirty languages and authors such as the Swedes Henning Mankell, Stieg Larsson and Liza Marklund, the Norwegian Jo Nesbø and the Dane Jussi Adler-Olsen are selling millions of copies of their crime novels outside of Scandinavia (Nestingen and Arvas 2011; Forshaw 2012).

The wave of Scandinavian crime fiction, which initiated in the 1990s and intensified in the first decades of the twenty-first century, conforms to Franco Moretti's theory about the transnational spread of novelistic genres, emanating from the literary and cultural centres and influencing the peripheries through translations, adaptations and mimicry, eventually resulting in original local variants that add to and innovate the global form of the genre itself (Moretti 2000). The phenomenon of Scandinavian crime fiction demonstrates that crime fiction is a particularly mobile and adaptable genre, able to spread and take root throughout the world of literature. It may be argued that the popularity of Scandinavian crime fiction has played a central role over the recent decades in opening up the doors for crime writers around the world to the global and much coveted yet notoriously impermeable Anglo-American markets. According to an article in the *Wall Street Journal* about 'Fiction's Global Crime Wave', published at the height of the Stieg-Larsson craze, 'Detective novels from Japan, Nigeria, Germany and Korea are pouring into the U.S. as publishers hunt for the next "Girl With the Dragon Tattoo"' (Alter 2010).

Local crime-writing in the European semi-periphery of the Nordic countries arose out of the generic forms, originating, for the most part, in Anglo-American traditions. In the post-War period, Scandinavian crime writers absorbed and imitated the American hardboiled detective novel and the British clue-puzzle, notable examples being the Swedish queen of the whodunit, Maria Lang, the Dane Else Fischer and the Norwegian Gerd Nyquist (Egholm Andersen 2010; Skei 2008: 79; Wendelius 1999a: 46). Since the early 1970s, Scandinavian crime fiction has become more than adaptations in the periphery of Anglo-American predecessors. Crime fiction began to find its particular local expression in Scandinavia where the 'social work' of the crime genre became acted out, mediated and consumed on the stage of the Scandinavian welfare state. Since then, Scandinavian crime fiction has become a dramatic form that both adopt central concerns in crime writing and seek to present content and forms specific to local social realities and traditions.

Curiously, in the first decade of the twenty-first century, this local Scandinavian variant became a new centre from where not only translated novels but also subtitled TV drama would spread to the rest of the world, notably with the success of original Danish TV series, Swedish and Anglo-American adaptations of novels by Henning Mankell (*Wallander* with Kenneth Branagh as Inspector Wallander; Left Bank Pictures/Yellow Bird, 2008–2016) and Stieg Larsson (*The Girl with the Dragon Tattoo*; David Pincher 2011); TV series such as *Forbrydelsen* (*The Killing*) and the Danish–Swedish co-production *Broen/Bron* (2011, 2013, 2015, *The Bridge*) were remade to serve other local contexts when, for instance, *The Bridge* was relocated from the Öresund Bridge between Sweden and Denmark to the tunnel connecting the UK and France in *The Tunnel* (2013) and the Bridge of the Americas between Mexico and the United States in FX's *The Bridge* (2013–4). The success of Nordic Noir TV drama in the United Kingdom has arguably influenced series such as the Welsh and bilingual *Y Gwyll/Hinterland* (S4C/BBC One Wales, 2013/2014), and Nordic Noir has been taken up by UK-based crime writers such as Torquil MacLeod with his Malmö Mysteries and in Quentin Bates's Gunnhildur series, as well as in Simon Donald's TV crime thriller *Fortitude* (Sky Atlantic, 2015) set in Arctic Norway. These recent examples demonstrate that Scandinavian crime fiction, while still mostly set in a Nordic country, preferably in cold, snowy landscapes, does not necessarily need to be written in a Scandinavian language by Scandinavians.

As such, Scandinavian crime fiction can be viewed as a new kind of centre in the global network of crime fiction and world literature. Itself an imitation of or a new accent to popular forms originating in the Anglo-American global centres, it has given rise to new accents at home and further afield. This new centre of popular fictions may only hold for a while, yet as a global commercial, cultural and literary phenomenon, thoroughly localized in national and regional settings but addressing widely shared concerns relevant to our fluid, fast-paced globalizing world, it is worthwhile, as I hope this book will demonstrate, to pause and consider what Scandinavian crime fiction, written and read over the past five decades, may tell us about our world, seen, as it always is, from a particular, recognizable yet foreign location.

1

Scandinavian crime fiction and the welfare state

In 1960 it felt as if the utopia of wealthy, egalitarian and progressive welfare societies were becoming a reality in Scandinavia. The general perception was that these had become societies where, in the words of the Danish nineteenth-century clergyman and politician Grundtvig, 'few have too much and fewer too little.' Prime Minister Per Albin Hansson's vision in 1928 of an idyllic Swedish 'people's home' (folkhem), which would replace a society mired in class divisions, had, in the eyes of many, materialized in a near-perfect nation-family characterized by equality, mutual understanding, low unemployment and a general optimism for the future following steady economic growth during 'the record years' (*rekordåren*) in the decades following the Second World War. Sweden, in particular, had become internationally acclaimed as a functional utopia, 'a middle-way' to arise out of the polarized Cold War between capitalism and communism.

Make good times better

In Denmark at the height of this golden age of the welfare state, the Social Democratic Party went into the general election of 1960 with the slogan: 'Make good times better' – a phrase also used by its Swedish sister party (Petersen et al. 2012: 71). One of the election posters carrying the message of 'comfort [tryghed] for the family', which has since become a symbol of the optimism characterizing the 1950s and 1960s, portrays a smiling, modern, middle-class nuclear family lounging in front of their new TV set. Until then a curiosity in Danish living rooms, one-third of households owned a TV in 1960, and more, it is suggested, would own one if the Social Democratic Party was to be elected. The focal point allotted to this new wonder of information technology and family entertainment tapped into the growing consumer desires of the still more affluent citizens in the welfare state. On this occasion of a general election, it was also an appropriate choice for illustrating the bright future ahead, the progress towards a modern democracy, as this was the first election day to be transmitted live on Danish TV. The expanding middle class could look forward to a welfare state that not only provided close to full employment, social security, universal health- and childcare, pensions and other tax-funded universal benefits, but, more importantly, even better times for the consumers, whose smiles widened with the prospect of increasing leisure time and wider access to new luxuries such as TVs, household appliances, cars, modern homes and package holidays to Mallorca.

While the Scandinavian welfare state certainly was, and still is, based on largely shared beliefs in social equality, solidarity and the central role of the state in providing individual and universal security, the new reality of the modern consumer society became a mass phenomenon in the post-War expansion and consolidation of the welfare state. In 1950s Scandinavia, consumption became a central concern to the rapidly modernizing welfare societies following the persistent rationing of the 1940s. As Sara Kärrholm asserts: 'consumption grew in step with the shaping of the welfare state, and it contributed simultaneously to its shaping' (Kärrholm 2005: 276). In a Swedish context, according to Kärrholm, 'to be able to freely consume was almost seen as a national duty' (276). Consumption was central to the success of the welfare state and it materialized in the new homes and urban spaces that were being constructed for the modern citizens in the carefully planned and well-managed modern society.

Welfare urbanism

As seen in the election poster, the private became, to a large extent, a matter of public policy, and it was ingrained in the welfare state that social planning or engineering by scientific means could lead to an efficient, healthy and progressive society for all. New independent economic forums and social research institutes sprung up to provide the foundation for political actions (Petersen et al. 2012: 33). In Sweden, for instance, the Research Institute for the Home (Hemmets Forskningsinstitut) was tasked with rationalizing housework chores, which turned the home into a well-oiled machine for the production of efficient workers, who found evidence of their upward social mobility in the commodities they came to possess.

While the scientifically based design of the welfare state was comprehensive in all the Scandinavian countries and reached every corner of society, from kitchen appliances, public broadcasting, furniture design and support for the arts to the labour market, policing and penal system, health-, child- and elder care, arguably the most visible monuments to the modern welfare state and its radical restructuring of the everyday lives of its citizens were its comprehensive urban renewal schemes and ambitious housing programmes.

As in many other aspects of the welfare state, Sweden submitted Stockholm to the most radical urban 'sanitation' programme immediately following the Second World War, a period in which other European nations such as Britain were busy rebuilding city centres scarred by war, tearing down unhealthy and crime-ridden urban slums and building idyllic New Towns for the socially mobile working class. This was, what David Harvey has called, the era of the 'Keynesian city': 'shaped as a consumption artifact and its social, economic, and political life organized around the theme of state-backed, debt-financed consumption' (Harvey 1989: 37–8).

The ambition in Sweden went beyond meeting the increasing demands for more and better housing. Urban renewal was to improve the connection of the city centre to the suburbs with a new underground service, improve the city's infrastructure by adjusting to the drastic increase in car ownership and to replace larger areas of derelict buildings and slums with new office buildings and commercial spaces. According to Ericsson et al., the term 'urban sanitation' used in Sweden for the renewal programmes also suggests wider discursive implications of social engineering reminiscent of social, even racial, hygiene. The new society that was envisioned would be one in which the utopian desire for progress towards a sanitized or 'clean' future society involved the abolition of backward traditions and represented a vision of a 'mono-cultural' society without 'dreg'. Urban sanitation was, then, more than a rational response to an immediate housing crisis. It was a 'symbolic gesture' towards a future society inhabited by a modern welfare-man who had dispelled all social and cultural ambivalences and conflicts (Ericsson et al. 2000: 26). According to Alexandra Borg, the sanitation also targeted areas, which housed artists, writers, small retailers and craftsmen such as tailors and shoemakers in the name of progress and modernity. The demolition of an entire urban culture, which had allowed arts and crafts, creative communities and established traditions to thrive in the urban centres did not go unanswered at the time. There was, according to Borg, a heated debate about the loss of cultural memory and history embedded in the old buildings and urban areas doomed for demolition (Borg 2012: 134).

Post-War urban developments in Scandinavia were, of course, a necessary socio-geographic response to an immediate housing crisis and a rational response to changes in demography and consumption patterns as the industrial welfare state sought to maintain its high level of growth and social progress. Larger, healthier and more efficient homes and urban spaces were needed rapidly, yet the pace of progress that rolled over Scandinavia during the golden age of the welfare state resulted in wider cultural conflicts and mental crises. The recent history of Scandinavian crime fiction, I shall argue, can to a large extent be understood as a multifaceted, popular cultural response to the broader sociocultural upheavals prompted by the progressive welfare state, the years of rapid modernization and economic growth, the wider consequences of the affluent consumer society and its crises from the early 1970s onwards.

If the birth of the crime novel is generally perceived to coincide with nineteenth-century urbanization and the social and psychological pressures and conflicts it produced, including high levels of crime, overcrowded urban spaces, social depravation and impoverishment (Worthington 2011: 1–15), Scandinavian crime fiction, as we have come to recognize this particular regional contribution to the crime genre today, was borne out of the dreams and anxieties arising in accord with the spatial and social transformations of the modern welfare state.

Where American hardboiled detectives could still walk down the 'mean' streets of a modern American city depicted as 'a wasteland devastated by drugs, violence, pollution, garbage, and a decaying physical infrastructure' (Willet 1992: 5), the Stockholm of Stieg Trenter's crime novels from the forties and fifties seems an unsuitable place for a classic hardboiled sleuth. The amateur detective Harry Friberg notes how tidy and ordered the newly built part of the city is with its bright facades bathed in the afternoon sun and their long lines of colourful awnings. In fact, the city was 'all too tidy and ordered. Here were no mysterious nooks, no seedy backyards – no picturesque or bizarre elements to the buildings. Here everything was made to measure and cast in the same form' (Trenter 1945: 121). While there is a good deal of nostalgia for the old city threatened by urban renewal and conformity in Trenter's Stockholm crime novels, his is mostly an idyllic depiction of the Swedish people's home, as was the trend in the post-War Swedish clue-puzzle tradition, according to Kärrholm. We will have to wait for Sjöwall and Wahlöö to return the urban environment to its generic noir condition: as an illusion of the capitalist welfare state, a polished and sanitized facade that hides a more 'real' and mucky social dystopia.

One of the most lauded innovations of the urban plans of the 1950s was the new urban centres of satellite cities. These were to materialize the welfare state's grand vision of producing well-functioning, healthy and democratic citizens and efficient, educated workers by giving access to fresh air, light, strong communities, public services within easy reach and, not least, modern housing with ample space and time-saving appliances. An early Swedish example of such a satellite city was Vällingby outside of Stockholm – the first example of an 'ABC City', an acronym for *Arbete-Bostad-Centrum* or Work-Dwelling-Centre. This was not to be a sleepy, purely residential suburb, but instead a new urban centre, a microcosm of the people's home, wherein residents would have access to shops, restaurants, a cinema, childcare, schools, work and nature within easy reach of Stockholm by the new transit system and arterial motorway. Similar urban plans were conceived in Denmark as the Finger Plan (1947) and in Norway as the Great Master Plan for Oslo (1960). These holistic designs for living, as it were, in the future, 'reflected the general spirit of the 1950s and 1960s: urbanization of the countryside, a complete clearance of the old blocks and a comprehensive redevelopment, high plot ratio, motorways through central areas, clearance and redevelopment of old urban structure replaced by technically and hygienically [effective] modern housing' (Kolbe 2006:138). The residents who moved into these new ABC cities, which had seemingly grown out of the plain fields overnight, found themselves in an utterly idyllic yet also rather uncanny future. It is in one of these suburban centres outside of Copenhagen that Anders Bodelsen set his first welfare-crime novel, *Think of a Number* from 1968. In this novel, the urban space becomes a sounding board for the individual crisis of a stereotypical welfare-man as he derails into a life of crime as a response to pressures of consumption and the welfare state's corrosion of meaningful social relations.

Perhaps the most ambitious plan to deal with the post-War housing shortage through urban development was the 'million-homes programme' (*Miljonprogrammet*) in Sweden. The unprecedented ambition was to build a million new dwellings for a population of merely eight million over a ten-year period between 1965 and 1974. These suburban areas became to a large extent the quintessence of the welfare state's vision for a modern, egalitarian and community-based society that could produce democratic and productive citizens (Ericsson et al. 2000: 31). Some, but far from all, of these homes were brutalist concrete tower blocks, and were already criticized at the time as representing 'betong-socialism' (concrete socialism). Many of the new housing areas became seen as symbols of failed social engineering; though, as Göran Hägg describes the belief at the time, 'Rationality and public information would sooner or later convince the general population' (Hägg 2005: 210). However, even if the new inhabitants had been given everything they could possibly need, it became apparent that these urban areas had become geographically and mentally segregated from the rest of society. Instead of fostering normalcy, these modernist urban environments soon became associated with deviance and antisocial behaviour. Reading Gunnar Staalesen's Norwegian detective novels from the late 1970s, it becomes clear that the sensible public housing projects of the welfare state had come to materialize social segregation instead of collectivism, alienation instead of democratic participation, economic, social and cultural marginalization and stagnation as soon as the residents had moved into their well-managed welfare-state homes.

Scandinavian crime fiction from the late sixties and seventies responded to the ambitious social engineering programmes of the welfare state and their social impact by using the crime genre as a 'scalpel' with which to forensically examine the welfare state, which, in Per Wahlöö's metaphor from 1966, had become an ideological corpse (Secher 1984: 374); to examine the existential alienation produced by the urban environments and consumer culture in an age of affluence, as in Bodelsen's use of the detective and thriller genres as determined by a 'poetics of facts' (Bodelsen 1970: 168); or, finally, in Staalesen, to use a phrase coined by his fellow Norwegian, Kjartan Fløgstad, to employ a 'dialectical detective' to investigate crimes that are, in the vernacular crime novel, linked to the material conditions of private ownership in the capitalist society (Fløgstad 1979).

In other words, by employing the clue-puzzle's foregrounding of rational, fact-based crime investigation and the detective novel's penchant for the uncanny yet realistic social and geographical environments of the modern consumer society, these new Scandinavian voices used available subgenres (psychological thriller, police procedural and hardboiled detective novel) to examine the darker sides of life in the well-managed welfare state and to present counter-discourses to its idyllic, rational and progressive image of the future where the 'good times' seemed to be only getting better.

Noir consumers

The central critical preoccupation in Scandinavian crime fiction of the 1970s, with the social welfare state presented as inherently a capitalist consumer society, owes much to the American hardboiled noir tradition. Erik Dussere's study of the American Noir tradition in the post-War era, *America Is Elsewhere: The Noir Tradition in the Age of Consumer Culture* (2014), argues that the post-War crime novel can be seen as a direct response to 'the unprecedented rise of consumer culture' that 'reshaped American national identity in important ways' (3). While the impact of consumer culture on an imagined national identity came later in Scandinavia and the cultural responses were significantly different due to societal dissimilarities, there are, however, parallels in the ways in which the American Noir tradition and 'Nordic Noir' have used crime genres as a critical response to the increasing conflation of consumption and citizenship.

According to Dussere, 'American cultural productions expressed a newly urgent desire to discover or rediscover a version of the nation imagined as authentic and opposed to consumerism' (3). In Scandinavian crime fiction a few decades later, 'noir' fictions similarly respond to a national self-image of comfort and affluence. However, in the first generation of new Scandinavian crime writers it is explicitly the consolidation of the welfare consumer society rather than a national self-image, like the 'American dream', that is viewed as an illusion and has led its citizens into an inauthentic existence as, what Per Svensson termed, 'comfort junkies'.

In Dussere's account, the hardboiled crime novel and Noir film confronted the shiny surfaces of an affluent consumer society with its 'gritty-realist aesthetic' and used these 'authenticity effects' to evoke 'particular commercial spaces, which take both literal and symbolic forms' (5). The new American landscape of automobile culture, suburban living and supermarkets in the forties and fifties suggest 'the commodity as the dominant structure' underlying national space. It is a society, with reference to Marcuse, where '[p]eople recognize themselves in their commodities; they find their soul in their automobile, hi-fi set, split level home, kitchen equipment. The very mechanism which ties the individual to his society has changed' (8). In Dussere's reading of the post-War noir tradition, it is these spaces in particular that offer a confrontation between 'the degraded, commercialized mainstream and the darker and more vital alternative offered by the noir aesthetic' (5). In this sense, the hardboiled crime genre can be viewed as performing a systemic analysis or as an example of a counter-culture critique of the anxieties produced by 'the omnipresent national consumer culture' where 'citizens come to feel that the nation they inhabit is pervasively artificial and inauthentic' (5).

Dussere shares with Lionel Trilling and others 'a structural understanding of authenticity as the desire for something that is perceived to be lost and perhaps unrecoverable', a longing for an America or an 'American dream' that is inherently 'elsewhere' (8). Therefore, the noir genre's search for authenticity, according to Dussere, may be defined as what he calls a 'false nostalgia' – a nostalgia for something that may never have been – which posits itself as 'the antithesis of society, artifice, imitation, modernity, conformity, or alienation' (6).

Perhaps the best example of false nostalgia as directly linked to the Scandinavian consumer society is to be found in Sjöwall and Wahlöö's *Mannen på balkongen* (1967, *The Man on the Balcony*, 1968). Here the advent and critique of the expanding consumer society is held up against a general anxiety about a changing urban and social environment and a nostalgia for a disappearing culture with its local communities, traditions and small shops giving way to mass consumption and supermarkets: 'Soon they'll vanish altogether [the small bakeries] and you'll be able to buy nothing but mass-produced bread in plastic wrapping and the entire Swedish nation will eat exactly the same loaves and buns and cakes, thought Police Officer Kvist' (Sjöwall and Wahlöö 2007: 172). Kvist is only in his twenties but already feels that his childhood is in a distant past. While no direct links are made from the disappearance of small shops and 'authentic' bread rolls to the criminal activities investigated, this aside filters into the novel's dystopian portrait of a conformist society in moral and social decline, with its paedophile serial killers, vigilante citizens, police violence, prostitution, alcohol and drug consumption among increasingly younger people, where '[a]ll that the police really succeeded in doing was to stir up the dregs – the homeless, the alcoholics, the drug addicts, those who had lost all hope, those who could not even crawl away when the welfare state turned the stone over' (135).

While the social ills of this novel are not explicitly linked to mass-production and the consumer society, Sjöwall and Wahlöö's urban space of Stockholm is one that produces anxieties about artificiality, modernity, conformity and alienation, what Dussere associates with the crime novel's diagnosis of the consumer society's production of 'inauthenticity'. Kvist, who had only the previous year completed his police training, is already longing for a more 'authentic' elsewhere that is relentlessly receding into the past, and we find in this welfare dystopia a portrait of a consumer society, where, eventually, it is the citizens themselves that are being consumed.

Consumption in the modern Scandinavian welfare state was figured as a central marker for its success. Good times were obviously getting better when more families could afford new TVs around which the family could gather and through which citizens could take part in the new democratic processes of the information society. New consumer practices were central to the urban planners when they created the new centres of utopian satellite cities. To become functioning new 'centres' the retail and entertainment sector had to be included in cooperative planning. Inside their homes, the welfare citizens were provided with functionalist kitchens that would enable families to engage in healthy consumption and save the housewife time as she went about her household chores. In an era that still maintained traditionally gendered divisions of labour, it was envisioned that well-managed and technologically assisted homes would enable the housewives to also become producers in a booming labour market in dire need of more hands. The progressive social state was actively producing and responding to the post-War consumer society. However, its responses were very much following in the footsteps of Nordic cooperatism and aided by rational social engineering and functionalist architecture.

Dussere's reading of the American hardboiled and noir tradition emphasizes the genre's critique of an increasingly commercialized mass society in which urban and commercial spaces exhibit the inauthenticity of a post-War national identity in the consumer society and a callous disregard for authentic and autonomous individual lives, their communities and traditions. Crime fiction in the American noir tradition responded to this 'crisis of affluence' by presenting particular 'authenticity effects' that could make an alternative vision for America and national identity visible. However, in the Scandinavian welfare state, the opposition between the mass and the individual was not as clear-cut. According to Helena Mattsson, this was already a crucial dialectic set out to be overcome by the functionalist architects in the 1930s, who held a central position in the physical as well as 'moral' formation of the new 'classless' welfare state in the decades following the Second World War, in which

the consumer became a figure whose desires must become essential for the making of the new society. Through the commodity the modern subject became part of a new collectivism, and the commodity came to represent a society without classes, rather than social status. This also entails a shaping of a new form of personality, whose desires will be geared towards the 'sound commodity'. (Mattsson 2010: 74)

The central struggle between the mass and the individual in the Western consumer societies, as viewed by many post-War writers such as Herbert Marcuse, resulted in a loss of selfhood: 'Mass-production and mass-distribution claim the *entire* individual' (quoted in Dussere 2014: 8). However, this dystopian vision of the effects of the consumer society was at an early stage of the formation of the Scandinavian welfare state countered by adjusting the individual desires of the citizens to the collective needs of the society. Modern functionalist architecture, for instance, was to respond to the growing desires of the working class for middle-class comforts while at the same time reigning in consumption through state-capital alliances such as the 'cooperative movements ... state subventions and regulations' (Mattsson: 76) together with state-funded consumer information (Aléx 2003:143). Mattsson names this welfare state consumer 'the reasonable consumer', and the new standardized homes and urban areas of the welfare state became places 'for the invention of a controlled consumption and its concomitant reasonable consumer' (Mattsson: 97).

Conspicuous consumption was seen as a threat to social cohesion, and the welfare state sought to encourage a particular kind of consumption in the reasonable consumer: an educated consumer who can influence production and supply not with subjective desires, leading inevitably to conspicuous consumption, but directed towards a common good: functional homes, household goods, child care, education and entertainments, where, according to Nanna Gro Henningsen, 'the act of "consuming" produces a new type of modern subjectivity, the good citizen of the welfare state' (Henningsen 2013: 30). Such reasonable consumers were to inhabit the functionalist 'middle-way' utopias of the welfare state's satellite cities that mushroomed in the 1950s; yet, however 'reasonable' these urban developments may have been at the time in their carefully planned response to a severe housing crisis and demographic migrations propelled by rapid industrialization, low unemployment and affluence, being a good citizen of the welfare state became fraught with existential and social crises perhaps best explored by the Danish philosopher of the welfare state, Villy Sørensen.

In the tale '*Købmanden*' (1955, 'The Grocer', 1991), he captured the individual and social challenges presented by an ideology of reasonable consumption set in an imagined new Danish satellite city. Sørensen's grocer embodies two competing positions regarding the relationship between the state and the individual. His business model is that he will only sell goods that individual customers need

and not what they desire. He will, therefore, not sell beer to build-
ers who might fall off the scaffolding or cigarettes to customers
who already have cigarettes. His philosophy is that maintaining the
health and well-being of his customers, so they can keep consuming,
will in the long run be better for business. On the other hand, the
grocer also represents 'the nanny state' (formynderstaten), which in
Danish has paternalistic connotations, and was a phrase used at the
time, as well as later, to criticize the expanding welfare state.

The end to the grocer's regime comes with new urban developments and a new kind of citizen: 'Prospective husbands who came
from the city to look for flats in the newly built tower blocks in the
outskirts, could hardly see [the grocer's] house where home and
business got on so famously without feeling quite sad' (49). With
the new residents and urban renewal, the grocer's monopoly as a
retailer is broken by the arrival of self-service supermarkets:

> [P]eople thronged in front of the new shop's gaily-lit windows,
> in which the whole shop was on show like an advertisement –
> abounding in goods that had never been seen in those parts
> before, because the old grocer hadn't thought them necessary
> ... There were enough shop assistants for everyone, for they all
> served themselves and took the goods they wanted, and to which
> coloured advertisements drew their attention. Helpful assistants
> strolled among the customers, bowing and showing the way ...
> Everyone paid up willingly, for all his wares were cheaper than
> the old grocer's; but their bills were bigger, for now they were
> allowed to buy things they didn't need. There were no customers
> in the grocer's shop. (Sørensen 1991: 75–6)

As Lasse Horne Kjældgaard has pointed out, the tale needs to be
seen in its cultural context where the number of supermarkets more
than quadrupled between 1954 and 1959, and, I would add, in
the context of the new urban living spaces of the modern welfare
state and its particular forms of 'socially engineered' consumption
(Kjældgaard 2009: 36).

The grocer expresses his realization of, what to him appears
as, 'the end of the world': 'It's the end of the world – people want
to serve themselves' (Sørensen 1991: 74); ['Det er verdens under-
gang, menneskene vil ekspedere sig selv' (Kjældgaard 2009: 36)].
Kjældgaard points out that the Danish word used by Sørensen

for 'to serve', *ekspedere*, denotes several meanings in Danish: 'to kill' and through its Latin root in *expedio*, 'to set free or emancipate' (36). The grocer's vision for the new welfare society is one in which consumers will want to service themselves leading either to their emancipation or destruction – a double meaning that also reflects disparate views on the Scandinavian welfare state as an utopia of individual freedom and social equality or, in Huntford's dystopian view, one that leads to dehumanization and an epidemic of suicides.

While critics warned against the dehumanizing and de-individualizing effects of 'the nanny state', Sørensen argued in his essays that the social security and comfort provided by the welfare state was not an end in itself but rather a means towards an end of existential liberation, enabling the citizens to pursue independent goals (Sørensen 1959: 221). In a similar fashion, 'The Grocer' can be read as a critical comment to the persistent critique of the welfare state as one that encroaches on individual freedoms and produces conformity, one that turns everyone into mindless shoppers. Instead, Sørensen's tale suggests, the welfare state is to be seen as a means towards existential emancipation making it possible for all individuals to 'serve themselves' with all the social and individual responsibilities and choices it entails – in this Sørensen is clearly inspired by Søren Kierkegaard's 'concept of anxiety' as a dizziness of freedom.

According to Sørensen, the idea of the welfare state is that 'everyone should feel safe as citizens, from which does not follow that they should feel safe as humans, for they shouldn't' (220). Whether individual consumption would lead to emancipation or doom was, to Sørensen, not the remit of the welfare state, but was, at least partly, a responsibility given to art and literature. By representing the inherent conflicts of the modern welfare consumer society, literature could assist readers in confronting their anxieties to become fully formed individuals and consumers in the modern welfare state. Sørensen did not think of crime fiction when considering the ability of art and literature to aid the welfare citizens towards their own emancipation by the means of a modern consumerist welfare state. However, one Danish crime novel came to demonstrate that crime fiction could be a particularly valuable generic form through which the desires, choices and anxieties of a modern consumer society could be negotiated.

'The harried welfare-man': Anders Bodelsen's *Think of a Number*

Anders Bodelsen used the realist crime thriller to explore the existential choices between emancipation and doom enabled by the materially secure and affluent welfare state in his *Tænk på et tal* (1968, *Think of a Number*, 1969). The novel became an instant bestseller in Denmark and has been translated into several languages such as Czech, French, German, Italian, Japanese, Russian and Spanish. It was adapted for film in Denmark in 1969 with an English language remake in 1978 as *The Silent Partner*, which included Elliott Gould and Christopher Plummer in the cast. The novel owes much to one of Georges Simenon's 'romans durs', *L'Homme qui regardait passer les trains* (1938, *The Man Who Watched the Trains Go By*, 1942), wherein an anonymous and respectable clerk of a shipping company, Kees Popinga, faced with the bankruptcy of his company and the loss of his savings just before Christmas, spirals into a life of crime and madness on the run from the authorities towards Paris.

As in Simenon's novel, the accidental criminal in Bodelsen's is an everyman. One evening before Christmas, the bank clerk Flemming Borck is tidying up the bank. He discovers an undelivered letter of demands written in a childish hand by a possible bank robber among the 'sinful' mess of dull bank forms and glossy travel brochures jumbled together on a table in the customer area. His gaze is consumed by the dreamy images of the brochures that 'featured color photos of sunburned people swimming or sunbathing – pale golden sands, an incredible blue sky, palms, little refreshment tents, a colossal Mediterranean sun about to set' (Bodelsen 1969: 3–4). As he walks home from the bank he realizes within himself an unspecified sense of opportunity that appears in the form of the mysterious word 'change'. The following days, Borck spends his time staking out the shopping centre for signs of the would-be robber, and his suspicion falls on a 'fake Santa Claus' standing outside the local supermarket when he realizes a similarity between the handwriting on his sign and on the letter of demands. In anticipation of the robbery, Borck secretly moves the large bank notes from his till into his blue lunch box with the word *Velbekomme* (bon appétit) printed in golden italics on the lid. Eventually the fake Santa robs the bank leading to a momentary identity crisis in Borck as he recognizes himself in the bank robber – they were not two separate minds but one. When the robber realizes that Borck has cheated him of a great part of the loot, a cat-and-mouse game ensues, and a novel of detection turns into a psychological thriller. The robber, together with his femme-fatale girlfriend who, true to the hardboiled tradition of the doomed sleuth, seduces Borck, pursues him all the way to Mallorca, the dreamscape of 1960s mass tourism, where they confront under a burning Mediterranean sun.

The question raised in both Simenon and Bodelsen's *romans durs*, or psychological crime thrillers, is what it takes for a regular law-abiding person to turn into a hardened criminal. How are we to understand the sudden change in roles and the seemingly unpremeditated erratic actions of a man leading a comfortable yet slightly tedious life in a bland small town? Obviously both suffer from suppressed desires for an unrealized 'elsewhere'. Popinga is a train spotter, who dreams of exotic destinations such as Paris. In *Think of a Number* the action is relocated from Simenon's Belgian province to the urban and commercial spaces of one of the welfare state's new satellite cities: Nærum Butikstorv (Nærum shopping centre) – a recognizable social environment that embodies the dreams and anxieties central to Bodelsen's ambition to situate and depict contemporary 'social disharmonies' and 'collective conflicts' in the 'private conflicts' that have arisen with the affluent welfare society (Bodelsen 1970: 166).

The well-ordered urban utopia with its shopping centre, bank, cinema, motorways, green spaces and functionalist apartment blocks is the stage upon which Borck attempts to liberate himself from his inauthentic life. When he opens the bank by unveiling the large plate-glass window to the gazes of the queuing customers in the morning, he thinks of himself as an actor on a stage about to play his expected role. In fact, the whole shopping centre is presented as a stage set, with decorations, wings, a proscenium arch, foot lights and a fourth wall looking out upon the motorway that brings in the audience to this Naturalistic play of the consumer society in the shape of Christmas shoppers.

The shopping centre consisted of three wings: in one of them was the bank and various shops; the opposite wing housed the cinema. Along the third, which connected the other two, ran a loggia which had been decorated since the end of November with festoons of spruce twigs and little lights. In the middle of the square, two middle-aged men in student caps were selling Christmas trees. The fourth side of the square was open, providing a view of the flat landscape and the highway that approached the square and went on past it; it was marked at this hour by an unbroken line of headlights. (Bodelsen 1969: 6)

While Bodelsen is describing an actual place in Denmark, the shopping centre in Nærum, it appears increasingly staged and artificial, abundant in advertisements for exotic holidays and other luxury goods on display. However inauthentic, it also appears as a place where 'anything can happen' and he can decide for himself (16).

Think of a Number draws on a contemporary 'fashion for bank robberies', widely covered by the media, and particularly the series of so-called Volvo-robberies, which culminated in 1968 with the arrest of the notorious Finnish bank robber Matti Markkanen, also known as Volvo Markkanen for his preferred brand of getaway cars (Nicolajsen 1977: 86). Contemporary readers of the novel would perhaps early on make the connection and suspect that the bank clerk might turn to crime when Borck walks past a car dealer and his consumer desires are stirred when he sees the new Volvo: 'that looked just like the rest of them but could shoot ahead whenever its owner wished' (Bodelsen 1969: 7). Borck's window shopping further confirms the novel's central concern with conspicuous consumption as a motivating factor for Borck's crime in a 'competitive society', where individual success is measured by an individualist desire and ability to get ahead of the pack.

The lure of consumption is displayed emphatically in the opening pages of the novel. From the bank, Borck can see the cinema and the tall Christmas tree through the large windows, and in front of him

sat a Christmas pixie, a cornucopia between its widespread legs. A stream of golden coins issued from the cornucopia's mouth. As long as the bank was open a little electric motor inside the pixie's body kept up a whirring noise and made its head nod with satisfaction. The pixie had been in the bank longer than Borck. (Bodelsen 1969: 3)

While functioning as a symbol for the central location of the bank in the seasonal consumer hysteria, the carnivalesque pixie, ejaculating coins with a satisfied nod, links consumption with uncanny auto-erotic pleasure and also hints at Borck's dormant desires that will not only show to be dangerous but also, as the mechanical doll, be mired in artificiality. As the mechanically driven fountain at the heart of the consumer utopia of the Paris World Exposition cannot quench the thirst of the dying wood nymph, in Hans Christian Andersen's tale 'The Wood Nymph' a hundred years before, the lurking doom of conspicuous consumption is materialized in the repetitive mechanical movements that drive the never-to-be-satisfied pixie and, by association, Borck's repetitive life in the bank from where he can stare longingly at the dream-factory of the cinema.

The accumulation of figures for Borck's growing consumer desires (the travel brochures, the Volvo and the pixie) together with the theatrical display of the shopping centre where everything and everyone are playing roles (Borck and the fake Santa, 'the most hackneyed picture of a bank robber imaginable', [33]), suggests that *Think of a Number* is the story of an everyman who lacks excitement in his life and finds himself unable to compete in the consumer society unlike those higher up on the ladder in the hierarchy of the bank. He then simply seizes the moment to accumulate wealth by illicit means, perhaps to be able to finally buy the new GT-model Volvo, which spins slowly and hypnotically on its platform in the tropical light of the car dealer's display room (49).

This is, however, only part of the story, the conflict that is enacted on the level of the individual, the private. Borck's criminal conspicuous consumption has, however, wider consequences related to the welfare state he inhabits. He is in many ways the embodiment of 'the welfare man'. He has a good white-collar job and can look forward to a secure and pleasant future where most of his basic material needs will be met. The welfare state has released him from most duties of care as his father is in a retirement home (Mai 2013: 210). All is, then, seemingly well in the Danish welfare state, which has enabled his liberation from the constraints of the market and familial responsibilities; however, Borck also appears lonely and unable to connect with his co-workers and his dying father. Bodelsen's hyperrealist narrative style emphasizes the superficiality of his life by its minute registration, through Borck's eyes, of

spaces, things and awkward social interactions – a well-ordered life
to which Borck appears as his own dispassionate observer.

Borck's turn to crime can be explained as a reaction to the unrealized dreams of a prosperous welfare society, which has not, in
his mind, provided him with the happiness he was promised from
childhood. At home when Borck lays down under his 'sunbed' – a
further reference to the world of artifice he inhabits – he is again
haunted by the word 'change', now directly associated with the letter of demands and in particular the bank robber's childish hand-
written letters: 'he wondered why the mere thought of them caused
him to feel something that bore a striking resemblance to happiness'
(Bodelsen 1969: 7–8). Later the association of his desire for change
to the promises of childhood gets clearer: 'a transformation which
throughout his childhood had seemed certain and just around the
corner, but which later had moved farther and farther beyond his
reach. Change. The word had a magic ring as he repeated it to
himself' (49).

According to Anne-Marie Mai, we can see this desire for change
and what drives Borck to crime as rooted in what the novel suggests about the welfare state's crisis of affluence: 'The inter-personal
relations as shaped by the material progress and dissolving family
ties inherent to the welfare state have to Borck become so weak
and indeterminate that selfishness easily trumps the ethics of the
welfare society' (Mai 2013: 211). Therefore, if he has not found
emancipation within the framework of the welfare state, his desire
for change is produced by the growing expectations to the progress
of the welfare state on a societal level where 'good times' should
always 'get better' – a critique similar in kind to what the Swedish
Prime Minister Tage Erlander in 1956 called 'the discontent of rising expectations' (quoted in Tapper 2014: 63).

It becomes clear that his 'self-serving' actions are suggesting two
potential existential outcomes of the 'the welfare man' as consumer,
as laid out in Sørensen's 'The Grocer', leading either to emancipation or death. Through his crime, he will be released from his life
of conformity, but he will also be doomed to living an unfree life.
While he does not eventually die from his self-serving acts, he is
nevertheless doomed far harsher than having to be endlessly on the
run from the authorities and the bank robber. While Popinga in
Simenon's novel spirals into chaos as he murders and revels in his

ability to elude the police before he is finally captured, *Think of a Number* does not end with Borck's capture – he eventually kills a Danish policeman and the bank robber gets hold of the incriminating evidence that he will only use if necessary – neither does it end with his emancipation.

Even if he in the end escapes with his life and his basic freedom intact by accepting the companionship of his threatening shadow under the burning Mediterranean sun (a reference, I believe, to Hans Christian Andersen's tale 'The Shadow'), very little has actually changed for Borck. He still works in the bank and is alone apart from the short yearly holiday he can spend in the house he managed to buy with his loot. By the end of the novel, Borck lives a life between his bank business, a 'suntanned girl in a white terry-cloth sunsuit' and a 'colossal Mediterranean sun' exactly as predetermined in the 'sinful mess' he found on the table in the bank at the beginning of the novel between bank forms and travel brochures (Bodelsen 1969: 4). He has not been able 'to tidy up the mess' of his own life and desires, which have become a mere copy of these accidentally conflated discursive worlds and experiences, just as he himself and the fake Santa have become a 'trivial' fiction, a cliché of a bank robber.

Think of a Number is a crime novel about one individual's inability to adjust his personal desires to the needs of the collective. His unethical self-serving actions, his conspicuous consumption signify his inability to maintain meaningful social relationships that, due to the welfare state's 'liberation' of the individual from social bonds, demand ethical choices that transcend the individual. Borck is in many ways still a child of the welfare state, as he hides the money in his school lunch box; a child who still has to grow into a welfare citizen, who is able to differentiate between the ephemeral dream world of advertisements and what makes for real happiness or an authentic life.

Such a representation of inauthentic life and the difficulty of adjusting to the demands of the modern welfare state could sensibly be the province of mainstream fiction or the then-fashionable style of neo-realist prose. Apart from possibly reaching a wider audience through the popular genre of crime fiction, Bodelsen found particular potential in the genre for negotiating the conflict between individual desires and society. In an article in the newspaper *Politiken* from 1971, Bodelsen characterized the critical potential of the thriller genre:

> According to me, the best thrillers are always political in their critique of a society promoting psychological, moral and social egocentrism. Potentially they are romances because they depict indirectly the longing for a collective ... The thriller, the novel of anxiety, is a novel about the need for a collective and love. (quoted in Hedegaard et al. 1981: 10)

However, Bodelsen's crime novel is not moralizing as such, neither is it offering an alternative 'elsewhere' to the conformist and selfish life around Nærum Butikstorv. His is a report from an age characterized by accelerated consumption and, what the Swedish economist Staffan Burenstam Linder in 1969 diagnosed as, 'the decadence of progress', with an empathetic portrait of 'the harried welfare man', who has become its victim. The title of Bodelsen's newspaper article cited above, 'It could have been me – it is me', further extends the portrait of Borck to a more universal experience of life in the welfare state. Burenstam Linder's harried welfare man grew up in a society where economic progress promised a new Arcadia but resulted in the opposite, a society where the instant gratification of consumer desires and a primary focus on material well-being had led to a hectic life wherein the scarcity of time deprived consumption of its potential value for material and spiritual welfare (Burenstam Linder 1969: 10). Good, or 'reasonable' consumption, takes time, according to Burenstam Linder, and the accumulation of wealth, the affluent welfare state, has produced a scarcity of time wholly taken over by the accumulation of material goods.

Bodelsen related, with some degree of sympathy, the individual conflicts of the harried welfare man to a larger social reality, marked by the welfare state's erosion of traditional collective bonds and an accelerating culture of selfish consumption, without posing an alternative elsewhere, neither in the form of a false nostalgia for a long-lost past nor in the shape of a new socialist utopia. In 1968, Sjöwall and Wahlöö had already begun writing their series of police procedurals whose critique of the liberal-capitalist consumer society and the failures of the welfare state were to become far more radical and activist in their depiction of an everyman police detective's growing political and social awareness and utopian alternatives embodied in vigilante bank robbers and political assassins. However, as the next chapters will demonstrate, the police procedurals of Sjöwall and Wahlöö and Gunnar Staalesen's Norwegian hardboiled detective novels can also be read as exhibiting a deep-felt longing for authentic and trusting relationships in what are presented as alienating, violent and corrupt welfare societies.

Bodelsen's welfare crime novel is in comparison subtle in its critique of society and playful in its use of a 'trivial' genre to portray the conflicts of 'trivial' detectives and criminals. In his own play of cat-and-mouse with his contemporary Marxist critics, who almost unanimously criticized the novel for merely reproducing a bourgeois ideology (Pittelkow 1971) and itself falling prey to a conformist commodity aesthetic (Nicolajsen 1977) through its use of a mass-market genre, Bodelsen performed his self-conscious choice of genre, which is as much a part of the welfare consumer society as other luxury goods, by signing copies of his bestseller crime novel in the bank in Nærum at the same table where Borck struggled to clear up the 'sinful mess' of bank forms and travel brochures.

2

Welfare crime: Sjöwall and Wahlöö's *Novel of a Crime*

With Maj Sjöwall and Per Wahlöö's ten-volume Martin Beck series (1965–75), collectively known as *Novel of a Crime* ('Roman om ett brott'), Scandinavian crime fiction was to add an emphasis on social realism and critique, gloomy Nordic locations and the trademark morose detective to the various subgenres of crime fiction. In the 1960s, Sjöwall and Wahlöö had translated several of Ed McBain's 87th-precinct novels, and found in his pioneering police procedurals a formula wherein police officers' private lives and personal struggles can be mirrored in the larger sociopolitical landscape of Sweden's people's home. From their Marxist–Leninist perspective the authors explicitly aimed to use their crime novels as a means to analyse the Swedish welfare state, to relate crime to its political and ideological doctrines and to reveal its perceived fascist nature. The novels' subtitle, *Novel of a Crime*, was, then, as much an indicator of the genre as it was a programmatic statement criticizing the 'criminal' subservience of the welfare state to capitalism, and referred to 'crime as an act of social frustration in a repressive society' (Tapper 2014: 82).

From *Roseanna* (1965, *Roseanna*, 1967) to *Terroristerna* (1975, *The Terrorists*, 1976), Sjöwall and Wahlöö's crime novels follow Martin Beck and his homicide squad from the sex murder of an American tourist to the murder of the prime minister in a Swedish police state, anticipating the murder of Prime Minister Olof Palme by a decade. In their investigations, Beck and his team are constantly faced with an impenetrable police bureaucracy, a metonymy for a brutal society that gradually overshadows the idyllic Swedish welfare state.

In 1960s Sweden, Sjöwall and Wahlöö were far from alone in using literature as a vehicle for social critique. This was a decade of growing political awareness, where authors used their novels, poems, journalism and documentary fiction for political activism. They dealt with international topics such as the Vietnam War, the apartheid system in South Africa, as well as local Swedish issues such as social justice for miners, juvenile delinquency and rehabilitation, sensationalist journalism, the state-owned alcohol monopoly, Western welfare and progress based on third-world exploitation and worker's rights and conditions (Wright 1996: 402–8). Several of these topics also appear in *Novel of a Crime*.

The crime series was an attempt at dealing with serious social and political issues in a popular, mass-market genre. The authors' ambition was to reach as wide an audience as possible with their increasingly more explicit social criticism and political agitation. Rather than providing readers with the comforting conclusion that Beck and his colleagues will restore faith in the just and harmonious society by catching the criminals, they paint an acidic picture of a fallen welfare state in the grips of class warfare, police brutality and festering criminality that will only deteriorate Swedish society further as the series progresses. As the Norrmalms Square drama suggested, the petty criminals might eventually be caught, but those responsible for the systemic violence that produce criminal responses in society are rarely put to justice.

The activist agenda disguised as genre fiction was a conscious choice, according to an interview with the authors published in the Danish newspaper *Information* in 1974:

> In 1963, we consciously decided to write books directed at crime fiction readers, and our intention was to, in the first three titles, describe the crimes and solutions in a pretty much apolitical way. From the start we planned to make the mask fall in the fourth or fifth novel. (quoted in Tapper 2014: 84)

Throughout the series their documentary mode is enhanced by basing several of the fictional crimes on crimes known from the press, the use of real locations and references to contemporary events.

The authors' background in journalism (as so many of their successors) is also detectable in their language, which is characterized by 'short sentences packed with causative verbs' and the typographic rendition of transcriptions of interviews and lists, 'authenticity effects' that further add to the reader's sense of reading a piece of crime journalism (Tapper 2014: 84). This blending of genres, fact and fiction was to become a hallmark of Scandinavian crime fiction in the new millennium, often characterized as entertainingly melodramatic yet with a dominant social-realist edge. Sjöwall and Wahlöö's critique of the systemic violence of the capitalist welfare state, its covert promotion of capitalism, consumption and individualism, while pretending to further social equality and justice, is rendered partly through the police procedural's other 'authenticity effects': the team of investigators represents a recognizable microcosm of social types with professional as well as personal lives; the investigative work is rendered as simulating 'real' police work in a recognizable and minutely described geographic and social environment and the procedural's association with the period's fashion for drama-documentary genres.

Sjöwall and Wahlöö's international breakthrough came with *Den skrattande polisen* (1968, *The Laughing Policeman*, 1970), the fourth instalment in the *Novel of a Crime*. The novel centres on the investigation of a horrific mass murder in a Leyland double-decker bus in Stockholm, one of the victims being a younger colleague of Martin Beck and his team of investigators, Åke Stenström. It turns out that he was murdered along with a suspect he was shadowing while conducting an independent investigation into a sixteen-year-old murder of a Portuguese woman.

An upper-middle-class migrant to Sweden with strict Catholic morals and assimilated Swedish virtues, Teresa Camarão had, according to her file, 'tumbled down the social ladder' (Sjöwall and Wahlöö 2002: 166) and ended up a 'whore' and a 'nymphomaniac' (162) – a sexually deviant woman portrayed as a conspicuous consumer of men and a victim of their consumption rolled into one misogynist whole. The sexually deviant woman as the victim of sex crimes was also central to the first novel in the series, *Roseanna*, where another foreign 'promiscuous' woman, an American librarian, became the victim of a sexually repressed serial offender and avid consumer of American movies. Sexual deviance and social regress are, however, only a few of the symptoms treated in the authors' 'forensic' investigation of a welfare consumer society that 'creaked at the joints' (182) and intensified the 'dull pain in [Beck's] stomach' (183).

The Laughing Policeman is in many ways a typical police novel. For most of its duration nothing really happens; clues are hard to come by, there are several false leads and the investigation stalls repeatedly leaving ample opportunity for the narrator to explore the diverse personalities of the investigators, to let them reflect on the case itself and, importantly, on pressing sociocultural and political issues such as the urban renewal of Stockholm:

> Inside the grounds of Sabbatsberg Hospital work was going on with the extensive rebuilding; the old buildings were to be torn down and new ones were already shooting up. At present they were blasting away the high rocks toward Dalagatan. As the noise of the explosion was still echoing between the house-walls, Gunvald Larsson said, 'Why don't they blow the whole of Stockholm to bits in one go instead of doing it piecemeal? They ought to do what Ronald Reagan or whatever-his-name-is said about Vietnam: Asphalt it and paint on yellow stripes and make parking lots of the goddam thing. It could hardly be worse than when the town planners get their way.' (Sjöwall and Wahlöö 2002: 70–1)

Urban renewal and the social geography of the welfare state is a recurring, gradually more explicit motif in the *Novel of a Crime*. The cultural violence committed by the urban planners in the name of the welfare state is compared to that of American neo-colonialist exploits in Vietnam, a parallel that adds to Sjöwall and Wahlöö's depiction of Sweden as a repressive, militarized and capitalist state, a society that has sacrificed traditional social virtues for progress and materialism.

In *Polis, polis, potatismos!* (1970, *Murder at the Savoy*, 1971), the rise in crime is directly linked to a 'loss of culture' in the wake of urban renewal. Despite the fact that unemployment has been eradicated, according to the novel's narrator, 'all varieties of crime flourished better than ever in the fertile topsoil provided by the welfare state' (Sjöwall and Wahlöö 2007: 88). The politicians and 'the experts who had the delicate task of trying to make the society function smoothly' appear puzzled by the inability of the welfare state to stem the rise in crime in Stockholm. However, as the narrator explains, '[b]ehind its spectacular topographical facade and under its polished, semi-fashionable surface, Stockholm had become an asphalt jungle, where drug addiction and sexual perversion ran more rampant than ever' (88). In the 'mean streets' behind the facade of the welfare state a new proletariat had been created to which 'fallen women' such as Teresa belonged as well as the elderly, who are unable to make ends meet in a society and a city with the 'highest costs of living in the world' (88). The narrator refers to 'the latest surveys' which showed that 'many pensioners had to live on dog and cat food'. While the political rhetoric here resembles that of populist right-wing agitation in later decades (outside forces threatening national harmony with the elderly as primary victims), the portrait of a Stockholm in social, cultural and moral decay, with its politicians and planners oblivious to reality, owes as much to genre conventions as to perceived contemporary social conditions.

In *Murder at the Savoy*, the narratorial voice filters into Kollberg's impressions of social and topographical change, as he visits the part of the city where he grew up of which 'not much was left':

> With the approval of the city planners, the steam shovels of property speculators and the bulldozers of the traffic 'experts' had devastated most of the respectable old settlement. By now the few sanctuaries of culture that remained were pitiful to look at. The city's character, atmosphere and style of life had disappeared, or rather, changed, and it wasn't easy to do anything about it. (Sjöwall and Wahlöö 2007: 89)

There is, as in the earlier quoted passage about the disappearance of small bakeries (Chapter 1), a marked nostalgia in these novels for an 'elsewhere' belonging to a selective version of the past – a 'false nostalgia' for 'respectable old settlements' and 'sanctuaries of culture' now threatened by the capitalist bulldozers, which reveals a strand of anti-modern cultural critique within the authors' socialist agitation. Later in the series, this critique of civilization takes the shape of an explicit eco-socialist critique of the capitalist welfare state. One could perhaps understand the wider appeal of the *Novel of a Crime* series as rooted in its ambivalent expression of socialist revolutionary rhetoric, ambiguous sexual politics and articulated national and cultural conservatism.

The Vietnam War, and particularly the police's brutal handling of demonstrators outside the American embassy, is also a recurring topic, as is the more local issue of the nationalization of the Swedish police force in 1965 (Søholm 1976: 128–45). Very much a hallmark of the extreme Left of the time, an expressed anti-Americanism that saw America as the embodiment of asocial capitalism, neocolonialism and conspicuous consumption, influences the investigators' discussion of the psychology of mass murder in *The Laughing Policeman*. The discussion refers to a text book annotated by Stenström, which will later prove to hold the key to unveiling the mysterious identity of the mass-murderer:

> 'Mass murders seem to be an American speciality', Gunvald Larsson said. 'Yes', Melander agreed. 'And the compendium [the text book] gives some plausible theories as to why it is so.' 'The glorification of violence', said Kollberg. 'The career-centred society. The sale of firearms by mail order. The ruthless war in Vietnam.' (Sjöwall and Wahlöö 2002: 94)

Even if, as it will turn out, the mass murder in the bus has no direct link to global capitalism and American imperialism – the association of mass murder with such Leftist, Cold War discourses about a violent, individualist and consumerist America brings home the point of the novel's outspoken Leninist authors: that Sweden's people's home has become an uncanny, *unheimlich*, American-style parking lot, a society given over to senseless violence and citizens pursuing their own antisocial desires as irresponsible consumers – committing, in fact, what in the novel is referred to as 'welfare-state crimes' ('välfärdsbrott') (Sjöwall and Wahlöö 2015: 183).

In the novel, Kollberg defines a welfare-state crime as intimately tied to conspicuous consumption. He relates a previous case of a man who had murdered his wife: 'Dreary story. Typical welfare-state crime. A lonely man with a status-poisoned wife who kept nagging at him because he didn't earn enough. Because they couldn't afford a motorboat and a summer cottage and a car as swell as the neighbours' (Sjöwall and Wahlöö 2002: 138). Clearly sympathies are with the poor man Birgersson with the 'status-poisoned wife'. Birgersson holds one of the keys to solving the crime not because of what he and his crime exemplifies, but because he has accumulated expert knowledge of car brands while walking the streets as an escape from his nagging wife. Ironically, he has learned to read the ciphers of the modern consumer society, while hiding from his wife's consumer demands. Therefore, Birgersson is able to tell Kollberg that with his help Stenström had discovered that the getaway car witnesses had seen in connection with Teresa's murder was a different brand than the one the first abandoned investigation had believed it to be.

Throughout the novel, the worst crime imaginable is not the mass murder itself – this is merely a horrific symptom of a systemic social ill. The most despicable criminal, according to Beck's colleagues, is one who commits a crime to preserve or increase social status as this is deemed to have a particular subversive effect on the cohesion of society. Thinking back on the case towards the novel's end, Larsson tells Rönn something he has never told anyone before. He reveals that he generally sympathizes with the criminals they encounter: 'They're just a lot of scum who wish they'd never been born. It's not their fault that everything goes to hell and they don't understand why.' Those really guilty are the 'smug swine who think only of their money and their houses and their families and their so-called status' (215). It is such 'welfare criminals', of whom we 'only see their victims', who 'wreck the lives' of the people the police regularly encounter in their job.

However, this final verdict is complicated by the novel's unsympathetic portrait of Teresa and female sexuality more generally. The mass murderer killed Stenström and the man he was shadowing on the bus because they were both on his trail threatening to reveal that he was the one who killed Teresa sixteen years ago. Teresa, who had migrated to Sweden and found a Portuguese husband, is described as combining 'strict Catholic upper class and strict Swedish bourgeoisie, with all the moral taboos inherent in each, to say nothing of the combined result' (165). Her social and moral fall is reported as resulting from her extramarital sexual encounter with a man who despite her repeated resistance at last 'simply lifted her out of the chair, carried her into the bedroom, undressed her and made love to her' (165). What to a modern reader appears to be a case of rape, is in the narrative presented as her sexual awakening: 'As far as is known, Teresa Camarão had never before shown herself naked to anybody, not even to women. Teresa Camarão had never had an orgasm. That night she had about twenty. Next morning the guy said "so long," and off he went' (165). It is a sexual 'awakening' that leaves her with an unquenchable desire for more. When he will have nothing to do with her, she leaves her home and departs into a life of depraved nymphomania that eventually becomes her livelihood in the 'underworld' of Swedish society. The murderer kills Teresa as she one night lets herself into his house and bed, threatening by her deviant desires to ruin his engagement to another (more Swedish) woman and his future career.

As Dawn Keetley has noted, the three women in the early volumes of the Beck series, who are punished for their promiscuity, are all foreigners (Roseanna is an American, Ari in *The Man Who Went Up in Smoke* is Hungarian and Teresa Portuguese). Through their foreignness and unruly sexuality they unsettle the Swedish society 'from beyond the boundaries of its rationalized constructs', thereby revealing, according to Keetley, 'an essentialism at odds with Sjöwall and Wahlöö's predominant social determinism' – 'a blind spot' of their 'trademark political critique' (Keetley 2012: 62). Tapper, who is also critical of Sjöwall and Wahlöö's reactionary views on gender and particularly the repeated focus on deviant female sexuality in the early novels, as well as being rightly critical of the general lack of critique of this generic and to some degree period-specific sexist undercurrent in the novels, notes the contrast between the deviant and conspicuous sexuality personified in Teresa and the police officers' (masculine) ability to reign in the promiscuity latent in their own wives. For instance, the always submissive wife of Kollberg, who poses naked for him following his instructions and says: 'You can do whatever you goddam like with me' (Sjöwall and Wahlöö 2002: 88). Stenström's widow Åsa Torell explains that she thought of herself as a nymphomaniac before she met him, but that they adjusted to each other and lived happily. Good female sexuality appears to be one tempered by masculine moderation and consumption, while bad female sexuality, portrayed as conspicuous consumption, will eventually lead to her social decline and death. In *The Laughing Policeman*, while we should not overlook the essentialism of the portrayal of foreign, unruly female bodies in Sjöwall and Wahlöö's early novels, this gendered dynamic is also presented as socially inevitable not simply because of a systemic male-chauvinist hegemony but as the result of the consumerist welfare-state crimes integral to a capitalist society, where men and women have equally suspended their moral obligations to society in their pursuit of individual gains and social status.

While Tapper and Keetley rightly point out Sjöwall and Wahlöö's sexist portrayal of the victimized and promiscuous 'femme fatale', revealing an important blind spot in early seventies' socialist discourse, where women's rights were not yet central to the revolutionary rhetoric of social justice, welfare-state crimes, as defined in this key novel, are also committed by police officers such as Stenström, whose death was the result of his own hunger for recognition and professional advancement – the reasons given for why he investigated the murder on his own. Martin Beck, although not driven by a desire for status or recognition, nearly kills himself and in a later novel decides to take matters into his own hands when he steps outside the community of the police team. Not only the 'scum' and 'dregs', victims and perpetrators, but also the 'good' police officers are victims of the 'career-centred society', the consumer society in which social status is achieved at the cost of others. Victims of crimes, the perpetrators and even police officers share the common predicament of being victimized by the systemic violence that upholds the consumerist welfare state – they are all consumers in the process of being consumed by the invisible forces of exploitation that reveal themselves in the effects of cultural, social and geographic change.

The virus of conspicuous consumption, aspirational materialism and resulting mores such as sexual deviance, violence and individualism, in other words, are threatening to weaken the 'reasonable consumption' that was supposed to uphold a healthy, egalitarian and communal welfare state. Mary Evans's suggestion that the paradoxical increase in anxieties about crime in a historically less crime-ridden society is a proxy for more general anxieties about the consumption demands and fantasies about the good life appears at first to be at the heart of the social scene depicted by Sjöwall and Wahlöö (Evans 2009: 16). However, in Sjöwall and Wahlöö's *Novel of a Crime* an anxiety about crime is not considered a mere 'proxy' for more systemic anxieties. Instead, the rise in crime and violence, despite the social and economic reforms of the welfare state, is the direct result of more general anxieties produced by the social and cultural changes associated with the affluent and consumer-oriented welfare state.

Christmas, it seems, is the time of year when notable Scandinavian crime novels from the late 1960s register that the affluent yet presumably egalitarian Scandinavian welfare societies are bursting at the seams. The art happening, the Santa Claus Army in Copenhagen in 1974, where fake Santas raided department stores and started giving out the merchandise as presents to surprised shoppers, exemplifies the centrality of the Santa figure in the period's negotiations of welfare and consumption. Anders Bodelsen's *Think of a Number*, which came out the same year as *The Laughing Policeman* in 1968, is a testimony to the centrality of this figure: the bank robber dressed up as a fake Santa. This novel focused, of course, on a 'welfare man' who became both a criminal, committing what Kollberg called a welfare-state crime, and a victim to the demands of the consumer society, wholly unable to transfer newly begotten wealth into a good life. One of Gunnar Staalesen's earliest attempts in the crime fiction genre was *Mannen som hatet julenisser* (1976, The man who hated Santas), the second instalment in his series about the police detectives Dumbo and Maskefjes, wherein a Christmas pixie and department store Santas are serially defaced and murdered.

The welfare state's inability to stem the tide of antisocial behaviour is in *The Laughing Policeman* best (or perhaps most humorously) expressed in the craze associated with Christmas in the affluent yet morally corrupt and distrustful consumer society. The lengthy, slapstick description of Christmas shopping that turns into a street fight between the police and members of the public in chapter 19 appears as an aside at a time when the police team led by Martin Beck is not getting anywhere with their investigation and 'the spate of useless tips' from what is referred to as 'The Great Detective the General Public' (Sjöwall and Wahlöö 2002: 78; 'den Store Detektiven Allmänheten'), 'had begun to dry up' (102). This is partly because the police are withholding information from the press and the public: 'The police had lied to the press and the public. If the press and the Great Detective the General Public were not given correct information, how could the police count on help?' (78); and partly because, although it was over a month to Christmas '[t]he consumer society and its harassed citizens had other things to think about ... the advertising orgy had begun and the buying hysteria spread as swiftly and ruthlessly as the Black Death along the festooned shopping streets' (102).

The Great Detective the General Public or 'Detectiven Allmänheten' was, according to Kärrholm, an important figure in the Swedish clue-puzzle tradition of the 1950s, where the productive collaboration between regular citizens and the police was a central motif (Kärrholm 2005: 69). The investigative practises of the golden-age detectives can be seen as related to more general social practises in the 1950s, where everyone was encouraged to become good detectives to ensure the safety of the state (64). Kärrholm offers the example of Astrid Lindgren's popular detective novels for young readers about the Master Detective Blomkvist (mästerdetektiven Blomkvist, a figure now well-known around the world through his namesake in Stieg Larsson's *Millennium* trilogy, in which the name is used derogatorily to belittle Michael Blomkvist), which led to a fashion for what was called 'blomkvisteri' (blomkvisting), where young people proved themselves as good citizens by assisting the police with crime investigations. More generally, we find frequent references to 'detektiven allmänheten' in the Swedish clue-puzzle of the 1950s, demonstrating both the crime novel and the welfare state's ideological predilection for cooperation. The everyman detectives common to the period and a mainstay in subsequent Scandinavian crime fiction, the young 'blomkvists' and 'the great detectives the general public' in the clue-puzzle of the golden age of the welfare state collaborated, driven by moral obligation and trained in rational deduction, to maintain the safety of what was considered by many to be the best and most modern society in the world. In this the detectives shared heroic status with the scientists, experts and urban planners, who became central to both the mental and physical design of the welfare state.

In *The Laughing Policeman* this collaboration and the moral obligations of the welfare state it represents has been suspended due both to a self-sufficient police system and the distractions of the consumer society, 'the buying hysteria' that spread as an 'epidemic', eating its way 'into houses and flats, poisoning and breaking down everything and everyone in its path':

> The gigantic legalized confidence trick claimed victims everywhere. The hospitals had a boom in cardiac infarctions, nervous breakdowns and burst stomach ulcers. The police stations downtown had frequent visits from the outriders of the great family festival, in the shape of Santa Clauses who were dragged blind drunk out of doorways and public urinals. (Sjöwall and Wahlöö 2002: 102)

The police busy themselves with drunken Santas, the 'sad foul-mouthed boozers', who are the embodiments of the 'great family festival', the consumer society itself. The citizens of this uncanny consumer society are harassed by the advertising orgy and buying hysteria, which is likened to the Black Death, and then by the police, who in their inability to stem the spread of the epidemic, resort to random violence with an old-age pensioner as collateral victim. The final observation by Melander, which can be read as a revolutionary premonition further explored in the following instalments of the series, claims that the consumer society and the representatives of the welfare state, the police, are in cahoots, and that it only takes a spark, or a drunken Santa, to ignite the violence of the masses representing all classes of society: 'It didn't look pretty and the police-haters were given grist for their mill. There's a latent hatred of police in all classes of society, Melander said. And it needs only an impulse to trigger it off' (102). The looming mass revolt against the police, and by proxy the rampant consumer society, reveals a complicated figure wherein the fake Santa, the side-kick to the welfare state, who brings gifts to the children and those less well off, has come to personify the 'legalized confidence trick' of the consumer society whereby welfare is eventually undone.

Sweden in the mid-1960s is 'a consumer society' that 'creaked at its joints', as it is elsewhere described, and the representatives or enforcers of the welfare state, the policemen, are no match for the zombie-like shoppers who are more akin to the dystopian welfare serfs described in Huntford's *The New Totalitarians* than the happy utopian welfare citizens of Childs's depression-era *The Swedish Way*. What is being consumed in this soon-to-be dystopian people's home, with its concrete cityscape and mass-produced consumer goods sold in the new supermarkets, is consumption itself, and it is already deteriorating the health of the citizens leading to 'a boom in cardiac infarctions, nervous breakdowns and burst stomach ulcers', not to mention the effect it has on the alcohol consumption of fake Santas. Alcohol consumption and burst stomach ulcers are, of course, reoccurring tropes of what Bo Lundin has named the Swedish 'ulcer school' of crime writing (Lundin 1981: 10). Beck's constant troubles with his stomach, later to be adopted by Henning Mankell for his police detective Kurt Wallander, includes the police force in 'the great confidence trick' that has been played on the 'great detectives the general public', and where the public collaborated

with the authorities to maintain the idyll of the golden age of the
welfare state, in Sjöwall and Wahlöö's police procedural of the late
sixties, the police and the general public are antagonized in more
or less comedic and accidental violent confrontations as victims of
a systemic violence perpetrated by the consumerist welfare society,
which as an epidemic disease infiltrates and spreads between their
bodies and minds. Consumption in the modern welfare state, in
the festooned shopping streets of the new urban environment, as
depicted in the carnivalesque scenes of *The Laughing Policeman*,
spreads social distrust which has led to a sick and violent society
that has wholly abandoned any moral sentiments as figured in reasonable consumption, 'blomkvisteri' and 'detektiven allmänheten'.

Contrary to most of their predecessors in the Scandinavian
crime novel, Sjöwall and Wahlöö's police officers are not described
as mere types. Though descriptions of Christmas shopping, social
scenes and secondary characters tend toward caricature, one of the
novelties of the *Novel of a Crime* was that readers could follow
the police officers as developed literary characters over an expanse
of time, allowing readers to develop sympathies with them despite
their flaws. While the late modern welfare society they inhabit and
represent gradually but surely deteriorates into a full-blown dystopia of concrete cityscapes, zombie-like consumers and political
terrorism, it is through the series' overarching portrait of Beck, in
the mode of a classic 'Bildungsroman' (novel of education), and his
'journey' from a stale bourgeois family life through a violent, urban
Stockholm to a new home with a more developed social awareness
that the series may be seen to offer a renewed (utopian or sentimental) vision for a social state to replace the consumerist Social–
Democratic welfare state.

The characters in the police collective develop throughout the
series and undergo both professional and personal crises. The
political or ideological work performed in the series relies heavily
on empathies developing between Beck and the practical-minded
socialist and mother figure, Rhea Nielsen, in the last three volumes,
as well as between Beck and the reader. The intended 'mask may
fall' mid-way through the series with the increasingly overt ideological social critique, as pronounced through various characters
and the omniscient narrator, but the novels' covert ideological work
as a work of literature pertains to its narrative use of sentimental
bonds that leads an apolitical police detective to enlightened social

awareness, reflecting a possible similar journey for readers, who might have started the series sitting comfortably in one of their 'million homes' and ended it, as Beck, reclining under a poster of Chairman Mao in a socialist commune.

Martin Beck is in the beginning of the series a typical monomaniac police detective who struggles in a loveless marriage with little interest in his colleagues and the world around him if not directly linked to the investigation at hand. In the eighth novel, *Det slutna rummet* (1972, *The Locked Room*, 1973), he realizes that the classic genre motif of the title, referring to a crime he is investigating, is as much his own 'locked room'. This personal crisis is initiated by Beck's near-death experience in the previous novel, *Den vedervärdige mannen från Säffle* (1971, *The Abominable Man*, 1972), where he was shot and severely wounded by 'the man on the roof' (later the title of Bo Widerberg's film adaptation) as he attempted singlehandedly to capture the sniper. The shooter was a former police officer seeking revenge for the inhuman treatment that led to the death of his wife by a ruthless and fascist policeman, 'the abominable man' of the title, while in his custody.

In *The Locked Room*, Beck, now forty-nine and recently divorced, has been made chief inspector and head of the National Homicide Squad. The novel begins with his return to the squad where, to his delight, he has been left out of the special unit to combat bank robberies led by the comical Bulldozer Olsson. He has, then, also been left out of his usual police collective and is instead given a curious and poorly investigated case of a man who was shot dead in his own flat, which was found locked from the inside with no trace of a gun at the crime scene.

Beck's usual stomach problem is now supplemented with an increasing feeling of loneliness. He was 'on his way to becoming a recluse who had no desire for others' company or any real will to break out of his vacuum. Was he turning into a serviceable robot, enclosed, as it were, under a casserole cover – a dome of invisible glass?' (Sjöwall and Wahlöö 2011a: 156).

However, as Beck becomes aware of his own isolation he also undergoes a social awakening that suggests he is not alone in finding himself as an automaton in a 'locked room':

Something was fundamentally wrong with his existence, something he wasn't prepared to accept as equably as he had before.

Observing people all around him, he gained the impression that many of them were in the same predicament he was, though they either didn't realize it or wouldn't admit it to themselves. (Sjöwall and Wahlöö 2011a: 235)

Everyone, it seems, suffer from anxieties created by the capitalist welfare state: 'the so-called Welfare State abounds with sick, poor, and lonely people, living at best on dog food, who are left uncared for until they waste away and die in their rat-hole tenements' (25). In this Sjöwall and Wahlöö's critique of the Swedish welfare society can be seen to reflect both leftist and right-wing critiques of the dehumanizing state that turns its citizens into welfare serfs (Huntford) or 'one-dimensional men' (Marcuse 2002 [1964]).

The society that surrounds Beck is turning into a full-blown dystopia recording a 'rising tide of violence, to which the only answer was ever more numerous and still better armed police' (Sjöwall and Wahlöö 2011a: 58). The police force is overworked and unable to attract good policemen despite mass unemployment, and the security police spend all their energy on keeping records of communists rather than fascist groups with whom they collaborate. Since the nationalization of the police force in 1965, the root of most evils in *Novel of a Crime*, it has become a fascist and power-mongering institution illustrated by the plans for its new headquarters in Stockholm: 'From this ultramodern colossus in the heart of Stockholm the police would extend their tentacles in every direction and hold the dispirited citizens of Sweden in an iron grip' (142). Despite the totalitarian power of the police, crime is still rampant in the welfare state. The penal institutions and retirement homes are described as inhuman and dysfunctional. Beck's own mother has in the novel become the victim of the latter. Elderly citizens had been 'condemned to it by a so-called Welfare State that no longer wished to know about them. It was a cruel sentence, and the crime was being too old' (68). It is a society where

[b]ig-time criminals profit from everything – from poisoning nature and whole populations and then pretending to repair their ravages by inappropriate medicines; from purposely turning whole districts of cities into slums in order to pull them down and then rebuild others in their place. The new slums, of course, turn out to be far more deleterious to people's health than the

old ones had been. But above all they don't get caught. (Sjöwall and Wahlöö 2011a: 86)

It is no surprise that the Swedish welfare society is one where suicide rates are escalating, social inequality is growing and one where a special task within the 'welfare machine' was performed by a few anonymous men in a van to uphold and sanitize the facade of the welfare state: 'Their daily task was to remove suicides and other unattractive individuals who had departed this life to more suitable surroundings' (150).

While there is little hope for the welfare state, as seen through Sjöwall and Wahlöö's dystopian prism, Beck is given renewed hope that he can break out of his isolation and alienation when he meets Rhea Nielsen. Rhea is the landlord in the building where the dead man in the locked room, Svärd, used to live. She overwhelms Beck with her straightforwardness and informality. She sees her relationship with her tenants as one of a 'caretaker' of both material and social needs, in opposition to the usual landlords including her own father: 'landlords in this country', Rhea says, 'are the last things God created ... But the system encourages them to exploit people' (167). Her vision for her own communal home in the centre of Stockholm is one where 'people who live in the same building must feel they belong together and that it's their home' (174). She is running a parallel society with a poster of Mao above her bed – an ideal socialist 'people's home', and, as her namesake the Greek 'mother of gods' suggests, she 'carries the future within her' and her own version of urban and social renewal (Tapper 2014: 97). Hers is a people's home based on mutual trust, assistance and solidarity, where there is room for difference ('Everyone's got his own little ways, naturally. But that's just fun' [Sjöwall and Wahlöö 2011a: 169]), where worn out TV sets are replaced by ones borrowed from friends and spaghetti bolognese is made from scratch to share. It is, in many ways, epitomizing all the virtues envisioned for Albin Hansson's folkhem and its 'reasonable consumers'. While Rhea may be seen as a Maoist superwoman in Sjöwall and Wahlöö's critique of the Social Democratic 'so-called welfare state', she is endowed with traditional values of caretaking and moderation that were central to what has, particularly from the political right, derogatorily been referred to as 'the nanny-state'; she is similar in kind to Sørensen's grocer, though less authoritarian, who was also under threat from the emerging self-servicing consumer society. It is not a coincidence that Rhea is depicted as a landlord, who, unable to finance the care of the building's facade, instead attends to the care of the inside, its inhabitants – in stark contrast to Sjöwall and Wahlöö's critique of the fake shining facades of the sanitized urban environment of the modern welfare state.

Apart from embodying a socialist future society, Rhea is an ideal and avid reader of crime fiction as her affection for jigsaw puzzles indicates. She helps Beck solve his clue-puzzle by first showing him an article about locked-room mysteries and then demonstrating, by accident, how a door can be locked from the inside when slammed too hard from the outside. Apart from giving Beck the solution to his clue-puzzle, Rhea has brought him out of his own locked room, as he falls in love with her and spends more time in her socialist utopia: 'At the same time he was breaking into Svärd's locked room he was also breaking out of his own' (277).

The locked-room mystery is central to the novel's sentimental narrative about Beck's character development, leading him to personal, sexual and political awakening through Rhea's sensual and practical Maoist Gaia character. The new home he finds with her is based on 'old-fashioned' social and moral obligations of cooperation and trust. While narrated in an outdated generic formula, Rhea, who provides the solution to the clue-puzzle, personifies a new version of 'detektiven allmänheten', the moral citizen who contributes to the good people's home by assisting the police in solving crime riddles.

This nostalgic or parodic citation and renewal of a largely defunct subgenre is weaved into the novel's two other plot lines, which both deal with bank robberies. These function primarily to provide the novel's social commentary. While the locked-room mystery can be seen as a parody of the clue-puzzle mystery with a sentimental narrative about Beck's sexual and social awakening, the bank robberies are part socialist sentimentalism and part police farce.

The first chapter of the novel follows Monita as she sets out to rob one of Stockholm's largest banks on Hornsgatan. Sjöwall and Wahlöö go to great pains to explain why she ended up a bank robber. She is a divorced single mother, unemployed with no education. Her unfaithful husband does not pay child support and her financial situation had deteriorated. She became steadily more depressed and lost confidence in the system: 'She'd begun to suspect that something more than higher wages and pleasanter working conditions would be needed before there would be much sense in participating in the industrial-capitalist system' (194).

The novel paints a picture of a victim of male exploitation, who can find no comfort in the social system, leading her to become a hardened, lonely, yet awakened socialist activist. Her home in a big suburban housing estate makes it impossible for her to break out of her isolation where 'everyone seemed to be erecting barriers around his own privacy … She felt like a prisoner in her own home', a victim to a careless society given material shape in the new housing estates of the million-homes programme (195). Monita's wishes for her daughter's future are formulated as a counter discourse to the 'welfare state crimes' as formulated already in *The Laughing Policeman*:

> She wanted her child to grow up in a warm, secure, humane environment – one where the rat race after power, money, and social status did not make everyone into an enemy, and where the words 'buy' and 'own' weren't regarded as synonymous with happiness. She wanted to give her child a chance to develop her individuality and not be shaped to fit into one of the pigeonholes society had prepared for her. (Sjöwall and Wahlöö 2002: 196)

Approximating a socialist libertarianism with a strong emphasis on anti-consumerism and individual freedom, Monita's image of Sweden in the negative is one of a dehumanized, threatening, consumerist and capitalist society that takes away the entire personality of its citizens. Monita's realization, formed by her sense of disempowerment and disillusionment with a society that pretends to be socially just, is that her hopes cannot be realized as long as she lived in Sweden: 'she had begun to hate this society, which boasted of a prosperity actually reserved for a small privileged minority while the great majority's only privilege was to keep moving on the treadmill that turned the machinery' (197). It is clear that the novel's sympathies lie with Monita. While she becomes a bank robber and a murderer, she is presented as a victim of the welfare state, and eventually she escapes to Yugoslavia where she can begin a new life with her daughter. She is depicted as a righteous vigilante who takes matters into her own hands in a society that offers no prospects for those who refuse to participate in the competitive, consumerist

and conformist society. Zygmunt Bauman has described the oppressive and seductive late-modern consumer society, which is gradually
corroding the welfare state from within, as one from which there
is no escape. Criminality may be the only option for those who
do not own the means to take part in a society wholly given over
to conspicuous consumption – and they are the ones feeding the
welfare state's 'prison industry' (Bauman 1997: 35–45). Monita is
a similar victim of the consumer society, who turns to crime out
of sheer desperation, but in Sjöwall and Wahlöö's imagination her
crime is just, and unlike the reality Bauman describes towards the
end of the twentieth century, she is given a free pass to a communist
utopia. While Rhea and her communal home represent the realization of the utopian society of which Monita dreams, she represents
a symptomatic revolutionary and violent response to the fallen
welfare state. In this, Sjöwall and Wahlöö's novel can be seen as a
premonition of the Norrmalms Square drama, which would capti-
vate the public the following year. The criminal would also here be
invested with curious sympathies that led to the popular diagnosis
of a Stockholm Syndrome. The criminal became the victim, and
the state and its representatives in the police viewed as those to be
feared. Monita is also a figure for the politically motivated violence
and terrorism that swept through Europe in the 1970s, the Rote
Armee Fraktion in Germany, which had killed a police officer in
a bank robbery in 1971, the Danish communist terror organization Blekingegadebanden (The Blekinge Street Gang), which committed several bank robberies in the seventies in support of the
Popular Front for the Liberation of Palestine and the murder of the
Yugoslavian ambassador to Sweden in 1971 where the perpetrators
were later released as part of demands made by the hijackers of an
airplane in Sweden the following year.

In *The Locked Room* the case of the possible political motives
behind the bank robbery is discussed in a conversation between
Gunvald Larsson and a witness, the communist metal worker,
Sjögren. It centres on the topic whether bank robberies can be
condoned if politically motivated. Larsson says, '"So you think
it's right to break into banks? And regard the police as the natural enemy of the people?" "Something of that sort, yes"', Sjögren
replies. '"Though not quite that simple"' (Sjöwall and Wahlöö
2011a: 210). The novel seems to be suggesting through its (and
Martin Beck's) sympathies with Monita that the systemic violence

of the society necessarily triggers subjective violence in those who suffer the social consequences the most. However, at the same time, the novel offers a nostalgic vision for communal living and reasonable consumption in the caring figure of Rhea, which promises to reinstall the rationality and cooperative virtues of the people's home and to curb the rise in crime and violence produced by social and economic segregation.

In the final volume of *Novel of a Crime* the Monita figure finds its double in another young mother who is wrongfully accused of a bank robbery but takes the ultimate step to become a political terrorist when she shoots the Swedish prime minister thinly disguised in the novel as Olof Palme, a decade before he was murdered on a street in Stockholm.

When Sjöwall and Wahlöö published the final instalment of the series in 1975, *The Terrorists*, they again tapped into the public craze for 'armed robberies, which were spreading across the land like a plague' (Sjöwall and Wahlöö 2011b: 18). The presumed culprit now being tried in Stockholm city court on a charge of armed robbery against a branch of the state-owned bank, Kreditbanken, was 'an eighteen-year-old girl named Rebecka Lind'. She is a young single mother who lived contently on small means until the American father of her child was lured back to the United States and imprisoned as a Vietnam War draft dodger. Knowing very little about society and in need of money to travel to the United States, she acts on the naïve impulse that a bank 'owned by the people' is there to help people like herself undergoing hardship. She turns up at the bank to ask for a loan, but the bank cashier panics, partly due to the media obsession with bank robberies, and mistakes her for a robber.

Rebecka is portrayed as the embodiment of a new individual with counter-culture and eco-socialist traits. In the first trial against her, she is described by a witness as having

a lot of ideas of her own, especially when it came to vegetables and natural foods. She was aware that our present diet is objectionable, that most of the food sold in supermarkets is in one way or another poisoned ... She grew her own vegetables and was always prepared to gather what nature had to offer. That was why she always carried a gardening knife in her belt. (Sjöwall and Wahlöö 2011b: 38)

She is a young person who distrusts the authorities and the welfare system, who may appear unable to understand the society around her, but who is throughout the novel emphatically considered not only the real victim and an alien body of the capitalist welfare society, but also one who understands more than most in her naiveté and position as an incorruptible outsider. Her legal counsel maintains that she 'sees the corrupt rottenness of society more clearly than thousands of other young people. As she lacks political contacts and has little idea of what is involved in a mixed-economy government, her clarity of vision is even greater' (266). As the little boy in Hans Christian Andersen's tale 'The Emperor's New Clothes', her innocence gives her a clearer vision of the 'legalized confidence trick' committed by the politicians running the country, who are described by her spirited lawyer as 'criminals, who from a lust for power and financial gain have led their peoples into an abyss of egoism, self-indulgence and a view of life based entirely on materialism and ruthlessness towards their fellow human beings' (266).

Rebecka's other-worldly predispositions, her refusal to accept the society in which she lives and her obliviousness to how it functions (as illustrated by her lack of knowledge of who the prime minister is and her naïve belief that the bank would give someone like her money), lead Rhea and Beck, who have from the very beginning showed sympathy for her situation, to empathize with her. When Beck eventually finds her held by the police following her shooting of the prime minister, he shows, curiously, no sympathy with the now dead prime minister, recalling instead what Kollberg had said about the little revolver Rebecka had used: 'you could hit a cabbage with it at a few inches' range, providing that it held absolutely still. Martin Beck looked down at the dead Prime Minister and at his shattered forehead and thought that was roughly what Rebecka had succeeded in doing' (241).

Where Monita was driven to her crime by an alienating society symbolized in the segregated and anonymous concrete tower blocks in which she lived as in 'a locked room' of her own, Rebecka's radicalization is partly linked to her eviction from her flat in south Stockholm:

> The building was old and run down, and now it was going to be demolished, to be replaced by a new block of flats from which the landlord could extract at least three times the rent after installing

all kinds of substandard but modern conveniences, and unnecessary decorative touches of poor quality but luxurious appearance. (Sjöwall and Wahlöö 2011b: 135)

The innocent young mothers in Sjöwall and Wahlöö's final volumes
are portrayed as the ultimate victims of a 'mixed-economy' welfare
state that has uprooted its citizens from their traditional communities and natural environment through an urban sanitation that
is figured as mere 'decoration' and 'luxury appearance' deepening
the social and economic differences in the welfare state. Monita's
dream of a society not dominated by competition and consumerism
is in the Rebecka figure radicalized into a dream of an eco-socialist
utopia where consumers have been turned into self-sustaining producers as a final negation of the welfare state's inability to rein in
conspicuous consumption.

Rebecka Lind, who symbolically links to the American victim
of sexual assault in the first novel, *Roseanna*, is perhaps the most
exaggerated and period-specific character in the Decalogue to con-
clude the most influential series of crime novels in Scandinavia that
has throughout been challenging the binaries between perpetrator
and victim, as also noticed by Tapper in his comprehensive investigation of the Swedish police procedural tradition: 'As in the novels
of Sjöwall and Wahlöö, the capitalist welfare state was the ultimate
perpetrator, while the convict was the victim of the class society and
its repressive mechanisms (conformism, discipline, consumerism)'
(Tapper 2014: 53).

Martin Beck has in this final volume become part of the social
Stockholm Syndrome as he clearly empathizes with Rebecka partly
under the influence of his lover Rhea. As Rebecka's name suggests, she is a surrogate child of this new couple, Rhea and Beck
(Søholm: 269). It is perhaps the series' strongest expression of
its revolutionary commitment that a surrogate child of the chief
inspector, the embodiment of innocence and a future (eco-)socialist
society, turns out to be the assassin of the Swedish prime minister.
Tapper suggests that Sjöwall and Wahlöö here tap into contemporary derogatory descriptions of Olof Palme as feminized. The new
perceptions and anxieties so dramatically and publicly figured in
the Norrmalms Square drama, were, therefore, both radicalized in
the subsequent and final instalments of *Novel of a Crime*, but were

also prepared in the many volumes that preceded the robbery in Kreditbanken.

The portrait of the single mothers as sentimental victims of an unsympathetic and morally corrupted welfare state is a figure that fits in with a more general critique of modernism and the welfare state and their relation to crime in the novels. The *locus criminis* is not only the bank but involves the greater people's home, its new welfare institutions, buildings, cityscapes and homes – all in one way or the other refracted through the lens of consumption. The grounding or location of criminality in the welfare state is noticeable in narratorial comments such as the already quoted: 'crime flourished better than ever in the fertile topsoil provided by the welfare state.'

Throughout the *Novel of a Crime* the urban environment is described and figured as representing a degenerate welfare state through its sociocultural and concrete architecture. As suggested by the Stockholm syndrome, in Sjöwall and Wahlöö's seminal Scandinavian police procedurals the criminals and murderers are considered the victims of society, of ingrained class structures, the state's covert subservience to capitalism and its promotion of an individualized, competitive consumer society (Hausladen 2000: 106). While in the first volumes Beck appears as a mere spectator to a society festering with violent crimes, he is finally released from his life of conformity and isolation by Rhea, who is on the one hand a mythological socialist figure and on the other representing the civil and moral virtues traditionally associated with the Swedish people's home. In employing the crime genre to portray a 'truer', more authentic vision of the Swedish welfare state, Sjöwall and Wahlöö eventually release Beck from his alienated existence into a more authentic or 'original' familial life in Rhea's communal people's home.

3

The hardboiled social worker: Gunnar Staalesen's Varg Veum

Gunnar Staalesen's Bergen-based private detective Varg Veum has appeared in a series of, so far, seventeen novels and two collections of stories from *Bukken til havresekken* (1977, The fox takes the goose) to *Ingen er så trygg i fare* (2014, No one is so safe in danger). Spanning thirty-seven years, the series chronicles a Norwegian society in the midst of dramatic social change. In *Begravde hunder biter ikke* (1993, Buried dogs don't bite), the journalist Ove Haugland sums up the period as: 'the Maoist 1970s, the right-wing wave of the 1980s that washed us all ashore with shattered limbs and broken necks in the 1990s' (Staalesen 1993: 190).

It has been claimed that Staalesen's detective novels, in contrast to Sjöwall and Wahlöö's Swedish procedurals, resist being explicitly political in their portrayal of life in the twilight of the Norwegian welfare state (Skei 2008: 115). Viewed mostly through Veum's melancholic hardboiled temperament, Bergen is rendered as an alluring and decadent microcosm of a wider society, where social dysfunctions, criminality and widespread misanthropy reflect a hostile urban environment, petroleum-infused consumerism and a society undergoing rapid modernization. As the novels, true to the genre convention, are focalized through 'the lone wolf' Veum, who is divorced with a son he struggles to relate to, his view of the external world is coloured by his own increasingly morose inner life, in the grip of loneliness with a bottle of aquavit within easy reach.

Despite this, to some extent, implausible relocation of the hard-boiled detective novel from Los Angeles to Bergen, Staalesen's series is thoroughly embedded in and makes references to the American tradition of Chandler, Dashiell Hammett and Ross Macdonald, as also pointed out by Staalesen himself (Forshaw 2012: 121–2), whose 'stubbornly democratic heroes of a post-heroic age' are 'righting wrongs in a fallen urban world'. Staalesen's adaptation of the genre to reflect a specific post-utopian period in Norway shares traits with the emergence of the American private eye novel in the 1920s and 1930s, which, according to Dennis Porter, 'depended on a particular historical, socio-economic and cultural conjuncture', which marked the end to 'old agrarian America'. Simpler times had given way to 'a new, fast evolving social and material environment characterized by monopoly capitalism, unprecedented wealth especially for the few, the struggle between capital and labour, heightened class conflict, and the progressive massification of everyday life' (Porter 2003: 95–6). In Staalesen's late-modern Norwegian detective novels a similar historical dynamic makes up the fictional world of Bergen where greedy capitalists, welfare dystopian concrete blocks and the oil boom violate not only society's most vulnerable and the natural environment but also the detective's sense of traditional values rooted in a diffuse imagined past of childhood memories, war-time solidarity and a premodern idyll.

The hardboiled subgenre became popular with the readers in Scandinavia already in the post-War years. Chandler's first novel *The Big Sleep* (1939) was published in Danish in 1942, in Swedish in 1947 and in Norwegian in 1954. However, the lack of Scandinavian epigones before Staalesen's renewal of the genre may relate to the fact that its melancholic world view and individualist lone-wolf detective still appeared too exotic in the optimistic and collectivist Scandinavian welfare societies of the fifties and sixties. However, as the welfare state with its modernized cityscapes began to lose its aura, as the shadows encroached upon its utopian ideals towards the end of the sixties and in the seventies, the sentiments of the private eye novel as well as its formal characteristics became easier to adjust to a particular perspective on Scandinavian social reality. Considering the plausibility of a hardboiled Norwegian detective novel, Staalesen has pointed out that: '[i]t helped that the oil industry had transformed Norway into such a rich country, although the immense wealth brought many problems. Our life-style became much more like that of the west coast of the USA' (Interview: Gunnar Staalesen, author 2010).

While the social-realist police procedural has proven to be the predominating subgenre in Scandinavian crime fiction (Nestingen and Arvas 2011: 5), Staalesen's 'domestication' of the detective novel was followed in Denmark by Dan Turéll's 'murder series' (1981–90) and, although technically police procedurals, Jo Nesbø's series featuring the alcoholic police detective Harry Hole, shares many traits with both Staalesen's Veum and his American prede-cessors. Nesbø's hardboiled police novels and dominant feminist hardboiled writers such as Liza Marklund, Anne Holt and Susanne Staun, who began to appear in the 1990s, not to mention the tough TV detectives Sarah Lund and Saga Norén in the 2000s, suggest that the subgenre continues to be a relevant format in which to reflect a Scandinavian noir mood.

The Nordic social worker detective

In order to make the essentially individualist private detective more plausible within a Norwegian context, Chandler's prescription for a lone, proud man of honour, who will go down these mean streets to make the world a bit safer, is replaced by a cynical and tough-talking former social worker. While Veum the social worker was deemed unfit to represent the welfare state when he resorted to physical violence, he decided to 'privatize' his social services to continue to protect, on his own terms, the victims of, what the defence attorney Paulus Smith in *Din, til døden* (1979, *Yours Until Death*, 2010) describes as, 'a class system which turns out winners and losers, even in our welfare state', where 'the losers always end up in court' and the 'winners paper over their crimes with money' (Staalesen 2010: 181).

As a private detective positioned outside the collective and the regular justice system, from where he is able to establish a social trust denied the police (Staalesen 2008a: 113), Veum's social worker detective figure is a reflection of a welfare state unable to provide justice for the victims of an increasingly distrustful, competitive and consumerist society. Paradoxically, as an American-style private eye, he is also himself frequently part of the problem, a representative of the growing individualism that is corroding society from within. He is a hard-headed and at times uncaring truth-seeker, who, in his own words, behaved as 'a swarm of locusts' who 'consumed everything [he] found ... left lives picked clean and nights emptied of their secrets behind [him]' (Staalesen 2010: 242). As a counter-weight to this paradoxical position, Veum is presented with the 'golden heart' of an empathetic social worker, and has been equipped with a moral codex that bids him to turn down lucrative cases of infidelity and, in the early novels, to resist a proposed merger with a large Oslo-based detective agency, which has no such scruples. Varg Veum is a complex literary figure whose internal moral struggles reflect wider social and political conflicts in his contemporary Norway.

The period leading up to the publication of Staalesen's first instalment in the Veum series in 1977 was dominated by optimism and progress: low unemployment, generous tax policies, wage increases, a veritable boom in consumption and production and an expanding public sector that gave rise to, what has been called, the 'takeoff phase of the blue wave' in Norwegian politics, more austere times for many following deregulations and a deflation of the welfare state (Fagerberg et al. 1990: 73). Veum is witnessing the social effects of these harder times everywhere. His is 'the time of the wolf' ('ulvetider'), as also suggested by the detective's own name (varg is Norwegian for wolf), a period marked by unrest and insecurity, where time itself like the mythological Fenris wolf at Ragnarok runs through the streets devouring everything in its path. According to Veum in *I mørket er alle ulver grå* (1983, *At Night All Wolfs are Grey*, 1986):

> [The Wolf] belonged here in the streets that awaited us outside. They had made the wolf extinct in the forests and on the plains. Yet, it is hunting in the city, hunting on the asphalt covered city streets, on the glistening cobblestones and along gaping gutters – the wolf, the time. It was probably best to stay indoors. (Staalesen 2011: 16–17, my translation)

According to Staalesen, the symbolism of Varg Veum's name derives from its Old Norse association to the concept 'varg i veum (meaning the wolf in the sanctuary, an outlaw)' (Staalesen 1995: 178).

It is a fitting name for a detective who often takes the law into his own hands, a flâneur equally at home in the mean streets of Bergen and, as a long-distance runner, in the forests and on the marshlands. His name signals both Veum's local Nordicness as well as his inheritance from a family of hardboiled detectives who are, according to Staalesen, 'in nine out of ten cases lone wolfs' (Staalesen 1995: 178). Staalesen's transplantation of the American popular genre to Norwegian soil comes with a heavy dose of a Nordic mythological past, which both adds to the novels' quality as self-reflexive storytelling and, in their confrontation with late-modern urbanism, to a 'false nostalgia' for a time before the wolfs were let loose in the streets of Bergen.

While Sjöwall and Wahlöö employed the realist police procedural to interrogate an increasingly more inauthentic and dystopian society, Staalesen's approach is the opposite. His novels constantly point to their own status as genre fiction thereby insisting, according to Willy Dahl, 'that Veum as a realistic figure in the Bergen of the 1970s and 80s is unthinkable. He is a literary construction – unreal – yet placed in a reality the author wishes to say something about' (Dahl 1995: 65). According to Hans Skei, Staalesen's use of genre with a detective who has a past as a social worker in a new age and a new environment turned his novels almost, but only almost, into a parody, which allowed him to play consciously with and against the limits of the genre to create new meanings for his own purposes (Skei: 114). While employing and writing up against an American genre convention, Skei continues, 'Staalesen is so much a Norwegian, a democrat and egalitarian in his way of thinking that the American popular genre is so fundamentally changed that the parody has serious consequences' (115).

The particular consequences for both the genre and the society it seeks to frame have to do with what Staalesen, tongue-in-cheek, has called 'sosionomskolen' (the social worker school) within Norwegian crime fiction (Staalesen 1995). The detective is related to the social worker, according to Veum, as 'just another way of doing the same job' (Staalesen 2010: 61). However, to be a detective of moral standing in the welfare state means first of all to be a good social worker; in fact, he claims, '[p]rivate detectives can't ever be social workers' (60).

As such, Veum extends the characteristic of conventional first-person narratives of hardboiled detectives that have always portrayed, what Stephen Knight has called, a 'double man', split into two narrative voices: the ironic, insightful narrative voice and an aggressive dialogic voice (Scaggs 2009: 132). John Scaggs describes this as a split between an external tough-talking 'Private Eye', who hides the inner motivations of 'the Private "I"' (133). The hardboiled detective is, Scaggs maintains, always, in one sense or the other, a 'double agent' (133). On the one hand, Veum wears an impenetrable mask when confronting victims, perpetrators and authorities, on the other his inner dialogues reveal strong empathies and often sentimental ruminations about his private anxieties and his observations about a city and a society that have changed beyond recognition and salvation.

As a 'sosionom', Veum often gets embroiled in cases concerning broken families, with children as the main victims, and, according to Forshaw, the 'broader role of government in such cases' (Forshaw 2012: 122). While crimes in the Veum novels are mostly committed by corrupted individuals, criminality is related to a wider sociocultural and moral change in Norwegian society, which has taken place since the Second World War. Veum's is an uncertain time where a teenage gang preys on single mothers in an isolated Norwegian high-rise suburb (*Yours Until Death*), where children of affluent, dysfunctional families end up as prostitutes in Istedgade, 'the gutter of Copenhagen' (*Tornerose sov i hundre år*, 1980; Sleeping beauty fell asleep for a hundred years) and where a small child has disappeared decades ago in a secretive hippie-commune outside of Bergen (*Der hvor roser aldrig dør*, 2012; Where roses never die). From this select list it is clear that Staalesen's Veum novels portray the social dysfunctions of the post-War Norwegian family as a condition that transcends social classes, but is nevertheless mapped as a social epidemic that expresses itself in different ways as conceits particular to separate classes.

Dahl has written that Staalesen used the hardboiled detective novel to critique the physical and moral changes associated with the petroleum-infused welfare society even before sociologists started talking about the crumbling solidarity (Dahl 1993: 185). However, it is not impossible that Veum's pessimistic view of his contemporary Bergen and Norway has been influenced on the one hand by generic hardboiled traits, and on the other, already widely read and debated publications in Norway that challenged the general perceptions of the welfare state's superior social policies such as the anthology *Myten om velferdsstaten* (1970, The myth about the welfare state). The general view is that the expansive welfare state has created an 'invisible Norway' through partaking in a '*renovation* of the "normal" society', by making those who cannot live up to the demands of the modern society invisible through institutionalization (Lingås 1970: 14). The crisis in the Norwegian welfare state is in the anthology diagnosed by the medical sociologist Yngvar Løchen, whose attention-grabbing article 'Velferdsstatens krise' raised the question, why it is that the expansive and expensive welfare state seems to produce more health problems and social inequalities. According to Løchen, the reason is that the social policies of the welfare state have always benefitted and secured the 'normal and functional' while the marginalized and weak have been left behind (Løchen 1970: 208). The continuing and growing pressure on the social services is, according to Løchen, produced by a growth in internal migration from the provinces to the cities, the concomitant breakdown of local communities and the associated individual and mental consequences of living in an urbanized and postindustrial society.

Veum himself and the people he tries to save are embodiments of this social crisis of internal migration, which takes on symbolic meaning in the novels to signify a more widely shared temporal migration from an idyllic rural past into a modern welfare state where city planning as a social policy has broken down human solidarity, local environments and authentic lives. According to Dahl, there is in Staalesen's novels a connection between Veum's anxieties about an erased past, the material development of the welfare state and what has happened in the relations between people (Dahl 1995: 69). Nowhere is this diagnosis more pertinent than in *Kvinnen i kjøleskapet* (1980, The woman in the fridge). Veum returns to the Norwegian oil capital of Stavanger, where he once studied to become a social worker. It was inevitable that Staalesen should base one of his Veum novels in Stavanger with the oil industry's physical, social and moral impact central to the plot and to Veum's growing sense of dislocation and alienation from the present.

In his essay 'Den dialektiske detektiv' (the dialectic detective) published in 1976, a year before the appearance of the first Veum novel, Norwegian author Kjartan Fløgstad assessed the relevance of using the hardboiled crime genre to describe his contemporary Norway:

> Without exceptions, the best American crime novels take place in California on the West Coast of North-America. The centre for oil activities on the Norwegian continental shelf is Stavanger on Norway's West Coast. Stavanger and North-Jæren will, over the next few decades, become one of the most densely populated urban areas in the country leading to a strong accentuation of the social problems that always follow when old agrarian societies undergo shock-urbanization. The symptoms gradually show: an increase in crime, violent robberies, nouveau riche speculators, rising rents, the country's highest land prices on Hinna and Sunde, a disregard for human life and opposition to unionisation of the oil industry, neo-fascist tendencies amongst young conservatives. (Fløgstad 1979: 268–9)

While the relationship between the oil industry and the welfare state is a complex one seen from the perspective of the twenty-first century, Stavanger and the 'black gold' has come to symbolize the effects of affluence, mass consumption and urban change on the social structure and culture of Norway in late modernity. The historian Karsten Alnæs writes in his five-volume *Historien om Norge* (2000, History of Norway) that in the period from 1910 to 1976 consumption quadrupled in Norway. He draws a picture of a consumer society towards the end of the twentieth century where 'many worry' about overconsumption and affluence in terms similar to those of Burenstam Linder. While politicians in Norway had many visions for how the oil could help create a 'qualitatively better society', and the new begotten wealth could help create 'a more equal society, prevent social problems, develop a more environmentally friendly industry, strengthen local communities and foster more reasonable consumption', when Alnæs looks back at the visions from the point of view of the year 2000, he sees a welfare society that has crumbled despite its affluence and grand visions. He sees widening social and economic inequality, individualism instead of collectivism is the order of the day supported by global consumerism and neoliberal policies, and the health and social services are leaving those most in need behind, which has resulted in a growing distrust in the political system (Alnæs 2000: 561–76). According to the sociologist Trond Blindheim, the wealth has turned Norwegians into apathetic shoppers, powerless, hedonistic and alienated consumers, who use shopping as therapy against anxieties that have arisen with the loss of traditional values and ideals of solidarity and practicality (380).

Alnæs, whose *History of Norway* was adapted for a sixteen-part series for Norwegian TV, is almost as bleak in his portrait of the Norwegian welfare society at the end of the twentieth century as Sjöwall and Wahlöö were of the Swedish three decades before. While Alnæs might be right in his diagnosis of the contemporary Norwegian consumer society, a diagnosis which might fit most other developed nations in an age of globalization, the portrayal of an oil-infused hedonistic Norway, which has lost contact with traditional ways and values, is a fitting description of Staalesen's Stavanger in *The Woman in the Fridge*.

As Veum makes his way from the ferry to his hotel, he thinks about how Stavanger had changed since he attended 'Sosialskolen' in the late sixties when it had still been a sleepy small town. Now the old fashioned picturesque houses had been taken over by exotic restaurants, discos and boutiques, 'modernist concrete buildings with Los Angeles facades' had sprung up between 'terrified wooden houses', and everywhere one heard foreign tongues as much as the local dialect (Staalesen 2008b: 27). As Veum is searching for an oil worker who has mysteriously disappeared, the dead bodies start piling up in Stavanger, and one of the bodies Veum finds decapitated and stored in the fridge of the missing man's flat. It is a city smelling of 'rot and death', seething with organized crime, gambling and prostitution. A preacher gives a fiery sermon about a city he no longer recognizes, a present-day Sodom and Gomorrah, where only oil and mammon are worshipped. The oil industry and its confusingly global culture is certainly central to the novel's depiction of a fallen society; however, the most startling image of a changing society comes upon Veum when he spends a night with Elsa (a promiscuous student of sociology who lost her son in an accident leaving her emotionally frigid) on the ninth floor of a tower block overlooking the North sea and its oil installations:

As the result of some town planner's absurd imagination, the three tower blocks in Ullandhaug were placed right by the protected Iron Age settlements by Hafrsfjord overgrown with lichen. Or perhaps, by the irony of fate, no one had given it a second thought before the three blocks were suddenly lying there snapping at the sky like three lone teeth in a half-open mouth. (Staalesen 2008b: 115)

An actual place in Ullandhaug, the modern tower blocks rising above the barely visible remnants of a deep past symbolize an unhealthy urban environment and an amnesic society produced not by immoral businessmen or criminal gangs but by careless town planners, the engineers of the modern welfare state.

Hardboiled sentimentalism

As a hardboiled social worker committed to hunting down the truths hidden under the veneer, the false 'sanctuaries', of families and the wider society, Veum does, to some extent, fulfil the role of the traditional 'moral' hardboiled detective, who, in Leonard Cassuto's view makes his way

> in an indifferent world that he navigates by establishing a code of behaviour that substitutes for the morals of the society he occupies. The code emphasizes self-preservation and a nihilistic sense of duty that arises ... because one is supposed to do something. (Cassuto 2009: 4)

Cassuto aligns this trait with what he calls 'hardboiled sentimentality' – a mode which compares to Dussere's notion of the hardboiled novel's longing for an 'elsewhere', an 'authenticity' with which to counter the alienating commercial surfaces of the post-War American city. Often, this 'sentimentality' expresses itself as a longing for a less complex rural past (4), or, as in the case of Hammett's Lew Archer, whom Staalesen upholds as a strong influence, a hardboiled detective who gradually rests his fists and instead spends his time 'tenderly piecing together families broken by past trauma'. As Cassuto laconically points out, '[i]nside every crime story is a sentimental narrative that's trying to come out' (6). This was the case in the arching storyline of Martin Beck's social and familial awakening in the *Novel of a Crime*, and, as Toft Hansen suggests cautiously, without referring to Cassuto's particular use of the term, 'sentimentalism is not a useless concept with which to characterize Staalesen's detective' (Toft Hansen 2012: 140–1).

A good example of hardboiled sentimentalism in Staalesen's Veum series is *Din, til døden* (*Yours Until Death*), which in its Norwegian title plays explicitly with hardboiled sentimentalism in its reference to the phrase 'till death do us apart' from the Christian marriage liturgy. The comma inserted after 'Din' ('Yours') suggests not only that this novel will be preoccupied with marital problems but also that death will play a central role in the novel's treatment of relationships. In the novel, Veum grows fond of Wenche Andresen, a divorced single mother. She lives in a housing estate with her son Roar, who initially sought out Veum's help to retrieve his stolen bicycle from a violent gang of juveniles. Veum, himself divorced and estranged from his son, finds in Wenche and Roar a surrogate family, and his wanderings and thoughts in the novel often go to his childhood in Bergen's Nordnes quarter, which has changed beyond recognition. It is a novel, as several other Veum novels, about the loss of innocence, about Veum's personal loss of a simpler past and the loss of his own family. When Veum tries to help Wenche reclaim part of a life insurance owed to her by her ex-husband, he unknowingly sets in motion a string of events that leads to the ex-husband's murder in Wenche's flat. As she was found holding the murder weapon, the police are in no doubt about the identity of the killer while Veum maintains Wenche's innocence.

The following investigation takes him deep into the private lives and social world of the estate with its alcoholism, deceit, blackmail, failed social workers and broken relationships. In the end, while Veum with the best intentions tried to repair Wenche and Roar's family and in the process discovered most of the sleazy facts that led to two murders, he must in the end realize that he was wrong about Wenche. Staalesen's Veum is a hardboiled sentimental detective in the genre's tradition. He is determined that his quest for the truth will piece together broken lives and families, including his own, even when such a sentiment is doomed from the start – as doomed as the fight against the ravages of time that cast his idyllic childhood and Old Bergen into oblivion.

Urban crimes

Hans Skei is, to some extent, right in claiming that the crimes of the Veum novels are not directly linked to the failures of the welfare state, at least in comparison to the explicit ideological project of Sjöwall and Wahlöö. However, as Toft Hansen points out, 'if society is not to be blamed in Staalesen's novels, then at least the big evil businessman is to be blamed as the personification of capitalist rationalism and consumerism' (Toft Hansen 2008: 35). Such a conflation of individual and social guilt is expressed by Veum in his heated discussion with two businessmen in *Buried dogs don't bite*: '[Y]ou represent utter misanthropy ... The same disregard for human life saturating the new cities in which we have to live – and which have taken the life of the old!' (Staalesen 1993: 290). As noted above, Veum's cases mostly centre on missing and violated children who have been abandoned physically or emotionally by their dysfunctional families. They are easy prey for morally corrupt individuals, who represent a wider misanthropic spirit of the age made legible in 'the new cities' that have 'taken the life' of the old.

As in Bodelsen and in Sjöwall and Wahlöö's late-modern Scandinavian crime novels, Dussere's notion of a 'false nostalgia', the dream of an 'elsewhere', as a characteristic of the hardboiled mode, runs as a continuous commentary throughout the Veum series. In *Buried dogs don't bite*, Veum's diagnosis of the age shares obvious sentiments with his Swedish counterparts' depiction of a fallen Swedish welfare society:

> It is a civilisation in an advanced state of dissolution, a perverse affluent society constantly looking for new ways of titillation, a need for entertainment beyond all proportions. It is adjusted to a world wherein money is power and life no longer has any intrinsic value. (Staalesen 1993: 190; my translation)

The Veum series is a chronicle of fin-de-siècle Norway, but the novels are perhaps better understood in a longer historical perspective as present-day Norway is constantly held up against a turbulent past anchored in the early post-War years. In *Yours Until Death*,

Veum condenses the post-War history of Bergen into a parable of rapid modernization:

> For some reason I thought of 1946. 1946. That was sort of the beginning for all of us. The war was over but the city was still paralysed. It wasn't until the fifties that it rose out of the ashes, set square high-rises on its crooked spine and let the past fall into ruins. The America-bound boats gave up sailing and they built Flesland Airport. The Laksevåg ferry was shut down and they built a bridge over Puddefjord. They dug holes through the mountains and built housing developments where there'd been farms and forests and marshlands. But that hadn't begun in 1946. (Staalesen 2010: 84–5)

The sentimental recall of a past pastoral is narrated in such 'Private "I"' inner monologues with a convoluted sense of temporality. The 'beginning for all of us', coinciding with the birth of Veum's post-War generation, is characterized by the paralysis of a nation and a cityscape scarred by war out of which an age of progress was borne. However, a more fitting beginning to the novel's contemporary environment is suggested by that which 'hadn't begun in 1946', namely the housing and infrastructure boom of the affluent and progressive welfare state that took shape in the following decades. In Veum's perspective, the affluent welfare state produced alienation from the past that materialized, for instance, in square blocks of social housing. In the last line of the quoted passage, 'But that hadn't begun in 1946', Veum expresses a longing for a time and a city before the arrival of the modern state, which he associates with the work of anonymous others: before *they* built a bridge and *they* dug holes through the mountains. In this way, a contemporary dislocation from an idyllic past is demonstrated by the narrative's own temporal 'fall into ruins', and, by association, Veum's own temporal and social dislocation. Holed up in his shabby office, resisting the winds of change that have swept through his city, Veum's loneliness extends beyond the need for human and familial relationships to a deep sense of alienation from the city itself: 'My city still lived outside the windows, but it lived without me' (28).

Veum contemplates urban renewal through lenses tinted with nostalgia, as also noted by Dahl, but also as a figure that unites

Veum and the novels' victims in a common destiny (see Dahl 1995: 66): 'I walked around Nordnes on Sunday. Once there'd been little wooden houses leaning against each other. Now there were dreary concrete cubes people lived in' (Staalesen 2010: 28). In the Norwegian original, the little wooden houses are given human characteristics as they are leaning tiredly ('trette') against each other, stressing their symbolic reference to harder but also more communal times, whereas Veum's view of their modern substitutes expresses his disbelief ('utrolig nok') that people can actually live in the 'heavy concrete blocks' (Staalesen 1981: 28). To him, these new presumably 'social' housing projects materialize the disregard for human life, the misanthropy, which characterizes the Norwegian capitalist consumer society that has abandoned traditional values of togetherness and social responsibility.

The figure of the 'concrete giants' is recurring throughout the series, and the high-rise housing estate is associated with social segregation and alienation in a way similar to its representation in Sjöwall and Wahlöö's series. In *Yours Until Death*, Wenche dismisses Veum's question whether no one on the estate could have helped her retrieve Roar's bike from the gang:

> 'Have you ever lived in a place like this? How many flats are there? Fifty – sixty? Almost two hundred people. I do say hello to some of them who live on this floor. Sometimes to other people in the lift. But it's like an anthill. Do ants say hello?' She shook her head again. 'I don't know a soul. We're as isolated now as we've always been.' (Staalesen 2010: 25)

The concrete blocks are viewed as generating the social isolation, which not only fosters crime but also leaves the community itself unable to counter its transgressions, to care for its most vulnerable inhabitants, in a social environment and an age where fathers are conspicuous by their absence. Wenche's son Roar appears to intuitively understand this condition, which is why he searched for a generic private detective in the phone book and not the representatives of the state, the police. Possibly inspired by detective shows on TV, the situation seemed to demand a 'mean' detective preferably with a gun. While Veum, to Roar's regret, does not have a gun, his hardboiled posturing, confronted with the juvenile offenders, does help him retrieve the bike. However, his subsequent interferences into the lives of Roar and Wenche will have dramatic consequences for the boy and his family. Although he has succeeded in uncovering the truth, we are in the end left with a situation where justice might have been done, yet the underlying social and historical processes, the detective's personal sense of isolation and alienation as well as the future fate of the actual innocent victim of the whole story, Roar, are left shrouded in Bergen's darkness, victims of an age of amnesia and social disintegration.

Consumer crisis in paradise

The historic development in the Scandinavian countries from the optimism of the 1960s to the conflicts of the 1970s initiated an age of uncertainty that led to continuous debates over the welfare state in crisis, which, several similar crises later, are still being negotiated today (Jónsson and Stefánsson 2013: 15). In 1970s Scandinavia, we arrived at an age of uncertainty, which Zygmunt Bauman has termed our 'liquid modernity'. This was an age characterized by the wide-ranging consequences of globalization, the demolition of the social state and its utopian promises of collective progress towards a reliable, trusting and secure world. Apart from social degradation and growing inequalities the visible symptoms of this post-utopian society were a ubiquitous politics of fear, 'the personal safety state' and a thoroughly 'individualized consumer society' (Bauman 2007: 15, 104).

Within Scandinavia, the ideological and economic crisis that challenged the hegemonic welfare ideology was particularly significant and shattering in Sweden, mainly due to its forty-four years of unbroken Social–Democratic rule (1932–76). The seemingly natural right of the Social Democratic Party to the government offices was broken in 1976. The election was lost partly due to a heated tax debate fuelled by Astrid Lindgren's publication of the 'fairy-tale' 'Pomperipossa in Monismania' in the newspaper *Expressen*, wherein she attacked the government and its taxation policies, and Ingmar Bergman's farewell letter to Sweden following charges put against him for tax evasion.

While the political left in Scandinavia became more vocal about the shortcomings of the Social–Democratic welfare state and its failure to deliver on its promises of a more social, equal and just society, the hitherto glossy image of the Swedish welfare state became viewed, from the political right and from outside of Scandinavia, as a failed state most scathingly in the British journalist Roland Huntford's book *The New Totalitarians* (1971).

An age of optimism had been replaced by an age of uncertainty and crisis – utopia by dystopia. To some, the welfare state became increasingly seen as an enemy to individual freedom, a socialist, bureaucratic enterprise that eroded traditions and family structures through the politicization of the private sphere. To others, the third-way politics of the welfare state had succumbed to the demands of international capitalism. They sought escape from the dehumanizing forces of the consumer society in new utopian free-cities such as Christiania in Copenhagen (1971) or, inspired by the student rebellion in Paris in 1968, sought to overthrow the authoritarian bastions of knowledge and power at the universities through demonstrations and occupations. On the left, the values of democratic progress and the moral fabric of the welfare state were seen as compromised on a geopolitical scale with the war in Vietnam and the growing consciousness of the role of industrialization, unlimited consumption and a Western way of life in environmental degradation (Swenarton et al. 2015: 14). These conflicts figure prominently not only in the crime fiction of the 1970s but are also central to the social consciousness or 'authenticity effects' that became associated with Scandinavian crime fiction in the new millennium.

The global crisis early in the 1970s and the waves of social change that washed over Europe did not bypass Denmark and Norway. The general election of 1973 in Denmark, commonly known as the landslide election, introduced five new political parties to the parliament. The new political-ideological situation represented a growing distrust in the traditional political landscape and scepticism towards the legitimacy of the ever-present welfare state and particularly the high level of taxation (Petersen et al. 2012: 742). However, more general discussions of the legitimacy of the welfare state had been initiated earlier, as in the example of Løchen's critique of the growing health issues in the Norwegian welfare state.

The slogan on the Social Democratic election posters of 1960, 'make good times better', also demonstrated, apart from the incurable optimism of this golden age, a social and political revolution that had outlived itself. More existential questions about life in the welfare state arose with the realization of what had for the better part of a century been, as in all good utopias, 'a horizon of expectations'. Now that the welfare state was more or less a reality, the question asked was: what to do with it? (74) The discussion only intensified and polarized with the crisis in 1973 and, in Denmark, 'we do not have to get far into the 1970s before the golden age is being replaced by the twilight of the welfare state [velfærdsstat i tidehverv]' (123). According to Mary Hilson, the ideological crisis of the Social Democratic parties across Scandinavia came down to the paradox also pointed out by Løchen: 'why did inequality persist after two decades of more or less undisturbed economic growth and the construction of a comprehensive welfare system?' The expansion of the economies and the welfare state now became increasingly seen

as the source of new social problems that were articulated with a new vocabulary: alienation, social exclusion, environmental degradation. The redesigned town centres and new functionalist housing blocks constructed through the Swedish 'million homes' programme came to stand not for the rational, efficient and cosy people's home, but as a concrete and brutal symbol of social alienation. (Hilson 2008: 107)

Three of the central Scandinavian crime writers discussed here, from Denmark, Norway and Sweden in the period between 1968 and 1980, took as their setting these 'redesigned' urban spaces of the welfare state and submitted them to a social critique, which emphasized the alienating effects of welfare modernization, affluence and consumerism in the process of severing traditional trusted relationships. The alienating effects of the engineered welfare state and its urban living spaces have also received much attention in Scandinavian literature and film beyond crime fiction. The Danish author Tage Skou-Hansen described, in several novels from the 1970s and 1980s, the alienated inhabitants of a Danish suburbia depicted as ghettos of individualism; in Michael Buchwald's novel *Blokland* (1975) it is the modern tower blocks and the social consequences of the welfare state's housing policies that have created social and individual alienation; and in the Swedish director Jan Troell's documentary *Sagolandet* (1988, Land of dreams) a decaying, alienating welfare state is portrayed with contrasting images of the modern consumer society and its destruction of nature and creativity.

There can be no doubt about the influence of Bodelsen, Staalesen and Sjöwall and Wahlöö on subsequent generations of Scandinavian crime writers. Their plain, yet biting social realism, bleak views of life in the otherwise idyllic Scandinavian welfare states and their nonconformist use of available international crime genres have left their mark on most Scandinavian crime writers – at least since Henning Mankell reinvigorated the Swedish police procedural in the 1990s and made it an international phenomenon. Staalesen's Varg Veum has, as mentioned, found many new 'sentimental' hard-boiled siblings in Scandinavia; Bodelsen's neo-realist preoccupation with existential conflicts in the most mundane of life worlds amplified by a sudden criminal disturbance is recognizable in later crime series by Danish writers such as Elsebeth Egholm, Gretelise Holm and in Norwegian Karin Fossum's series featuring the detective Konrad Sejer. Most Scandinavian crime writers will cite Sjöwall and Wahlöö's police novels as formative for their own work. Most obviously their influence is palpable in Swedish police procedurals by Mankell, Haakan Nesser, Leif G. W. Persson, Åke Edwardson and Arne Dahl, but also across Scandinavia in hardboiled procedurals by Jo Nesbø and Jussi Adler-Olsen. The iconic status of Sjöwall and Wahlöö's *Novel of a Crime* in contemporary Scandinavian crime fiction is demonstrated by continuous reprints and translations; by the ongoing production and success of films, TV adaptations and spin-offs, such as the Martin Beck series; and the subtle and playful traces of their series in, for instance, the name of Sejer's dog in Fossum's series of crime novels, named after Beck's colleague Lennart Kollberg, and in the Danish writers Dorph and Pasternak's first police novel set in the 1970s, *Om et Øjeblik i Himlen* (2005, In a Moment in Heaven), which begins with the phrase: 'Then I say X, X as in Marx', a phrase borrowed from the last line spoken by Kollberg in Sjöwall and Wahlöö's last novel, *The Terrorists*.

The central preoccupation with the rise of the consumer society associated with an age of affluence and the golden age of the welfare state has also been a persistent theme in the subsequent tradition of Scandinavian crime fiction. Perhaps the best example of a nostalgic response to the pressures of the consumer society similar to Sjöwall and Wahlöö's is found in Mankell's sixth book in his Kurt Wallander series, *Den femte kvinnan* (1996, *The Fifth Woman*,

2000). Here we find a scene where Wallander's daughter Linda asks him why he finds it so difficult to live in Sweden. He replies with a cryptic parable of sock mending:

> Sometimes I think it's because we've stopped darning our socks ... When I was growing up, Sweden was still a country where people darned their socks. I even learned how to do it in school myself. Then suddenly one day it was over. Socks with holes in them were thrown out. No one bothered to repair them anymore. The whole society changed. 'wear it out and toss it' was the only rule that applied to everybody. (Mankell 2012b: 223)

Wallander's memory of a time before the modern consumer society, which he admits might just be an expression of every age seeming worse than the one before, is an example of a persistent experience of his throughout the series: of his sense of alienation and displacement in time and space, of somebody who cannot adjust to the new society around him, and particularly of his anxieties about an increasingly more violent society. 'As long as it was just a matter of our socks, the change didn't make much difference', he continues', [b]ut then it started to spread, until finally it became a kind of invisible but ever-present moral code. I think it changed our view of right and wrong, what you were allowed to do to other people and what you weren't. Everything has gotten so much more difficult.' The younger generations have no memory of 'a time when we darned our socks. When we didn't throw everything away, whether it was our woollen socks or human beings' (224). To Wallander, the Sweden of the 1990s has become increasingly dehumanized and demoralized, a society in which human beings have themselves become consumables, a country which has not improved much since the bleak portrait painted by Sjöwall and Wahlöö.

The individualized consumer society and its dehumanization of the social state was already a present condition in the realist detail of Bodelsen's crime fiction as illustrated in the bank clerk's window shopping for the latest and fastest Volvo. In more recent crime fiction, details of consumer spaces and brand names have become ubiquitous as 'authenticity effects' and continue to function as markers of conspicuous and individualized consumption, which not only leads to criminal behaviour but also prevents characters in novels such as Nesbø's *Hodejegerne* (2008; *Headhunters*, 2011) and Jens

Lapidus's *Snabba cash* (2006; *Easy Money*, 2012) from creating and maintaining meaningful social relationships and stable identities.

Perhaps most iconic is the figure of the consumer in Stieg Larsson's *Millennium* trilogy (2005–7). Lisbeth Salander's struggle to reclaim her independence from her state-appointed guardian in a dysfunctional, violent and corrupted welfare system is mostly concerned with her access to independent funds. When she cannot be liberated through the corrupt legal system, she takes the law into her own hands and secures access, through threats and computer hacking, to illicit funds placed conveniently in off-shore accounts. Her consumer desires are few, restricted mostly to technological gadgets and coffee made on her Jura Impressa X7, but as several contemporary crime novels, Larsson's is abundant with recognizable consumer products and brands. Salander famously lives almost exclusively on Billy's Pan Pizzas from the local Konsum store. When we go shopping with her in IKEA in *Flickan som lekte med elden* (2006; *The Girl Who Played with Fire*, 2009), in order to furbish her new upmarket flat, the narrative is taken over by an extended hyper-consumerist shopping list:

> She bought two Karlanda sofas with sand-coloured upholstery, five Poäng armchairs, two round side tables of clear-lacquered birch, a Svansbo coffee table and several Lack occasional tables. From the storage department she ordered two Ivar combination storage units and two Bonde bookshelves, a T.V. stand, and a Magiker unit with doors. She settled on a Pax Nexus three-door wardrobe and two small Malm bureaus … She paid with a card in the name of Wasp Enterprises and showed her Irene Nesser I.D. She also paid to have the items delivered and assembled. The bill came to a little over 90,000 kronor. (Larsson 2015b: 83–4)

This list obviously holds very little importance to the crime plot of the novel, but it is significant both as a 'realism effect' and to the narrator's portrait of Salander as a consumer who knows how to construct or furbish a home, but very little about actually living in it. Her flat will remain an empty, impersonal IKEA-catalogue home, a front or disguise, representing her own uncanny, or, indeed, *unheimlich* family situation.

When we go shopping with Salander in IKEA it is not insignificant that she is dressed up as her alter ego Irene Nesser. She is her vengeful global jet-setter alter ego with bank accounts in tax shelters and breast implants, whose disguise Salander uses to take her revenge over corrupt and misogynist industrialists, financiers and state bureaucrats. Salander's revenge comes in the disguise of that very same impersonal, capitalist and misogynist system she will eventually help to break. In other words, a major part of Salander's heroic powers is her ability to out-consume the very worst and conspicuous of consumers.

Crime fiction, according to Gill Plain, once sought to allay the anxieties of its readership, in the new millennium it seems designed only to satisfy their appetites (Plain 2001: 245). When we consume Stieg Larsson's blockbuster crime trilogy, some of the most popular crime novels internationally of the 2000s, we are, however, also consuming a particular grim vision for our late-modern consumer society, wherein conspicuous consumption may only be fought by its own means.

4

Crime fiction in an age of crisis: Henning Mankell's *Faceless Killers* and Stieg Larsson's *The Girl with the Dragon Tattoo*

In 1990 it felt as if the utopian dream of the harmonious Scandinavian welfare state had become a distant memory. Nothing quite was what it used to be. In the past lay the hopes and dreams of economic and social progress, which had materialized in weighty state bureaucracies and the ambitious social and urban engineering programmes of the 1960s and 1970s. Several financial and political crises later, these monuments to the modern welfare state were crumbling, both literarily and symbolically, as the ideological and historical winds of change swept in from a turbulent world and an increasingly neoliberal West, demanding leaner, more competitive states and citizens who could adjust to and survive in the expanding, fast-moving and more opaque transnational markets of a multipolar world. The new millennium beckoned with anxiety and melancholia for what had been lost in the past and the loss of footing in a constantly shape-shifting landscape of the present.

Where Scandinavian crime fiction in the seventies responded to the emerging individualistic consumer society that threatened traditional social structures from within, the crime novels that appeared at the threshold to the new millennium, still true to the realist tradition of the Scandinavian crime novel, held up a mirror to a dramatically more opaque and insecure world beyond the horizon of what once was the golden age of national welfare utopianism.

'There can be no doubt', Eric Hobsbawm writes in his history of the twentieth century, *The Age of Extremes*, 'that in the late 1980s and early 1990s an era in world history ended and a new one began' (Hobsbawm 1995: 5). A post-War golden age of economic and social progress had ended in 1970 giving way to 'a new era of decomposition, uncertainty and crisis' (5). In many regions of the world such as Africa, the former USSR and the formerly socialist parts of Europe, the uncertainties of a new age, Hobsbawm observes, spiralled into catastrophe: famine crises and civil war in Ethiopia and Somalia, the Rwanda genocide, the outbreak of ethnic conflicts and war in the former Yugoslavia and the first Gulf war.

Globalization became the ubiquitous catch-all term by which this new, increasingly hostile 'runaway world' (Giddens 2002) was named. Crucial to the widely shared experience of having migrated – without leaving one's couch – into a distorted version of Marshall McLuhan's 'global village' were electronic and new digital media networks. Near and distant events, conflicts and disasters were brought into the relatively peaceful Scandinavian homes 'in real time', via satellite TV and twenty-four-hour news coverage. Yet, in Scandinavia, the uncertainties of a globalized world did not remain a mere virtual reality.

In 1986, the unprotected Swedish Prime Minister Olof Palme was assassinated in central Stockholm as he walked home from the cinema with his wife. Across Scandinavia the murder came to stand as a watershed for what may have been left of the self-perception of living in an idyllic periphery of an increasingly more hostile and wayward world. Easy access to politicians, even the prime minister, once the pride of Scandinavian democracies and an emblem of their peaceful nature, suffered a deadly blow suggesting that Sweden and the rest of Scandinavia were, indeed, less exceptional nations and more like everywhere else. While Scandinavia had not been spared ideologically motivated terrorism in the recent past, the unsolved murder sparked conspiracy theories that cited a long list of agents that seemed to have jumped out of the pages of the popular spy-novels and thrillers by Jan Guillou and Leif Davidsen: a South

African spy, the PKK, left-wing extremist groups, Chilean fascists and the Yugoslavian security services.

Criminologist and crime writer Leif G. W. Persson's 'Fall of the Welfare State Trilogy' (Välfärdsstatens fall, 2002–7), represents the most extensive attempt at dealing specifically with the Palme murder, the relentless social trauma that followed and its wider connection to the perceived fall of the welfare state. The trauma inflicted upon Sweden had symbolic and cultural consequences for the way in which citizens related to the political system and how social trust in the welfare state had begun to wither from within. Persson's trilogy is an exploration of a Sweden suffering from what resembles a collective post-traumatic stress syndrome. However, contrary to most conspiracy theories, Persson's 'docu-drama' investigation in the form of a crime series does not implicate external forces or foreign criminals in the murder. Instead, the guilty are to be found among local Swedish police officers and particularly the security services, which, true to the tradition from Sjöwall and Wahlöö, are portrayed as forming a brutal and cancerous neo-Nazi cell at the very heart of the welfare state.

Scandinavian crime fiction towards the new millennium needs to be seen against this background of 'crises, conflicts, break-up, disorder and broken illusions about the political opportunities' of the welfare state in an age of globalization – developments that polarized society and threatened the very identity of the nation (Tapper 2011: 406). Andrew Nestingen reminds us that the universal welfare state had created a 'homology between state and nation', which is a central tenet for understanding why the period's diminished welfare state, under the sway of neoliberalism, growing individualism, demographic change and a loss of trust in the political system, had such deep resonance in the 'imagined communities' of the Scandinavian countries, perhaps most deeply felt in Sweden and Denmark, where austerity led to more far-reaching political reforms than in Norway. According to Nestingen, '[t]he changes of the 80s and 90s caused a problem for national definition, for they undermined the idea that the Scandinavian nation-states were unique unities of people and state' (Nestingen 2008: 8).

In Denmark, even the Social Democratic coalition governments led by Prime Minister Poul Nyrup Rasmussen (1993–2001) continued the neoliberal restructuring of the welfare state through privatizations of the public sector, which increasingly turned citizens into individualized consumers of welfare services (Mathiesen 2000). While the literary fashion in Denmark, since the very politicized social realism that dominated the 1970s, had been more preoccupied with formal and aesthetic concerns, exemplifying a general postmodern scepticism towards 'grand narratives', in the 1990s and 2000s Danish authors such as Jan Sonnergaard (*Radiator*, 1997), Jacob Ejersbo (*Superego*, 1999) and Christian Jungersen (*Undtagelsen*, 2004; *The Exception*, 2006) turned their attention to the dark side of the neoliberal 'competitive society' (Pedersen 2011), which had replaced the welfare society with its narcissism, inauthenticity, corrosion of cultural and social bonds, fluid morality and identities (Bunch 2010; Stidsen 2010).

While Norway was less affected by the economic and political winds that blew from the West and the rest of Europe, Thomas Hylland Eriksen has described similar political and sociocultural changes in his book *Typisk norsk* (1993, Typical Norwegian). His view of Norway in the early nineties is similarly bleak in the description of the welfare society as a collective project that had capitulated to external and internal forces of change: 'Globalisation, opaqueness, the incessant white noise of the media and a lack of control with the basic social processes create confusion, political numbness and despair' (146). The welfare state's trust in social progress had been substituted with an almost religious belief in individual progress, which is a development Hylland Eriksen relates to a growing sense of lack of collective purpose. Since, by the end of the eighties, the Social-Democratic welfare project seemed fully realized, there was no longer a collective project, a national project, around which a new generation could gather. The abstract collective or the 'imagined community' of the nation was disappearing in a haze of apathy: 'As long as the Social-Democratic spirit of progress and the ideology of togetherness could create a subjective sense that life was improving it could foster trust and a sense of a national community.' In the competitive society of the nineties it had become 'each man for himself' (147). While few Norwegian crime writers engaged explicitly with the loss of solidarity, the breakdown of national and familial relations, in the eighties and early nineties (several socio-critical crime novels would appear later in Norway), Norwegian novelists such as Erlend Loe, who described his generation as 'we who didn't build Norway' (*L*, 1999), Jan Kjærstad's Wergeland trilogy (1993–9) and Hanne Ørstavik's *Kjærlighet* (1997, Love) explored the anxieties produced by the decomposition of national and familial identities and collectives (Andersen 2013).

Foreigners in the welfare state: Henning Mankell's *Faceless Killers*

While the murder of Palme buried any illusion of the idyllic, exceptional Scandinavian welfare societies, around 1990 the Scandinavian countries underwent dramatic demographic, political, economic and cultural changes, which added to the sense that a new era had indeed arrived. Refugees from wars, humanitarian and economic crises around the world found safety in the Scandinavian countries in large numbers, which challenged a national imaginary in whose self-perception cultural and social homogeneity and political consensus still formed the foundation for harmonious and equal societies. By 1990, according to Allan Pred, crisis 'became a commonplace part of everyday Swedish' (Pred 2000: 12). The assassination of Palme made many Swedes believe that their country had become unrecognizable; the closing of factories, disposable incomes in decline and escalating unemployment meant that for many 'Sweden was becoming less and less like what people liked to remember' (14). This distorted image of the once affluent welfare state produced deep individual and collective identity crises in the nineties: 'What in the world is going on here? Where in the world am I, are we? Who in the world am I, are we?' (17). While driven by a deep recession, the Swedish crisis in this 'age of extremes' found its most dramatic expression in the response to immigration:

> For many Swedes, perhaps nothing has become more unrecognizable, perhaps nothing has become more disorienting ... than either the large-scale presence of non-Europeans and Muslims or the assortment of racisms that have constantly risen to the surface among a very small minority of right-wing extremist Others – and less consciously – themselves. (18)

Racism as a pervasive crime and the question 'What was happening in the Swedish welfare state in the 1990s?' provided the impetus for Henning Mankell to write a series of nine police procedurals (and one collection of short stories) from *Mördare utan ansikte* (1991, *Faceless Killers*, 1997) to *Den orolige mannen* (2009, *The Troubled Man*, 2011), featuring the police inspector Kurt Wallander and forming, in the tradition from Sjöwall and Wahlöö, a collective 'novel about the Swedish anxiety' (Mankell 2009: 1). The Wallander novels mostly take place in and around the provincial southern Swedish town of Ystad on the shore of the Baltic with various sections and storylines set abroad (Latvia, the Dominican Republic and South Africa). Mankell intended the Wallander series as an investigation into the deterioration of social consciousness in Sweden. While set in a provincial Swedish borderland, Mankell's crime series is global in scope, confronting the attitudes of a provincial microcosm towards border-crossing phenomena such as immigration (*Faceless Killers*); organ trafficking in the developing world (*Mannen som log*,1994; *The Man Who Smiled*, 2005); human trafficking (*Villospår*,1995; *Sidetracked*, 2000); Swedish mercenaries in the Congo (*Den femte kvinnan*,1996; *The Fifth Woman*, 2001); and an international conspiracy to destroy the financial system to right the wrongs of worldwide economic inequality in *Brandvägg* (1998, *Firewall*, 2004).

Reading the first Wallander novel *Faceless Killers* in 2015, the year Mankell passed away, and nearly twenty-five years after the novel was originally published, leaves one with an uncomfortable sense of its continued if not increasing relevance. As a divided and fragile Europe finds itself in what has been called the worst refugee crisis in modern time, Sweden's majority consensus has sustained a laudable humanitarian stance when it comes to welcoming and providing security for refugees from war-torn countries like Syria, until also the Swedish government eventually succumbed to the pressure of mass-immigration by introducing stricter border controls. The country's image as a successful multicultural society dedicated to global solidarity is in 2015 being tarnished by a rise in support for the anti-immigration party Sverigedemokraterna, now rivalling, as similar parties in the other Scandinavian countries, the established parties in popularity; a spate of arson attacks against refugee centres across the country; the knife-stabbing of a mother and her son in an IKEA shop in Västerås committed by an asylum seeker who had been denied residence permit; and a racist hate-crime attack by a xenophobic young man with neo-Nazi sympathies leaving two dead at a multi-ethnic school in Trollhättan.

The attack in this industrial town north of Gothenburg sends uncomfortable reminders of neo-Nazi skinheads assaulting Somali refugees, burning down a mosque and ethnic clashes on 'million-home' estates in the early nineties, where Trollhättan, in one newspaper headline in 1993, was dubbed 'the capital of Swedish racism' (Pred: 203). Then, the industrial town had been severely hit by the recession, by closures and cutbacks at major Volvo and Saab plants (206), and groups of disenfranchised youths found their scapegoats in the newly arrived non-European residents. When *Faceless Killers* was published '[t]he fact that people who were regarded as "different from us" immigrated to Sweden was a new experience for the Swedes, and probably contributed to a growing xenophobia' (Byström and Frohnert 2013: 229). Dramatic occurrences of racist hate crimes committed by 'The Laser man', who shot eleven people and killed one, mostly immigrants, in Stockholm and Uppsala in 1991 and 1992 and neo-Nazi skinheads who were responsible for the 1986 murder of Ronny Landin, which has been called the first racist-motivated murder in Sweden, inaugurated a new age of national divisions along social and ethnic lines.

Inspector Kurt Wallander is a Swedish everyman, whose anxiety about this new age, an age he repeatedly admits he does not understand, makes him a reflector for a wider national confusion about morality and solidarity in the multicultural society. The novel begins with a 'senseless and savage' double murder of an old couple in their 'whitewashed' farm house in the rural village of Lunnarp outside of Ystad. Wallander drives to the scene of the crime worried about the approaching winter, and anxious about his recent divorce as he fends off the traumatic memory of a stab wound he received as a young policeman with the incantation '*A time to live and a time to die*'(9). In our first encounter with Wallander's frequent internal monologues, we are presented with a constellation of anxieties making up both his private and a wider social map of insecurities that will follow him throughout the series: a landscape of foreboding, traumatic memories of the past, broken relationships, loneliness and the repeated eruption of senseless violence in the most unlikely, bucolic and peripheral of places.

The woman, who was found with a noose around her neck at the crime scene, turns out to be still alive. Her deathbed testimony, which describes the perpetrator as 'foreign', adds a further node

to the anxieties that will drive the meandering plot and investigation of the novel. Wallander and his colleagues are fearful of what
will happen if it becomes publicly known that the killers may be
'foreigners' – refugee camps in the area had already been the focus
of attacks, crosses had been burned and buildings had been spray-
painted with slogans. At the same time, the police are aware that
some of the asylum seekers 'had been caught red-handed breaking
into a business that rented out farm machinery', an incident that
had been hushed up and the perpetrators eventually denied asylum
(44). Wallander's fear about the public reaction is confirmed when
the clue of foreigners' involvement is leaked to the press: a local
vigilante militia is formed ready to take the law into its own hands,
a refugee centre is attacked and set on fire, and a Somali refugee is
murdered in broad daylight by a neo-Nazi group, which turns out
to include a former policeman.

While most of the crime investigation sees the police following
false leads and having to deal with associated hate crimes and a
dysfunctional immigration system, the killers do in the end turn
out to be foreigners, though perhaps not 'visibly' so, as they are
two fair-skinned Czech criminals, who have exploited Sweden's lax
enforcement of immigration laws and porous borders by posing as
gypsy asylum seekers. The ruthless killers, who have disturbed the
Swedish harmony are, nevertheless, 'foreigners' and may be seen to
endorse Wallander's and the public's fear of border-crossing Eastern
European criminal gangs.

According to Michael Tapper's critical reading of Mankell's
series, the Wallander novels tap into and reproduce xenophobic
prejudices through narratives that constantly depict crime and violence as something that arrives in an idyllic and innocent Sweden
always from the outside:

> Rather than countering or even analysing the roots of paranoid
> and racist narrative, *Faceless Killers* confirms it in every detail.
> Even the vigilantism and other transgressions among Swedes
> are triggered, and thereby explained, by the alien invasion of
> refugees, drugs and crime. The implication, as in the old colo-
> nial detective stories, is that crime itself is something foreign and
> barbarian. It is not really in our blood, not really in our culture,
> but something by which we have been contaminated. (Tapper
> 2014: 170)

As such, Tapper reads Mankell's crime novel in line with John Scaggs' identification of a common trait in the subgenre of the police procedural, wherein the monstrosity of the killer isolates the criminal's instincts '"from all social, political or economic causes", exonerating the social order of all responsibility regarding its "deviant" citizens ... [I]t returns to the clarity of black and white distinctions in which evil ... is a pure "other" that is uncomplicatedly monstrous and inhuman' (Scaggs 2005: 99). The police and the detective in the police procedural, then, come to function as 'a powerful weapon of reassurance in the arsenal of the dominant social order' (98). However, as I shall argue and as also pointed out variously by Anna Stenport and Nestingen, 'Swedishness' and 'foreignness', the inside and the outside, detective and criminal, are presented as complicated and ambivalent figures in Mankell's version of the police procedural (Nestingen 2008: 244; Stenport 2007: 3).

The ambivalence or the difficulty of detecting what is domestic and what is foreign is already suggested when the investigative team is debating what the old woman could have meant by the word 'foreign'. Wallander's mentor Rydberg suggests: '"Maybe they looked un-Swedish. Maybe they spoke a foreign language. Maybe they spoke poor Swedish. There are lots of possibilities." "What does an 'un-Swedish' person look like?" asked Wallander' (Mankell 2011b: 43). When the detectives finally hone in on the two fair-skinned Czech migrants, Wallander's scepticism about the possibility of ethnic identification and cultural coding of what appears as Swedish and foreign is confirmed as they do not 'look' as stereotypical ethnic others. Wanting their real names, the police instead give them the nick-names 'Skallmannen' ('Skinhead') and 'Lucia' for their 'Swedish' appearance: one has a shaved head and the other long fair hair. Stenport explains the significance of their nicknames:

The name Lucia is self-explanatory to most Swedes and poignant in its association with one of the most cherished Christmas traditions (the Saint Lucia procession on the morning of December 13) while 'Skallmannen' ['Skinhead'] ties the murderer's appearance to the Anglicism used for neo-Nazis in contemporary Swedish parlance. (14)

The foreign criminals, the monstrous Others, are thereby labelled in the novel 'as iconic representatives of Swedish culture, but in culturally conflicting ways' (13). While the contradictory or post-modern ironic double-coding of Skinhead is clear (signifying simultaneously a foreign criminal and a home-grown racist), the name Lucia can also be read as a figurative contradiction, since the name refers to a popular national custom deeply ingrained in 'Swedishness' and 'whiteness'. Where the name Skinhead associates border-crossing crime with Swedish racism, the name Lucia adds further ambivalence to Wallander's question about what a non-Swede would look like by coding the criminal foreigner as indistinguishable from a 'white' Swedish heritage. However, in the immediate sociopolitical context of the novel, the name Lucia also recalls an iconic change in Swedish post-War immigration policies known as the 'Lucia Decision' of 13 December 1989, which essentially restricted asylum policies. The change in policy from one that had historically been far more generous than the Geneva Convention prescribed meant that

> It would no longer be possible to be granted asylum as a *de facto* refugee or a war refugee unless there were particularly strong protection needs ... The Lucia Decision was justified by what was said to constitute an emergency situation for the reception of refugees, or, in the words of the Social Democrat minister for immigrants at the time, Maj-Lis Lööw: 'The Swedish reception of refugees is facing a crisis.' (Borevi 2012: 49)

Not 'merely' an administrative adjustment deemed necessary at a time of crisis, Byström and Frohnert suggest that the policy should be seen as a political response to a more abstract and widespread anxiety about a new borderless Europe and a 'flood of refugees from Eastern Europe when the [Berlin] Wall came down' (Byström and Frohnert 2013: 229). In giving the name of Lucia to one of the monstrous Eastern European killers, Mankell seems to be alluding not only to the recent restriction of asylum policies in Sweden, but also to this particular critical assessment of the Decision as a symptom of an anxiety about a new world order, porous national borders and Sweden's vulnerable, peripheral position against the rising tide of change.

Located on the Swedish border to the rest of Europe, Scania (Skåne) became the geographical area where refugees were first received and many settled, and the region became associated with racial tensions and unrest which influenced the Lucia Decision. The naming and double-coding of the opportunist Czech criminals by the police allows for at least two readings of the representation of immigration and Swedish racism in the novel: one that sympathizes with a Swedish anxiety about the porous borders of a globalizing world, the threats from the outside that are corrupting a harmonious and ethnically homogeneous welfare state in the European periphery (such a reading necessarily takes Wallander's anxieties and his perspective as the novel's ethos) and one that insists on the novel's ambivalent presentation of the killers' 'foreigness' and Wallander's own xenophobia in a narration that refers to real and present, national and regional, ethnic and political conflicts without posing, as Nestingen has it, 'a rosy social democratic solution to the problems' (Nestingen 2008: 249).

According to Byström and Frohnert's discussion of how Sweden responded to mass-migration around 1990, '[x]enophobic sentiments flared at intervals. When in 1988 a rural district in Skåne in the southernmost part of Sweden arranged a local referendum on refugee reception and the result was a no, it caused a media storm and political concern' (229). Stenport argues that this local event permeates *Faceless Killers* and turns Mankell's Ystad and Skåne into more than just another eccentric, peripheral location: 'Skåne's countryside had by the early 1990s become iconic in the popular imagination' (7), partly due to the referendum in the small town of Sjöbo:

> After several years of significant increases in asylum seekers and refugee immigration, the rural Skåne municipality of Sjöbo adopted a drastic measure to voice popular protests against the effects of large-scale immigration. The municipality voted in a referendum in 1988 not to accept any immigrants or refugee seekers within its borders ... Sjöbo is located just up the road from Ystad, yet it is never mentioned by name in *the novel*. Its silent presence nevertheless looms over the text. (7)

The political context is significant and helps us understand that while Skåne and Ystad are in many ways European and Swedish peripheries, the 'refugee crisis' and its local reactions have turned the landscape of *Faceless Killers* into a centre for national and global conflicts. Especially the major Scanian city of Malmö has

become, since the early nineties, a multicultural society with its concomitant political, ethnic and social challenges. Malmö, Sweden's
'third city', has about 40 per cent foreign-born residents and unemployment rates exceeding 50 per cent in some neighbourhoods
(Stenport: 7). However the presence of Sjöbo and its xenophobic
referendum is not as 'silent' in the novel as Stenport claims, though
it is subtle. It is curiously 'commemorated' in the market ('Sjöbo
marknad') where Ebba, the receptionist at the police station, has
bought an old-fashioned music box that catches Wallander's eye
(Mankell 2011b: 283, 293). In their attempt to locate Skinhead
and Lucia, Wallander's colleagues have encountered various 'workers from Eastern European countries without work permits' (284)
being exploited by local businesses. The music box and possibly
Ebba's comment that one can find something wonderful among all
the junk at the market has stirred in Wallander's subconscious all
day and provides him with a vague intuition that the killers are to
be found at a similar market. The next day they are apprehended at
the market in Kivik.

While perhaps dissatisfying to crime fiction readers as an exercise in carefully plotted detection, the coincidental capture of the
killers at the market must be viewed as part of the ambivalent
double-coding of locations and characters in the novel: the killers
embodying both the feared Other and domestic xenophobia as the
'market place' figures both local xenophobic policies in its reference
to Sjöbo and the location of illegal migrant workers. Going back
to the question, what was happening in the Swedish welfare state
in the 1990s, with the ambivalences of the novel's ethos in mind,
suggests that while the police may more or less accidentally stumble
upon the criminals, the deeper causes for the crimes are shrouded
in a Scanian fog leaving the investigation necessarily inconclusive,
in this 'new era, which demanded', Wallander realizes, 'a different
kind of policeman' (298).

There seems little doubt that Mankell intended the readers of
Faceless Killers in early-nineties Sweden to explore this connection
between widespread xenophobic fears of the subjective violence of
immigrant Others and the systemic violence of xenophobic policies
that are turning a formerly and famously progressive solidaristic
and humanitarian nation into a peripheral, anxiety-ridden anachronism. However, as this conflict is merely suggested and never prop-
erly analysed in the novel, the reader is left with an ambivalence

that does not lend itself to any easy resolution. The reason why we are not offered a proper analysis of contemporary racism in the novel is mainly because the ambivalences and contradictory anxieties are embodied in the figure of Wallander himself.

While fearful of the racist reactions to the news about the 'foreign' killers, he also wonders to himself, like the majority of voters in Sjöbo, whether Sweden should accept immigrants and is angered by the political system, which does not seem to address the problem:

> It again occurred to Wallander that a change was taking place in Sweden. He sympathised with some of the arguments against immigration that arose in conversation and in the press while the trial was in progress. Did the government and the Immigration Service have any real control over which individuals sought asylum? Over who was a refugee and who was an opportunist? Was it possible to differentiate at all? How long could the current refugee policy operate without leading to chaos? Was there an upper limit? Wallander had made half-hearted attempts at studying the issues thoroughly. He realised that he harboured the same vague apprehension that so many other people did. Anxiety at the unknown, at the future. (268)

Furthermore, we are introduced to Wallander's xenophobia and racism when he sees his daughter with her new Kenyan boyfriend and in his erotic dreams of a faceless black woman. These recurring dreams form a narrative frame of the novel, as if embedding the otherwise social-realistic narrative within an overdetermined colonial fantasy of the subjugation of the feminized and exoticized Other:

> When the telephone roused him, he was deep in an intense, erotic dream ... he was alone in the bed. Neither his wife, who had left him three months ago, nor the black woman with whom he had just been making fierce love in his dream, was there. (7)

And again at the very end of the novel: 'He forced himself to push these thoughts aside [that fear will be on the rise] and sought out the black woman of his dreams. The investigation was over. Now he could finally get some rest' (298). Rather than referring Wallander's bigotry to the overall ethos of the novel, as Tapper does, it is an essential aspect of the narrative, according to Nestingen, that Mankell 'goes out of his way to impute to Wallander antisocial and racist attitudes ... In depicting a discomforting and reactionary anger in Wallander's questions and attitudes, the novels provoke the reader to disagree with the complex Wallander' (Nestingen 2008: 249–50).

This is one of the ways in which Mankell revised a central generic aspect of the crime novel and the police procedural by portraying Wallander as an ambiguous hero – not a new policeman for a new era, but instead a new police novel. Traditionally, the detective genre rests on a contract between the hero and the reader based on identification and trust. Though fundamentally anti-heroic, detectives such as Martin Beck and Varg Veum conformed to the crime genre's establishment of sympathies for their hard-headed protection of social justice and morals in a world beset with conspicuous consumption, brutality and a dysfunctional and sterile state. In the Wallander figure, however, the genre contract is broken as the detective is presented as much a part of the problem as part of the solution to the central conflict in the novel regarding the presence of ethnic Others in the 'homogeneous' Swedish social landscape, which in turn reveals the breakdown of a solidaristic ethos traditionally associated with the welfare state before the crisis. While the reader is invited to question the morality of Wallander and the police through the overdetermined portrayal of him as harbouring racist and sexist inclinations, this fissure in the trust between reader and hero is replicated in the novel's portrayal of the 'everyman' Wallander and his representative lack of trust in the ability of the state to secure the nation against border-crossing crime.

While *Faceless Killers* does not deliver a straightforward answer to the question of what is happening to Sweden by analysing the sociopolitical reasons for xenophobia and racism, it does deliver an unsettling portrait of a criminal periphery where guilt appears evenly distributed between the inside and the outside, and where anxieties about the foreign and unknown are as much anxieties about an uncertain future in a disempowered and peripheral state. The rift in social trust between the citizen and the state is part of a more extensive, complex and opaque shift in attitudes towards the welfare state in an age of neoliberal restructuring and globalization. The lack of faith in the ability of the state to 'engineer' a way out of the imminent crisis is a result of globalization itself and, not least, the Swedish financial crisis in the early nineties – the true silent context to the novel – and the neoliberal restructuring of the welfare state that 'has eaten into the state's symbolic authority' (Nestingen 2011: 173). An analysis of the systemic reasons for the violence and racism in the shape of a crime novel, a lack that Tapper has staunchly criticized in Mankell's work, is consciously hidden from view. Wallander is perhaps equipped with an unrivalled intuition for criminal investigation but is not armed with an ability to see the connections between the ideological, economic and demographic developments that underpin his own anxiety. His thinking and investigation needs to be as diffuse as the world that surrounds him – a world which is to him a constantly nagging mystery. The absence of an explicit critique of the welfare state and the systemic violence it veils, as opposed to the one we find in Sjöwall and Wahlöö, is conspicuous to the extent that we can understand its absence as a sign of the 'national' welfare state's diminished relevance in an age of globalization, reminiscent of a traumatic absent cause:

> Absent from the text is also the significant deconstruction of Welfare-State policies during the late 1980s and early 1990s when less money was available for ambitious integration programs while unemployment rates skyrocketed from a comfortable 3–4 percent to a staggering 10 percent in 1992, unheard of in modern Swedish history. The unemployment rate of immigrants quickly established itself at over 20 percent, where it has since remained. Segregation, marginalization, and the proliferation of negative stereotyping of immigrants quickly followed. (Stenport: 9)

It was a new age of widespread pessimism and crisis in the Swedish welfare state, and the flourishing of racism shattered both the internal and external image of 'a paradise of social enlightenment, as an international champion of social justice, as the very model of solidarity and equality, as the world's capital of good intentions and civilized behaviour towards others' (Pred: 9). While the flare of hate crimes and evident social and ethnic segregation was perhaps more deeply felt in Sweden due to its almost impenetrable self-image, developments in Sweden have been similar to elsewhere in Western Europe:

> Because of a parallel fiscal crisis of the state and an erosion of welfare provisions the majority of people in European countries live

at least intermittently with a sense of insecurity, of uncertainty or trepidation about the future, of frustration at unfair treatment and unrealized desires, of powerlessness, and, enmeshed in all this, a sense of dissatisfaction with their levels of consumption that is often accompanied by fears of social demotion, loss of status, and possible marginalization. (9)

Xenophobia and racism necessarily need the presence of ethnic Others to fuel already existing anxieties and a minority's irrational hatred. The flare of racism in the 1990s and in the present, however, should lead us to explore what Wallander appears incapable of, namely the policies, economic and systemic failures that lead to social insecurity, marginalization and segregation in the first place.

The experience of crisis, conflict and the decomposition of the Swedish welfare state found its way to the rest of the Scandinavian countries and seeped into the new millennium, where it became fuelled by fears associated with global terrorism and wars and a financial crisis which did not leave the Scandinavian countries unscathed. While an absent cause in Mankell's first Wallander novel, Stieg Larsson's global bestsellers draw explicitly on the financial crisis of the early nineties to frame a dystopian portrayal of millennial Sweden eroded by immoral border-crossing speculators, Swedish Nazis, Eastern European spies and misogynistic, rapist guardians representing a welfare state wherein the symbolic authority of the state and the police has completely vanished.

Financial crisis and trust capital in Stieg Larsson's *The Girl with the Dragon Tattoo*

Deregulations of the financial sector, loan-financed overconsumption and a speculative boom based on property and foreign loans on top of an international recession led to the dramatic banking and financial crisis of 1990 in Sweden, not dissimilar to the global financial crisis in the first decade of the new millennium. While the government intervened to save the banks, Sweden suffered years of negative growth, and unemployment rose to over 9 per cent by 1993

(Hilson 2008: 82). According to Mary Hilson, it was not only the global winds and migration flows that prompted a re-imagination of the national welfare state in the 1990s and beyond:

> the crisis marked a major social, political and cultural watershed, when many aspects of the Swedish model and Swedish identity itself seemed suddenly to unravel. The Social Democratic government's announcement of its intention to seek membership of the European Community in 1990 was seen by many of its critics as a partial admission of defeat and an acknowledgement that the traditional tenets of the Swedish model had failed. (82)

Stieg Larsson's *Män som hatar kvinnor* (2005, *The Girl with the Dragon Tattoo*, 2008) has rightly been read as a prime example of social realist Scandinavian crime fiction in its depictions of a seemingly realistic Swedish social and geographical environment. The novel's epigraphs reference statistical data of men's violence against women, which call into question the commonly perceived progressive egalitarianism of the Swedish welfare state and lend a degree of authenticity to the crime novel. Widespread violence against women is depicted as having deep roots in the past represented by Swedish Nazi serial killers and contemporary amoral representatives of the paternalistic welfare state, including lawyers and doctors, who abuse their roles as guardians and protectors of a traumatized and alienated, yet immensely resourceful and resilient, young woman, Lisbeth Salander, the girl with the dragon tattoo. The novel's critical depiction of the welfare state's well-polished facade hiding widespread moral and political corruption exemplifies a widely accepted view of Scandinavian crime fiction as depicting 'the comprehensive failure of the world's most comprehensive welfare system', as it is poignantly formulated by Ian Macdougal in his review of Larsson's *Millennium* trilogy entitled 'The Man Who Blew Up the Welfare State' (Macdougall 2010).

The novel has much in common with the genre Katy Shaw has defined as Crunch Lit, 'a body of writings that collectively function to represent the 2007–8 financial crisis' (Shaw 2015: 8), though Larsson's blockbuster crime novel, which took over the bestseller lists around the world at the same time, takes place in 2002–3 with references to the Swedish financial crisis in the early nineties. We might speculate that at least part of its international success, especially following its 2008 publication in English translation, could have something to do with its coincidence with the global financial crisis around that year. A global readership, who might not have known about the previous Swedish crisis, could be excused for believing that the amoral financial speculators in the novel were thinly disguised portraits of stockbrokers and bankers on Wall Street and in the City of London. As the wave of Crunch Lit in the United States and United Kingdom, Larsson's novel also 'grapples with the fallout from the financial crisis and dissects the wreckage left in its wake' (9).

The wreckage in the beginning of the novel is Michael Blomkvist's career as a trusted journalist specializing in 'investigative reporting about corruption and shady transactions in the corporate world' (Larsson 2015a: 54). When the story begins, he has just been convicted of libel against the financier Hans-Erik Wennerström by publishing undocumented exposés about his fraud with government aid money in the magazine *Millennium*, of which Blomkvist is also the co-owner and publisher. Wennerström is a speculator who 'deals with property, securities, options, foreign exchange … you name it' (35). Blomkvist learned that Wennerström had taken money he received from an assistance programme in the 1990s meant for helping industries in the former Eastern Bloc countries get back on their feet. Instead of building a factory in Poland, he kept the funds for himself at a time when loans were hard to come by 'just as the bottom was about to drop out of the market' in 1992. Blomkvist remembers well that year: 'I had a variable-rate mortgage on my apartment when the interest rate shot up to 500 per cent in October. I was stuck with 19 per cent interest a year' (35–6). It is a, by now, familiar story of dubious financial speculators, enabled by a deregulated market to exploit the 'little man' while themselves incurring fat bonuses derived from public funds.

Blomkvist rose to stardom as the journalist who helped capture a notorious band of bank robbers first dubbed the Donald Duck gang by the police, as they wore masks from the world of Disney (perhaps a nod to the bank robbers wearing Donald Duck masks and escape justice in Sjöwall and Wahlöö's *The Locked Room*), but later renamed as 'the Bear Gang' by the press (more appropriately translated as the Beagle Gang), 'which sounded more sinister' (18). We are also told that Carl Michael Blomkvist was frequently mocked with the nickname 'Kalle' after his namesake the Master Detective

Kalle Blomkvist in Astrid Lindgren's detective stories for children, known as Billy Bergson in English. Michael Blomkvist's fame and notoriety in journalistic circles, however, relates to his later book *The Knights Templar: A Cautionary Tale for Financial Reporters*, which, as the title makes clear, suggests that there is a good deal of hubris involved in his own verdict.

We learn about Blomkvist and his book mostly through the unlikely private investigator and 'Sweden's best hacker' Lisbeth Salander. She has been investigating Blomkvist on behalf of Milton Security, 'one of Sweden's most competent and trusted security firms' (38), on an assignment for a lawyer representing the old industrialist Henrik Vanger. We learn that he is considering hiring Blomkvist to work on an investigation into the mysterious disappearance of his niece Harriet Vanger from the then isolated island of Hedeby more than three decades ago under the cover of writing a history of the family-owned Vanger Corporation. In his book, which features a photograph of the Stockholm Stock Exchange floating in mid-air on its cover (98), Blomkvist made a 'declaration of war' against financial reporters who 'seemed content to regurgitate the statements issued by C.E.O.s and stock-market speculators – even when this information was plainly misleading or wrong' (99). In a quoted section from the book's conclusion, Blomkvist writes:

> In the world of financial reporting, however, the normal journalistic mandate to undertake critical investigations and objectively report findings to the readers appears not to apply. Instead the most successful rogue is applauded. In this way the future of Sweden is also being created, and all remaining trust in journalists as a corps of professionals is being compromised. (100)

Blomkvist is portrayed as a whistle-blower with high moral standards who called out his own profession of business journalists as complicit in the financial crisis and its deteriorating effects on Swedish society. The most critical effect of the crisis is the spread of social distrust.

When asked by Vanger's lawyer whether Blomkvist can be considered an honest person, Salander replies, 'That's his trust capital [förtroendekapital], so to speak. His image is to appear as the guardian of robust morality as opposed to the business world' (55). However, now that he has been exposed as not living up to his own high professional principles in his reporting on Wennerström, he must reluctantly withdraw from the public eye and *Millennium*, so that his declining level of 'trust capital' will not endanger the magazine's survival any further: 'It was a matter of trust. For the foreseeable future, editors would hesitate to publish a story under his byline' (24); 'his credibility was regarded as rather low' (523).

There are notable parallels in this part of the novel to the situation around the financial crisis of 2008, which saw public trust in the banking system and financial sector plummet as revelations of a greedy and immoral market saw the light of day, and called for subsequent scrutiny of how the worst crisis since the Wall Street crash and the Great Depression could happen in the first place and why no one saw it coming. Dean Starkman, a former business reporter with the *Wall Street Journal*, wrote a similar though factual book about the role of an uncritical press in the 2008 crash: *The Watchdog That Didn't Bark: The Financial Crisis and the Disappearance of Investigative Journalism* (2014). His opening words are striking in comparison to the centrality given to the earlier financial crisis in Sweden and the failure of business journalists in Larsson's novel:

> The U.S. business press failed to investigate and hold accountable Wall Street banks and major mortgage lenders in the years leading up to the financial crisis of 2008. That's why the crisis came as such a shock to the public and to the press itself. (1)

Apart from getting his revenge on Wennerström, Blomkvist's quest throughout the novel is to regain his lost trust capital in the public eye. Trust capital is the central battleground between the mediated public images of Blomkvist and Wennerström. In his story about Wennerstöm's illicit use of tax-payers' money, Blomkvist's 'deep-throat' Robert Lindberg says that Wennerström is 'presented in the media as a tremendous financial oracle. He thrives on that. It's his "trust capital" [förtroendekapital]' (Larsson 2015a: 33).

A reason for this repeated use of the term trust capital in the novel to describe the opposing sides of responsible critical reporting and financial speculators who, without state intervention, succeed in making money off the financial market crash by embezzling public funds, is the sociocultural investment in social trust as the kit that keeps the healthy welfare state together (Svendsen 2012: 11). According to Bo Rothstein, an important piece of the puzzle in the building of the Scandinavian welfare state is 'the lack of significant corruption and the high level of interpersonal trust in Scandinavian societies':

> It seems utterly unreasonable to think that it would have been possible to shape public opinion in favour of transferring such large economic resources to various public welfare administrations if the people had strongly believed that those administrations were basically corrupt and/or engaged in systematic abuse of power. (Rothstein 2005: 9)

The Girl with the Dragon Tattoo takes its starting point in an environment where trust in the corporate world and trust in a critical press have evaporated in the wake of a devastating financial crisis. To regain his trust capital, Blomkvist will have to leave his profession for a while and earn it back by going through a trial as criminal investigator. In his agreement with Henrik Vanger, he will be given the smoking gun on Wennerström if he succeeds in solving the mystery of Harriet's disappearance. Early in his career Wennerström had worked for Vanger, and we learn that Vanger cares very little for him. With this evidence Blomkvist will be able to provide documentation for his case against the financier, but he will have to commit himself to one year investigating 'a sort of locked-room mystery in island format' (Larsson 2015a: 93).

The updated folk-tale motif of undergoing trial as a private detective in a 'defunct' genre is part of the novel's self-conscious play with a wealth of crime-fiction subgenres (clue-puzzle, serial killer thriller, hardboiled detective novel, children's detective story, action thriller, financial thriller, procedural and true crime [Bergman 2014: 130; Tapper 2014: 251]), intertextual references to other crime novels (Blomkvist reads Sue Grafton, Val McDermid and Sara Paretsky and Henrik Vanger reads Dorothy Sayers [Messent 2013: 233]) and not least to the universe of the Swedish author of children's books Astrid Lindgren, where Blomkvist evokes the moral and rational Kalle Blomkvist and Salander is a grown-up yet still rule-breaking Pippi Longstocking (Leffler 2015).

This 'trial by crime fiction' is steeped in what Linda Hutcheon has termed postmodern parody, which 'signals how present representations come from past ones and what ideological consequences derive from both continuity and difference' (Hutcheon

2002: 89). In the detective novel and crime thriller that occupies most of the narrative, Blomkvist and Salander investigate the disappearance of Harriet Vanger and they engage in a role-play with identities that are similar to the juvenile Lindgren characters of which they have tried to rid themselves. Blomkvist is the Master Detective and, as his 1950s 'Blomkvistare', he is an amateur detective whose rational thinking and cooperative skills (demonstrated in his collaboration with the asocial, individualist Salander) will help him solve the crimes, where the police had failed in the past, thereby regaining and increasing his trust capital. Salander, on the other hand, whose anti-authoritarianism and individualism share traits with Pippi will have to learn to trust Blomkvist as well as she can (Larsson 2015a: 391), though as a victim of sexual abuse and a patriarchal welfare state, she has good reason to distrust most men she encounters. Leffler has suggested that Larsson's references to Lindgren characters 'undercut' the novel's bleaker if not dystopian presentation of a corrupt, misogynist and distrustful welfare society 'bringing into the trilogy an impulse toward positive change ... Like all children, they suggest, Larsson's protagonists have to be fostered and nurtured in order to become mature and independent individuals, socialized citizens and well-informed adults' (Leffler 2015).

In this there is a curious nostalgic element to Larsson's first novel. Trustworthiness is mainly invested in characters who represent values reminiscent of the golden age of the welfare state against opportunist, self-serving and criminal characters such as the Nazi sympathizers in Henrik Vanger's family, Salander's new rapist guardian Bjurman and the rapist speculator Wennerström. Opposed to the corrupt financier Wennerström stands the old traditional industrialist Henrik Vanger who represents the welfare state's agreement between industry and labour, perhaps best illustrated by the Saltsjöbaden Agreement (Hilson: 69). Founded on mutual trust and a sense of shared purpose, this agreement, embodied in Vanger, was a central driver in the success of the post-War welfare state:

> I'm proud that my name is a byword for a man who keeps his word and remembers his promises ... I've never had problems negotiating with trade unions. Even Prime Minister Erlander had respect for me in his day. For me it was a matter of ethics;

I was responsible for the livelihoods of thousands of people, and I cared about my employees. (Larsson 2015a: 86)

Henrik Vanger is clearly invested with a wealth of trust capital. He represents 'the backbone of industry in the welfare state' (72), both of which have fallen on hard times due to 'stock-market crises, interest crises, competition from Asia, declining exports and other nuisances' (72). Interpersonal trust is also a central marker of Salander's relationship with her first legal guardian Palmgren. A former member of the social welfare board, he is described as 'of the old school', a 'peculiar mixture of jurist and social worker' (153), who had 'devoted himself to troubled kids and other social misfits' (42). Salander is the most difficult 'misfit' he ever had to deal with, but as a good representative of the welfare state, his conviction is that 'everyone deserves a chance' (45). As her trustee when Salander was young, he gradually 'won not only a certain amount of trust but also a modest amount of warmth' from Salander (150). Palmgren eventually becomes her guardian following a district court hearing, in which the social services threatened Salander with internment in a closed psychiatric institution. This, again, recalls Pippi who was constantly under threat of being sent to an orphanage in Lindgren's stories. As Salander's lawyer, Palmgren succeeded in getting the court to consider guardianship as a compromise but on one condition, he says 'that Fröken [miss] Salander must be willing to trust me and accept me as her guardian' (152–3). She nods in agreement; bewildered as this was the first time anyone in the court had asked her opinion.

According to a lengthy description in the novel of the legal status of guardianship in Sweden, a guardian 'shall take over all of the client's *legal powers* ... Taking away a person's control of her own life – meaning her bank account – is one of the greatest infringements a democracy can impose' (210). Despite this infringement (the mention here of her 'bank account' as equalling independence is reminiscent of Pippi's suitcase full of golden coins), which surely is at odds with Salander's anti-authoritarianism, she is able to form a trusting relationship with her 'old school' guardian as he shows her respect, treats her as 'any other human being' and trusts her to 'take charge of her own money and her own life' (211). Under his guardianship she 'had not paid much attention to her legal status' – a situation which changes drastically when Palmgren suffers a heart attack and she is given a new guardian in Bjurman.

In Palmgren's absence, Salander, who now has no access to her own money and no one she can trust, is sexually abused by Bjurman. This experience turns her into a lone avenger. Salander does not turn him over to the police, as an 'ordinary citizen' would have done, because 'Salander was not like any normal person' and her 'faith in the police was generally exiguous. The police were a hostile force who over the years had put her under arrest or humiliated her' (211). The narrative of Salander's humiliations, assaults, loss of independence and trusting relationships runs parallel to her growing involvement in Blomkvist's case. In Blomkvist asking for Salander's trust in the exchange: '"Do you trust me?" Blomkvist persisted. "For the time being," she said', which is a repetition of Palmgren's earlier question in court, we are pointed in the direction of a larger symbolic narrative relevant to both protagonists about giving and earning trust capital.

In the novel, trust is associated with ethical values belonging to the golden age of the welfare state, the Swedish people's home, whose 'values of the good home' including equality, consideration, cooperation, helpfulness, were to replace social inequality and exploitation. The latter is of course associated with Wennerström, whose wealth is acquired at the expense of common people and the collective. The novel, then, is in the end a fairy tale about acquiring the trust capital that befits good welfare citizens, assisted by helpers who share the same traditional moral codex, and a tale about the well-deserved loss of trust capital in those who have taken advantage of others. This theme throws light on how *The Girl with the Dragon Tattoo* can be read as Crunch Lit and as a response to the fate of the welfare state in the wake of a financial crisis.

Rewarded for his and Salander's successful investigation and finding of Harriet Vanger alive and well in Australia, the novel ends with Blomkvist's exposure of Wennerström 'and his young stockbrokers, partners, and Armani-clad lawyers' in the pages of *Millennium* and his subsequent book entitled *The Mafia Banker*. The disclosure is a new threat to the Swedish Stock Exchange: it 'trembled as the securities fraud police began investigating' (524) and led to 'the biggest bubble to burst in the Swedish financial world' (525).

However, Blomkvist's comments, when asked by a journalist whether he felt responsible for crashing Sweden's economy, are illustrative of the novel's critique of the financial markets post-1990 and suggestive of the nostalgic hue, a fairy-tale dream of utopian permanence, in which the traditional, national, industrial welfare state is cast:

> The Swedish economy is the sum of all the goods and services that are produced in this country every day. There are telephones from Ericsson, cars from Volvo, chickens from Scan, and shipments from Kirona to Skövde. That's the Swedish economy, and it's just as strong or weak today as it was a week ago … The Stock Exchange is something very different. There is no economy and no production of goods and services. There are only fantasies in which people from one hour to the next decide that this or that company is worth so many billions, more or less. It doesn't have a thing to do with reality or with the Swedish economy. (528)

As noted by Peter Messent, Blomkvist 'is motivated by larger political and economic interests than Salander, and interests vital to the continuing health of the Swedish state' (Messent 2013: 232), and he is 'looking back to a more responsible business system and shared sense of social and national wellbeing' (239). However, as pointed out by several critics, we may question the means by which especially Salander helps restore the balance of social trust mainly through illegal hacking, international bank transfers, vigilantism, identity theft and vengeance, by, as Nestingen has formulated it, fighting 'neoliberalism by using its tools more skilfully and more ruthlessly than the corporations' (Messent 2013: 239, Nestingen 2011: 180; Stenport and Alm 2009: 175).

It is Salander's ambiguity that makes this first novel in the Trilogy more than a juvenile, fairy-tale of the restoration of an old welfare ethos, and will provide the storyline for the subsequent instalments. She is coded as an innocent victim whose well-founded lack of trust in the state leads her on the path of righteous vengeance. She avenges both crimes committed against herself and those committed by 'men who hate women', including Wennerström. Cast as 'the perfect victim' against Nazi serial killers and rapist representatives of the state, readers may be excused for empathizing with her choice of methods to obtain justice. However, Blomkvist's regained trust capital, through the exposure of Wennerström, does leave some questions, as his revelations of the illicit and unethical dealings of

Wennerström almost entirely depend on documentation hacked and stolen by Salander. In the end we are left with a novel that on the one hand endorses and nostalgically longs for traditional welfare ethics (trust capital) while on the other hand it illustrates that in the post-crunch era such 'capital' may only be restored by replicating the systemic (neoliberal) structures that crushed 'social trust' in the welfare state in the first place.

Compromised detectives

Mankell's *Faceless Killers* and Larsson's *The Girl with the Dragon Tattoo* use, revise and parody crime genres in order to explore the legitimacy of the welfare state in an era of social, political, economic and cultural crises. They do not, however, use crime fiction unambiguously to restore a past social order as in the clue-puzzle tradition (Scaggs 2005: 46), to contain the criminal Other as in the 'paranoid' hardboiled mode (75) or as a social placebo that will contain all threats to society and reinstall trust in the state typical of the police procedural (98). Both novels gesture towards such nostalgic recall of a more ethical, more harmonious, less violent and less complicated past but immediately deconstruct any utopianism through Wallander's dubious morals, Salander's illicit methods and, not least, their parodic play with crime genres, which demonstrates the continuity with and difference from a longed-for world that could be contained by 'a genre' while pointing out that an era of 'decomposition' also includes the 'decomposition' of stable narrative forms.

Mankell and Larsson's globalized Sweden of the early 1990s is in the midst of a deep financial and identity crisis, which gives rise to anxieties and a longing for a more harmonious past and present; a nostalgic elsewhere characterized by stable morals, lack of conflicts and trusting relationships that may never have existed. In the first novel of Mankell's series about 'a Swedish anxiety', Wallander already realizes that he has become an anachronism unable to comprehend the changes occurring in his own life and in the wide society. His is an existential anxiety which will, in the final instalment of the series almost two decades later (*Den orolige mannen*, 2009; *The Troubled Man*, 2011), end in complete amnesia as he withdraws into Alzheimer's disease.

In Stieg Larsson's crime novels, values inherent to the traditional welfare state are embodied not in amnesic but in dying representatives of the social state of the 1950s: Palmgren and Henrik Vanger. They function as role models for the novel's victims to the dissolution of morals in state institutions from journalism and finance to the social security system and the police. However, their people's-home morals are clearly outdated and nostalgic in the neoliberal and morally compromised society of the 1990s in which Blomkvist and Salander need to navigate. Social order and trust cannot be restored by abiding to or trusting outdated welfare institutions. It takes a 'foreign body' such as Lisbeth Salander to expose the systemic violence of the contemporary Swedish welfare state, a 'home' which has covered up her abuse and sheltered her abusers to maintain a facade of neutrality, incorruptibility and harmony. As a hacker she is working in the shadows of the modern digital age and is able to disclose incriminatory private documents to the public through a carefully selected and trusted media outlet such as Blomkvist's *Millennium* magazine – activities reminiscent of Julian Assange's WikiLeaks founded in 2006, one year after the first publication of *The Girl with the Dragon Tattoo*.

This is, however, also a personal story of what it takes to overcome the trauma of abuse, how to restore one's own trust in others, a trust which has been crushed successively since childhood. In the *Millennium* trilogy, Michael Blomkvist and his sister, the lawyer, Annika represent the characters of Tommy and Annika in Lindgren's children's books, with whose help Lisbeth tries to restore her trust in the justice system and finally gain her full personal and financial independence. Apart from friendships built on mutual trust, Lisbeth Salander uses stolen capital and information against violent and corrupt men in power in a private vendetta, which also serves a public purpose, as the wealth and information are used to provide justice for those countless others who are abused by men and to restore public trust in a traditional journalist, who is still bent on holding those in power accountable. As such, both Mankell and Larsson's crime novels let their readers face and work through breakdowns in interpersonal trust on both thematic and narrative levels and ask us to evaluate our own investment of trust in compromised detectives as well as in compromised welfare states.

5

Landscape and memory in the criminal periphery

The detectives we encounter in the post-1990 era of 'decomposition, uncertainty and crisis' (Hobsbawm 1995: 5; see Chapter 4) are in various ways trying to police and navigate their social and geographical landscapes without a reliable map. Set in the peripheries of a North European province, these crime novels became models for a particular Scandinavian take on, what John Sutherland has called, the 'hyperlocation' of crime fiction, which he defines as 'crime writers' practice of rooting their narrative not just in some metropolitan setting, but in one which is loaded with a "solidity of specification" (as Henry James called it) far in excess of what that narrative strictly requires' (Sutherland 2007).

Noticing this particular local genre trait in Henning Mankell's crime writing, Slavoj Žižek suggests that such a 'solidity of specification', or, to draw on a concept employed in Chapter 1, a genre-specific 'authenticity effect', should be understood as directly linked to the renewed significance of the local in an age of globalization:

> Henning Mankell's recent series of police procedurals set in the southern Swedish town of Ystad, with Inspector Kurt Wallander as their hero, is a perfect illustration of the fate of the detective novel in the era of global capitalism. The main effect of globalisation on detective fiction is discernible in its dialectical counterpart: the specific locale, a particular provincial environment

as the story's setting. In a globalised world, a detective story can take place almost anywhere. (Žižek 2003: 24)

Considering the recent decades of crime-writing in Scandinavia, one is tempted to agree that writers have indeed relocated their crime scenes from mostly urban centres to cover every inch of the map: Camilla Läckberg's Fjällbacka, Johan Theorin's Baltic island of Öland, Mari Jungstedt's Gotland crime novels, Åsa Larsson's Kiruna in northern Sweden, Karin Fossum's small-town Norway and Gretelise Holm's provincial Denmark – to mention just a few examples in support of Žižek's further suggestion that '[t]oday, the exception, the eccentric locale, is the rule' (24).

Scandinavian crime novels are ripe with 'overdetermined' eccentric locations, which are constantly refracted through a wider world of crime and insecurity. However, rather than providing a 'solidity of specification', beyond the mere stimulation of readers' desires for exotic northern landscapes, the very landmarks of their Scandinavian peripheries take liquid form: the earth under Wallander's foggy Scanian Ystad is slippery and unstable clay; Kerstin Ekman's Blackwater is a constantly shape-shifting marshland, and while Peter Høeg's Smilla is famously an apt reader of snow, her investigation becomes as much about her own fluid hyphenated identity and the colonial foundation underneath the crumbling Danish welfare state. Yet, the 'liquid' nature of the geographic locations, their inhabitants and communities and their sense of self and belonging – magnified, as it were, through the eruption and destabilization of violent crimes and their investigation in the crime novel – is, perhaps, exactly what made these novels global in nature as well as in reach. They demonstrate the volatility of the crime genre to respond to new and different pressures on individuals and collectives, to reflect the anxieties of a globalized age as it is absorbed into the specific geographic locations and generic traditions of a now much less stable Scandinavian imaginary.

The peripheral 'hyperlocations' in Scandinavian crime fiction are central social spaces for the negotiation of present individual and collective anxieties about belonging, solidity or rootedness in the era of the welfare state's political and ideological homelessness and more universal spatio-temporal dislocations. The fears represented in the Scandinavian crime novel around the new millennium are, not surprisingly, preoccupied with memories and the past – a past that appears at times as rootless, slippery and menacing as the clay, water and snow of the 'hyperlocal' crime scenes.

Welfare nostalgia

When looking back upon the dramatic changes that characterize the twentieth century and contemplating a global future from the vantage point of the mid-1990s, the mood is often marked by a growing '*fin-de-siècle* gloom' (Hobsbawm 1995: 6). According to Hobsbawm, the new global era introduced dramatic social, moral and cultural changes such as 'a-social individualism' related to 'the disintegration of the old patterns of human social relationships', the 'snapping of links between generations, that is to say, between past and present' (15):

> At the end of this century it has for the first time become possible to see what a world may be like in which the past, including the past in the present, has lost its role, in which the old maps and charts which guided human beings, singly and collectively, through life no longer represent the landscape through which we move, the sea on which we sail. In which we do not know where our journey is taking us, or even ought to take us. (16)

In Chapter 1, we have already seen how, to use Zygmunt Bauman's metaphor, the 'solid modernity' of the golden age of the welfare state expressed itself in a domesticated, controllable and rational cityscape envisioned to provide security for its citizens in their socially engineered homes, which promised a sanitized foundation for future progress (Bauman 2012). The crime novels discussed in Chapters 1 to 3 are all in different ways investigating the rifts that began to appear in these utopian 'concrete giants' of a harmonious welfare modernity: the consumer society's erosion of meaningful social relationships, solidarity, authenticity and a sense of both spatial and temporal rootedness. The modern welfare state's ideology of progress, with its dreams of an even better tomorrow and practice of social renewal through urban sanitation, had 'forgetting' inscribed into its very foundation as the dream of more egalitarian, wealthy and productive societies sought to sever themselves from stagnant class structures and festering poverty and to build a new and better future out of the physical and ideological rubbles of the Second World War. Scandinavian crime novels across subgenres by Sjöwall and Wahlöö, Bodelsen and Staalesen registered the individual and social consequences of societies bent on 'consuming' their way out of the past, and in various ways sought to establish more 'authentic', more 'reasonable' bonds through their detectives' development of communal responsibilities.

Crime novels towards the end of 'the golden age' of the welfare state reacted to the anxiety that the solid 'levees' of the welfare state might not withstand the pressures of the individualized consumer society by constructing, as in Sjöwall and Wahlöö's *Novel of a Crime*, fictional domestic utopian communities of a more authentic people's home in the ruins of the Swedish welfare state, or, as in Staalesen's early Varg Veum novels, by creating a sympathetic social-worker detective, whose nostalgia for a traditional solidaristic society is in stark contrast to the amnesic and violent consumer society he needs to navigate. While they explicitly presented a dystopian portrait of the welfare state in the 1970s, their detectives were inescapably carved out of the solid and progressive ideals of the post-War welfare state, and their nostalgia for a more authentic past was intricately tied to the symbolic realm of the solid welfare state, rooted in invented national traditions and values (see Chapter 2).

In Scandinavian crime novels, from the early 1990s, the rifts in the solid modernity of the welfare state have become wide-open wounds that characterize, to use Bauman's metaphors again, a 'liquid modernity', wherein social life is fundamentally conditioned by decomposed traditions, restless mobility and changeable communities made up of fluid, anxious identities. This next generation of crime novels, however, also expresses a persistent lament for a better, more solidaristic, more authentic, perhaps more sentimental society of close and trusting relationships perceived to having been forgotten in the wake of modernization and globalization – though, importantly, such bygone values are often coded as inherent to particular national characteristics of the Scandinavian welfare states.

This new era of anxieties about the waning relevance of the past – a local or national past that could anchor the present and provide comfort on the threshold to an uncertain, globalized future – has produced and been represented by crime novels that seem not only bent on investigating the effects of late-modern amnesia but also virtually obsessed with the past, with national histories, personal and familial traumas and even the deep pasts of myth and primordial nature. The central preoccupation in crime fiction is, however, still the present, even if set entirely in the past; yet, present anxieties and violent crimes are often linked to uncomfortable pasts, which need to be excavated to make sense of present conflicts.

This is the premise for Jussi Adler-Olsen's crime series about Carl Mørck and his Department Q. As the 'keeper of lost causes', Mørck oversees his 'dark' (*mørk* means dark in Danish) archival underworld in the basement of the police station, where unsolved cases from the past constantly erupt in the present to reveal brutal and immoral elements among the privileged upper class (*Fasandræberne*, 2008; *Disgrace*, 2012) and within a radicalized political landscape (*Journal 64*, 2010; *Guilt*, 2014).

The crime novel has become a privileged genre in which to process common anxieties connected to an impending loss of a better past or a present undermined by past crimes. Sally Munt reminds us that a central convention in crime fiction is 'Eden disturbed by chaos, loss, and conflict, the primary hermeneutic being the reinstatement of that paradisiacal unity' (Munt 1998: 135). However, as she also notes, we of course know that the 'return can never be completed, as evil has entered the garden for good.' Scandinavian crime fiction exploits this convention by exploring the bucolic, paradisiacal Scandinavian imaginary and its geographical peripheries suddenly exposed to violence that was previously associated with the global metropolis. The fallen landscape, the rural *locus criminis*, is presented as a small-scale model for a present ambivalent nostalgia for an idyllic welfare state of the past, with its hopes and dreams for an always better future now thwarted by the chaos and uncertainties of a globalized world. As David Lowenthal defines nostalgia in *The Past is a Foreign Country* (1985), it 'is memory with the pain removed. The pain is today. We shed tears for the landscape we find no longer [is] what it was, what we thought it was, or what we hoped it would be' (8).

The international success of Scandinavian crime fiction, initiated by translations of Peter Høeg's *Miss Smilla's Feeling for Snow* and Henning Mankell's Wallander series in the early 1990s, depended, to a large extent, on the fact that their various negotiations of particular, national pasts surfacing in recognizable Scandinavian hyperlocations could tap into more widely shared, even global anxieties and concerns that did not depend on local knowledge of specific histories and debates surrounding the fate of the welfare state. Andreas Huyssen has pointed out that the rise of nostalgic sentiments represents a widely shared perspective of the past at the end of the twentieth century, where 'the coordinates of space and time structuring our lives are increasingly subject to new kinds of pressures':

> One of modernity's permanent laments concerns the loss of a better past, the memory of living in a securely circumscribed place, with a sense of stable boundaries and a placebound culture with its regular flow of time and a core of permanent relations. Perhaps such days have always been a dream rather than a reality, a phantasmagoria of loss generated by modernity itself rather than by its prehistory. But the dream does have staying power, and what I have called the culture of memory may well be, at least in part, its contemporary incarnation. (Huyssen 2003: 24)

Generated by the pace of progress and the uncertainties arising from a globalized world which, according to Giddens, led to the 'end of traditions', Scandinavian crime novels at the end of the twentieth century can be viewed as popular instances of a wider 'culture of memory', a 'cultural obsession of monumental proportions across the globe', with a penchant for the nostalgic mode (Giddens 2002: 43; Huyssen 2003: 16).

The particular nostalgic mood captured in post-1990 Scandinavian crime novels, however, also reflects a wider Nordic experience related to specific reconfigurations of national and regional identities. The crises of the social state in the wake of globalization, financial crises and European integration produced a 'Nordic nostalgia', according to Ole Wæver. The crisis of the late eighties and early nineties led to a disintegration of the Nordic self-image of representing a future society, a middle way, between capitalism and communism: 'Suddenly the sources of the future are to be found not in Norden, but on the continent. The less-European identity of "Norden" is no longer a promise, but a threat – the threat of being periphery' (Wæver 1992: 77).

As a counter-reaction to this loss of national self-confidence, the 1990s witnessed a resurgence of nationalist sentiments in Scandinavia. According to Jenny Andersson, the utopian ideals of a Swedish 'people's home' became invested with 'a kind of nostalgia for a future lost, a nostalgia which might quite simply be called People's home nostalgia' (Andersson 2009a: 238). This nostalgia revealed itself in the 'rehabilitation of the notion of the People's home' or *folkhemmet*: 'everything from bars to television chat shows and interior decoration shops were suddenly named *folkhemmet*', in a vein similar to the 'Ossie' nostalgia in Eastern Europe (239). The recent phenomenon of a particular Scandinavian modern aesthetics and social consciousness embedded in everything from design furniture to Nordic food, Dogme film and 'Nordic Noir' is part of this nostalgic longing for a 'purer' and more harmonious golden age of a Scandinavian periphery, which today has found currency well beyond the Scandinavian countries.

The darker side to this reinforcement of the welfare state as a backward-looking national self-image, as coinciding unproblematically with a particular Nordicness or Swedishness, is that it hides a more problematic, exclusive and 'sanitizing' discourse about social values as if entrenched in national characteristics derived from specific locations and deep pasts, which can be 'elevated to the values of the "people" in response to the perceived threat of immigrant communities to these very defining values' (240). According to Andersson, this partly explains the rise of populist immigration-critical parties in Scandinavia in the same period, such as Sverigedemokraterna in Sweden, Dansk Folkeparti in Denmark and Fremskrittspartiet in Norway, whose political propaganda is shaped around a nationally ingrained welfare nostalgia that successfully taps into a growing sentiment of being under siege by an ethnically diverse and hostile world.

On the other hand, a welfare-nostalgic longing for values belonging to an inclusive, egalitarian and socially just society, a model that has been under threat from neoliberal policies and global capitalism since at least the 1980s, also represents a resurgence, in the wake of the 2008 global financial crisis, of a widely shared concern with growing social inequalities in a corrosive, competitive society. Since then, a more flexible Nordic or Swedish Model has again been the focus of attention as it is commonly seen to be producing prime examples of successful welfare states consistently ranging at the top of international tables and global wellbeing surveys (Wilkinson and Pickett, 2010).

The Scandinavian welfare state and its various national instanti-ations has, in this new age of crises, become a site of political, social and cultural struggle as perhaps never before; a struggle over its present and future values, its very legitimacy, in a globalized world, and, not least, a struggle over its past, its legacy, for understanding persistent and present conflicts. Crime fiction has since the early nineties been a product of and contributor to this ongoing negoti-ation of the welfare state with its generic predilection for investi-gating dependent individual and societal conflicts located in specific yet mutable social and geographic environments.

As argued in Chapter 1, nostalgia was a mode employed in the detective novel as a reaction to an increasingly inauthentic consumer-scape, and it carried into Sjöwall and Wahlöö's police procedural and Staalesen's hardboiled detective novel as symp-tomatic of their experience of urban homelessness in the modern consumerist welfare society. Similarly, the detectives in the post-1990 crime novel are often portrayed as, what Svetlana Boym has called, 'modern nostalgics' who 'can be homesick and sick of home, at once' (Boym 2001: 50). Crime fiction in the post-War period shares a pervasive discomfort with the present (welfare) state of affairs. The ubiquitous sense of displacement, as related through the crime genre, is inherent to the detectives' deep-felt though often abstract anxieties, prompting them to wonder what has gone wrong in society and in their own private lives. Anxieties of the present are expressed in a longing for a non-existent or imagined past ('false-nostalgia') or are related to the suppression of an uncomfortable memory or trauma shrouded by individual or collective amnesia.

One of the most successful Swedish clue-puzzle writers of the 1950s, Maria Lang, became influential in shaping the Swedish and Scandinavian crime novel's preoccupation with the idyl-lic spatio-temporal (dis)location of the traditional rural village. While Lang is rarely read today, and only a few of her forty-three Christie-inspired 'whodunits', featuring the amateur detec-tive Puck Ekstedt and police detective Christer Wijk, have been translated into English, the environment in which her novels take place is perhaps better known from the recent film and TV adaptation of six of her novels collectively given the title of her first novel, *Mördaren ljuger inte ensam* (2013, *Crimes of Passion*, BBC4 2014). Set mostly in and around the fictional small town of Skoga, the violent crimes in Lang's novels are usually caused by domestic conflicts, often with erotic undertones (the 'passions' of the English title), in enclosed middle-class environments. The mysteries are eventually solved through the collective workings of Puck's well-developed female intuition and the rational mind of the male police detective. While there appears to be a constant threat to the rural idyll (a central figure in 1950s Swedish clue-puzzle crime novels used as a small-scale model of the wider society), evil in paradise is always expelled and order reinstated (Kärrholm 2005: 53, 54).

Particularly in the recent TV adaptation of Lang's novels for a twenty-first-century audience, it becomes apparent that the idyll of the Swedish village is tinged with a 'false nostalgia' for a bygone age that may never have been. The nostalgic mode was already integral to the novels themselves and their time, written as they were in an age of rapid social and environmental change driven, for instance, by the industrialization of mining districts such as Bergslagen (Lang's childhood village of Nora in Bergslagen is the model for Skoga), and welfare modernization, which also swept through the rural districts. As urbanization created new consumer desires and necessitated a 're-imagination of communities', the idyll of the clue-puzzle came to function as a cultural anchor in a period of dramatic change to the readers' geographic, moral and mental sense of place.

The nostalgic sentiment implicit in both the original novels and their recent adaptation can be described as 'restorative nostalgia', to use a term coined by Svetlana Boym: a desire to revive a certain rose-tinted or prelapsarian moment in the past, which offers 'cultural intimacy', continuity with the past and collective belonging against present anxieties about displacement and criminal conspiracies that present the 'home' as 'forever under siege' (Boym 2001: 41–5). As we enter the 1990s, the possibility of an unproblematic temporal and spatial 'elsewhere' slips out of sight as the rural idyll, the safe enclosure of a national landscape, loses its figurative potential for grounding individuals and their nations in unambiguous and comfortable national histories framing commonly shared values.

The erased countryside: Henning Mankell's Wallander

In the urban welfare dystopia of Sjöwall and Wahlöö's *Novel of a Crime* the national periphery of Scania (Skåne) and even Malmö, still promised a national restoration and respite from the horrors, the violence, pollution and consumerism of the capital. In *Brandbilen som försvann* (1969, *The Fire Engine That Disappeared*, 1971), Scania is filtered through a 'staged authenticity' of a past 'elsewhere', an antithesis to the modern centre of Stockholm, prepared as for a 'tourist gaze' (Urry 2002: 9):

> Malmö is Sweden's third largest city and is very different indeed from Stockholm. It has less than a third of the number of inhabitants and sprawls over a flat plain, while Stockholm is built on a system of elevated islands. Malmö lies 360 miles further south and is the country's port to the Continent. The rhythm of life is calmer there, the atmosphere less aggressive, and even the police are said to be more friendly and attuned to society, just as the climate is milder. It often rains, but seldom gets really cold, and long before the ice begins to thaw around Stockholm, the waves in Öresund are rippling against flat sandy shores and limestone plateaux. (Sjöwall and Wahlöö 2011c: 157)

Two decades later, the rural periphery, Scania in particular, as seen from the centre has changed its meaning from a utopian border country, unsullied by the alienating welfare state, to a dystopian periphery contaminated by the urban centre and by its vicinity to a threatening European 'outside'.

In *Faceless Killers*, Wallander has a conversation with the public prosecutor Anette Brolin. She has just moved to Ystad from Stockholm and presents an idyllic view, or a 'tourist gaze', of 'the countryside', similar to the one presented in Sjöwall and Wahlöö's novel. Wallander, however, is anxious to explain that crime is getting worse even in the Swedish periphery, and, as if in an intertextual conversation with Sjöwall and Wahlöö, he turns the centre-periphery dichotomy upside down to such an extent that it becomes meaningless to speak of a more idyllic 'elsewhere' in a near-future Sweden:

'Tell me about this town', she said. 'I've looked through a number of criminal cases from the last few years. It's a lot different from Stockholm.' 'That's changing fast', he said. 'Soon the entire Swedish countryside will be nothing but suburbs of the big cities. There were no narcotics here twenty years ago. Ten years ago drugs had come to towns like Ystad and Simrishamn, but we still had some control over what was happening. Today drugs are everywhere. When I drive by one of the beautiful old Scanian farms, I sometimes think: there might be a huge amphetamine factory hidden in there.' 'There are fewer violent crimes', she said. 'And they're not quite as brutal.' 'It's coming', he said. 'Unfortunately, I guess I'm supposed to say. But the differences between the big cities and the countryside have been almost erased. Organised crime is widespread in Malmö. The open borders and all the ferries coming in are like candy for the underworld.' (139–40)

Wallander is here in his most nostalgic and melancholic of moods, no doubt influenced by his faltering investigation of the brutal killings in an old farm house in the idyllic Scanian countryside. As in the crime novels of the seventies, Wallander blames the spread of crime to the rural periphery on welfare urbanization, which, as discussed in Chapter 1, colonized the countryside by moving people out of the deprived city centres to the fresh air and modern flats of new suburban centres. At the same time, he channels new anxieties related to a borderless Europe, where the specific liminal location of Scania and Ystad is producing fears of border-crossing crimes (xenophobic fears that are both confirmed and undermined in the novel; see Chapter 4). Ystad, Wallander fears, located as it is in the intersection between rapid urbanization and Europeanization, is becoming uprooted, dislocated, suburbanized and globalized, and he is himself the victim of this historical process. However, it seems as if the historical processes are already inscribed into Ystad's geography and landscape, as the young police officer Lindman, who has recently moved to Ystad from Northern Sweden in the Linda Wallander novel *Innan frosten* (2002, *Before the Frost*, 2004), reflects when contemplating the Scanian landscape: 'I've never seen anything like this landscape before ... Here, Sweden simply slopes down into the sea and ends. All this mud and fog. It's very strange. I'm trying to find my feet in a landscape that's completely alien to me' (Mankell 2004: 258).

Wallander's own loss of footing in the societal landscape of the present makes him a modern nostalgic. He is both homesick, longing for a time when the countryside was countryside, when he was himself a young policeman with the future ahead of him, and sick of home, because it reminds him of his own dislocation in time and space. As he realizes, in an equally melancholic reflection, in *Den femte kvinnan* (1996, *The Fifth Woman*, 2003),

> [P]olice work ultimately had to do with being able to decipher the signs of the times. To understand change and interpret trends in society. And for this reason perhaps the younger generation of police officers were better equipped to deal with modern society. Now Wallander knew that he had been mistaken about one essential fact. It was no harder being a police officer today than it was in the past. It was harder for him, but that was not the same thing. (Mankell 2012b: 229)

It is not only Wallander whose nostalgic mood registers that the Sweden he once knew represents his own anachronism and 'lost future'. In Mankell's *Den vita lejoninnan* (1993, *The White Lioness*, 1998), the ruthless border-crossing ex-KGB officer, Konovalenko, who is working for a racist terrorist cell in South Africa plotting to assassinate Nelson Mandela and reinstate apartheid, hides out in the tower blocks in the Stockholm suburb of Hallunda. As he blends in with its multicultural community, he notices 'the lost ideals of the welfare state' written into the very facade of the tower blocks. Even for a criminal outsider, a 'victim' to the end of the Cold War and the decomposition of the Soviet Union, the architecture of the 'million-homes programme' signifies the fall of the utopian ideals of the Swedish welfare state:

> [H]e noticed that there were blemishes on the face even of this country, and it was supposed to be a model society. This grim suburb reminded him of Leningrad and Berlin. It looked as though future decay was built into the facades. (Mankell 2012a: 180–1)

While the racist Konovalenko is the nemesis of the conflicted Swedish 'every-man' detective Kurt Wallander, they both expound an anxious nostalgia for a less-complicated, more (ethnically) homogeneous past before an age of 'decomposition, conflict and crisis'. However, in letting Konovalenko reflect on the 'decay' of the welfare state we are also asked to reflect on the correspondence between two characters who have become, while located in various and far-apart regions of the globalized world, anachronistic peripherals of history, individuals with obsolete ideals who try to find their way in a new age with outdated maps. However, while Konovalenko and Kleyn, the leader of the Boer terrorist cell, actively seek to restore a past more fitting with their own racist ideals through conspiracies and assassinations (523), Wallander employs his nostalgic longing as a shield against present anxieties and the passing of time while simultaneously reflecting on the veracity of the 'past home' that is the object of his longing:

> Wallander realised that he was not alone in his feelings of uncertainty and confusion at the new society that was emerging. We live as if we were in mourning for a lost paradise, he thought. As if we longed for the car thieves and safe-crackers of the old days … but those days have irretrievably vanished, and nor is it certain that they were as idyllic as we remember them. (Mankell 2011b: 246–7)

Wallander's 'false nostalgia' for a lost paradise reveals the disturbing fact that an alternative 'elsewhere' has perhaps always been a 'nowhere' (a utopia proper), and that Ystad or indeed Sweden is not that different from a global 'anywhere'. The modern society, the progressive, solidaristic and future-loving post-War welfare state in which Wallander had grown up, 'was not as solid as they had thought. Under the surface was quagmire. Even back then the high-rise buildings that had been erected were described as "inhuman". How could people who lived there be expected to keep their "humanity"?' (Mankell 2012b: 228).

Wallander's longing is in the end not for a restoration of a more idyllic past in the present. His is a melancholic longing whose object seems to be longing itself, which he employs, much like his incantations in the beginning of *Faceless Killers* (see Chapter 4), as a defence mechanism against the ravages of time and to keep away personal traumas and wounds inflicted by a stabbing when he was a young cop, his teenage daughter's attempted suicide and his more recent divorce. The constant repetition in internal monologues of his longing for an imagined 'elsewhere', his fears for the future and his sense of alienation from the present are intimately related to his personal history and are symbolized in his father's compulsively repetitive painting of identical, bucolic landscape motifs. These not only provided the economic foundation for the family (throughout the series Wallander finds them hanging in many of the homes he visits), but formed from an early age Wallander's own melancholic mood. The repetitive idyllic landscape of his father's paintings mirrors Wallander's inherited response to personal trauma in the register of repetitive nostalgic laments (Wallander's trauma, according to Nestingen, is central to readers' fascination and empathy with his character; Nestingen 2008: 235).

Personal and national pasts are constantly haunting shadows in the idyllic landscape of the Wallander series, where they are not integrated into the present to make it possible for Wallander to deal with familial and social estrangement and Sweden to commit ethically to a globalized world. Mankell's criminal periphery of a contemporary Sweden remains traumatized, alien and muddy, where all that might once have been solid remain only in the shape of mass-produced and repetitive nostalgic landscapes.

Mankell's Wallander novels employ a trope common in Scandinavian crime fiction where individual conflicts and traumas are mirrored in the wider crises of small, secure welfare states portrayed as under siege in an unsettling and confusing globalized world. They also demonstrate a more subtle employment of this trope in which anxieties about the erosion of a national landscape are substitutes for more specific and personal anxieties about the failure to engage in trusting relationship, resulting in guilt, and the failure to adjust to a changing society.

Returning to the scene in *Faceless Killers*, discussed in Chapter 4, where Wallander is alone in his car on his way to the house in which an elderly couple have been brutally killed, it becomes clear that the anxieties surfacing while he is journeying into the idyllic landscape, soon to be revealed as an unrecognizable heart of darkness, are deeply personal, related to wounds on his own body and in his own family. The repeated mantra throughout the series, 'what is wrong with this country', functions as an 'anaesthetising of one fear by the other' – a 'troubled man's' sublimation of individual traumas into a wider social imaginary, where individual guilt is harder to locate and ascribe.

The 'anaesthetising of one fear by the other', is a phrase from Walter Benjamin's essay on 'Crime Novels, on Travel' (1930) (quoted in Salzani 2007: 166). It describes the way in which the popular reading of detective novels on trains, the 'new' and fictional anxieties arising from the 'freshly separated pages of the detective novel', helps the traveller distract from and overcome momentarily the 'anxieties of the journey' itself, understood as anxieties arising from the pressures, timetables, alienation and loss of direction in a modern urban age. Wallander does not find distraction in the reading of a detective novel as he drives towards Lunnarp; however, one senses that Wallander's all-consuming police work and his attendant worries about the fate of his contemporary Sweden – the influx of ethnic Others, racism, the rise in violent crimes and the general moral decay of the welfare state – function in a way similar to Benjamin's detective novels when read on trains, as anxieties that offer him momentary respite from his deeper personal crises and trauma.

Voices from the peasant society: Arne Dahl's *The Blinded Man*

In the opening pages of Arne Dahl's *Misterioso* (1999, *The Blinded Man*, 2012), detective Paul Hjelm finds himself in the backseat of a police car speeding towards a hostage situation in the local immigration office in the Stockholm suburb of Hallunda (the very same estate outside of Stockholm where Konovalenko was hiding in Mankell's *The White Lioness*); a Kosovar-Albanian man had taken three hostages because he was denied citizenship; he had been living with his family in Sweden for a long time and was now being 'sucked into the general wave of deportation'. Through the car's window Hjelm sees the street names 'Linvägen, Kornvägen, Hampvägen and Havrevägen' fly past, and they spark a collective memory of a prelapsarian state:

> The street names – flax, grain, hemp, oats – were like a textbook on agronomy. Everywhere loomed the antithesis of the agrarian society, the brutally unimaginative facades of the identical tall apartment buildings from the Sixties and Seventies. A breeding

ground, thought Hjelm without understanding what he meant. The extinct voices of a peasant society echoed through him like ghosts. (Dahl 2012: 8–9)

By the mid-1990s, the million-homes programme's ruinous monuments to the welfare state had not only become architectural eyesores, but the estates had also become associated with social, economic and ethnic ghettoization and segregation (Pred 2000: 98–125). Hjelm is channelling the 'ghosts of the peasant society' to his own discomfort and bewilderment, representing, we sense, a nostalgic xenophobic discourse that has come to see the housing estate as 'a breeding ground' for crime linked to the perceived infiltration of the nation state by 'foreign' Others.

In *The Blinded Man*, Paul Hjelm feels uneasy about the ghostly voices that speak through him from an undefinable past and his own place in this 'new' welfare society. He considers himself, much like Wallander, an anachronism unlike his new partner in the A-Group, Jorge Chavez, the son of Chilean immigrants, who navigates the multicultural and technological reality with considerably more ease. Their investigation of brutal serial killings of some of Sweden's top capitalists demands a new understanding of society – and a new kind of crime novel:

a fine old classic straight out of an Agatha Christie novel, had gone up in smoke – that type of puzzle intrigue belonged irrevocably to the past – and instead they had landed squarely in the present day: post-industrial capitalism, Eastern European mafia and the collapse of Sweden's financial regulatory system in the 1990s. (Dahl 2012: 151)

The Blinded Man is to some extent a representative Swedish procedural borne out of the social and political upheavals of the early 1990s. It is like Larsson's *Millennium* trilogy an austerity novel, which tackles the uncertainties of living in a new, less optimistic world. As the 'welfare-nostalgic' description of the novel on the author's website sums up its view of the state:

Misterioso is a book that dives straight into the contemporary problems of Sweden, a small but independent northern country that recently has been forced to give up its naivety and to surrender its virginity to a globalized world. It looks frenetically for the origins of the reduction of human values in a world that seems to have lost all connection with a decent life. ('Misterioso', The Official Homepage of Arne Dahl)

However, the cultural mood of xenophobia and anxieties about a globalizing world in the shape of violent asylum seekers and border-crossing Eastern European criminals are red herrings in the novel's crime plot – or to be understood more precisely as 'one fear anaesthetising another.' The serial killer is eventually revealed to be a home-grown avenger, a former bank clerk, who is taking out his anger of having been fired from his job on the board members, 'Sweden's top capitalists', who were responsible for implementing the bank's 'austerity' measures. In the novel, the avenger is spurred on by a public conversation in the media, which takes side against the bankers, whose sexual deprivations, as uncovered by Hjelm, do not give the reader much ground for empathy either. In this way, the actual crime plot shares many similarities with Sjöwall and Wahlöö's critique of the capitalist welfare state as reported in *Polis, polis, potatismos!* (1970, *Murder at the Savoy*), where our sympathies are with the avenging working-class killer who, driven by the present state of the credit market, inflation, the rising costs of living, sudden redundancy and eviction from his flat, takes out his anger and desperation on the 'big boss', Viktor Palmgren, now 'gone forever and missed by no one' (Sjöwall and Wahlöö 2007: 215). The difference is, however, that in Dahl's novel the evil and depraved 'home-grown' capitalists are presented as symptoms of a much wider world of injustices and insecurities that have encroached upon a helplessly unprepared welfare state.

If *The Blinded Man* is a crime novel about a small peripheral country's loss of naivety and virginity to a globalized world, the following 'reduction of human values' is rendered symptomatic of an obscure national political system that has decided to deny citizenship to a resident refugee (the employees in the immigration office feel almost as let down by the politicians as the hostage-taker) and in the obscure structures of global capitalism that have reduced employees to easily replaceable 'figures'. While no clear 'origins of the reduction of human values' are divulged in the novel, it is perhaps clearer in Dahl's police procedurals and in Adler-Olsen's Department Q series, where Mørck's partner is the mysterious

Syrian Assad, than in any of their counterparts in Scandinavia that the police collective itself can present a potential multi-ethnic, cross-generational microcosm able to dispel the ghosts of the past in order to deal at least with the violent symptoms of an opaque present (Kirkegaard 2010: 9).

The ghosts of history: John Ajvide Lindqvist's *Let the Right One In*

In the predominantly urban environments of the welfare-crime novels discussed in Chapters 1 to 3, the cityscape came to function as a figure for the erosion of a more authentic, communal rural past – a trope which has persisted in Scandinavian genre fiction. John Ajvide Lindqvist's horror fiction *Låt den rätte komma in* (2004, *Let the Right One In*, 2009) takes place in Blackeberg, one of the neighbourhoods that make up the suburban area of the showcase ABC city of Vällingby (see Chapter 1). The novel begins with the narrator looking back to the early history of 'the location', to thirty years ago when the welfare 'pioneers' first marched over 'Traneberg Bridge with sunshine and the future in their eyes' (Lindqvist 2009: 1). Throughout the novel, the location is depicted as a small-scale model of the Swedish people's home, its early progressive idealism and what had become of it in the novel's year 1982 as well as in the narrator's present in the new millennium.

Unlike the mythic pioneers on the 'Mayflower' (a reference to the Swedes who left in great numbers for the New World in the final decades of the nineteenth century), the 'Fathers are not carrying picks and shovels but kitchen appliances and functional furniture' into their new welfare-state settlements. Like the pilgrims the arriving residents are filled with optimism for the opportunities in this modern, 'unknown land'. Yet the pioneer spirit of the new residents, the welfare colonizers of the countryside, in their newly materialized 'people's homes' fades in comparison to the pioneers of the past as their homes come prefabricated: 'It was not a place that had developed organically, of course. Here everything was carefully planned from the outset. And people moved into what had been built for them. Earth-coloured concrete buildings, scattered about in the green fields' (Lindqvist 2009: 1). The propagandist or utopian image of pilgrims marching into a new land and a better future is replaced with a more 'realistic' or prosaic image of more or less mindless or disillusioned consumers, whose primary concern is not to build or produce but to fill their prefabricated homes with commodities:

> They came on the subway. Or in cars, moving vans. One by one. Filtered into the finished apartments with their things. Sorted their possessions into the measured cubbies and shelves, placed the furniture in formation on the cork floor. Bought new things to fill the gaps. (1–2)

The modern welfare settlement of Blackeberg has created state-supported consumers, whose dreams of material progress have resulted in collective amnesia. What the new welfare colony of Blackeberg lacked was essentially a past specific to its landscape:

> Where the three-storeyed apartment buildings now stood there had been only forest before. You were beyond the grasp of the mysteries of the past; there wasn't even a church. Nine thousand inhabitants and no church. That tells you something about the modernity of the place, its rationality. It tells you something of how free they were from the ghosts of history and of terror. It explains in part how unprepared they were. (2)

What they were unprepared for was, of course, the arrival of vampires in their midst, the uncanny reappearance of a suppressed past intimately linked to a landscape in which the 'welfare migrants' cannot take root – as in Mankell, forgetting seems to be built into the very architecture of the welfare state. At the same time, the arrival of these premodern vampires represents anxieties arising from the less ethnic homogeneous and less solidaristic welfare state that had already arrived by the early 1980s.

Importantly, the anxieties of the present as figured in *Let the Right One In* are linked to the modern society's dislocation from a rural and spiritual past. This is a dominant theme in Scandinavian popular culture in the decades around the new millennium. Lars von Trier's popular breakthrough TV series *Riget* (1994, The Kingdom) is another example. It also used the horror genre to 'undermine' the welfare state's faith in scientific rationality and progress. The series takes place in one of the most symbolic concrete buildings of the welfare state, Rigshospitalet (the Royal Hospital in Copenhagen), known popularly as Riget (the kingdom). In the opening vignette to each episode we are told that the hospital is built on old marshland where the bleaching ponds once lay: 'Tiny signs of fatigue are appearing in the solid, modern edifices' and the gateways to the Kingdom are again being opened.

Kim Toft Hansen has discussed this rather surprising wealth of spirituality and metaphysics as pervasive in recent Scandinavian crime fiction. He suggests that a renewed interest in the religious is a response to the processes of secularization and rational modernization and to widely perceived conflicts of a religious nature in the multicultural society (Toft Hansen 2012).

Let the Right One In and *The Kingdom* can also be seen as examples of a rich Gothic tradition in Scandinavian fiction, according to Yvonne Leffler, 'where characters are depicted as victims of the surrounding landscape, the uncontrollable wilderness' (Leffler 2013: 141). The wealth of 'Gothic topographies' in Scandinavian fiction and popular culture can be understood, according to Leffler, as a fictional response to an urbanized Scandinavian anxiety about the disappearance of a collective memory as rooted in local landscapes and belonging to 'original' 'communities of production'. Such idyllic landscapes figure as complex symbolic pasts, a simultaneously longed-for and feared 'elsewhere', to present-day Scandinavians' inauthentic relation to their natural environments, which have been reduced to places of leisure and tourism. What in a not-so-distant past provided the livelihood and social glue for local communities in Scandinavia had in the latter part of the twentieth century and in the new millennium become 'an unfamiliar and foreign environment, representing ambivalent ideas to many modern Scandinavians' (151). Whether the past represents folkloric occultism, communal utopias, forgotten traditions and values or traumatic events, suppressed in the frenzy of modern consumerism and progress, late-modern Scandinavian popular fiction constantly summons the past because, as Huyssen and others have suggested, there is so very little left of it in our rapidly globalizing urban world.

Particularly, but not exclusively, in Swedish crime fiction, the eruption of the rural past in the urban present has become a stock motif. Novels such as Åsa Larsson's *Solstorm* (2003, *The Savage Altar*, 2006), Camilla Läckberg's *Isprinsessan* (2004, *The Ice*

Princess, 2008), Johan Theorin's *Skumtimmen* (2007, *Echoes from the Dead*, 2008) and films such as Kjell Sundvall's *Jägarna* (1996, *The Hunters*) relate various detectives' present anxieties to a rural environment beset with social and private traumas. The common motif is the urban detective's reluctant return to her childhood village to assist in the investigation of a domestic crime, which necessitates the detective's confrontation with her own uncomfortable or traumatic past.

In the post-1990s crime novel, where grand national narratives have become suspect and all versions of the past are seen as dependent upon subjective perspectives, the past is at one and the same time imbued with a nostalgic hue and suggestive of something devious lurking in its shadows, which has been suppressed in order to maintain past hopes of historical, geographic and social cohesion and progress. The crime novel, then, comes to function as an investigation of the agents responsible for and victims to this temporal and spatial distance and dislocation that has opened up as a wound in time and in the landscape by violent crimes – an investigation often made problematic by the detective's own troubled history and homelessness, as in Mankell's Wallander novels and in Høeg's *Miss Smilla's Feeling for Snow*.

The nostalgic mode dominating several of the crime novels from the nineties is, in Boym's terminology, more akin to 'reflective nostalgia' (Boym 2001: 49). Contrary to 'restorative nostalgia', which represents a longing for the past-as-it-was, reflective nostalgia revels in the longing itself, reflects on the veracity of its object ('false nostalgia') and may form a productive way of engaging with anxieties in the present as related to individual or collective memories of the past. The crime novels of the seventies painted dystopian portraits of the present beset with conspiracy theories that cast the welfare state and the consumer society as indisputable evils. Against the homelessness and alienation of the present, crime writers sought to restore the embryonic virtues of a traditional (nation) state founded on the virtues of 'the good home'. While the nostalgic mood of particularly Sjöwall and Wahlöö and Staalesen's early crime novels can be described as restorative, the post-1990s crime novel is less certain about the relationship between the past and the present. The detectives are still hit by a pang of nostalgia when confronted with inexplicable violence and a country left unrecognizable in the wake of globalization; however, the object of the longing is less certain, fragmentary, even at times frightening, which leave the detectives 'homesick and sick of home, at once' (50).

Detecting uncomfortable pasts: Mankell and Nesbø

In Scandinavia the impetus to turn the gaze inwards and assess the historical context within which the modern nation took shape and was transformed, resulted in critical re-evaluations of the hegemonic ideals of progress, rationality, normalcy and ethnic homogeneity implicated in the social engineering efforts of the welfare state. Such national soul-searching provided crime writers with valuable material as they continued, in the wake of Mankell's popular novels, to come to terms with the social and individual consequences of crises in the welfare state. Across Scandinavia, practices of, for instance, eugenic programmes including forced sterilization of perceived 'asocial' or mentally disabled women have been documented, and historians, writers and film makers have uncovered the less-than-heroic past behind the persistent image of Scandinavia as uncorrupted by Nazism, imperialism and human rights violations before, during and after the Second World War. Crime writers such as Camilla Läckberg (*Tyskungen*, 2007; *The Hidden Child*, 2011), Gretelise Holm (*Under fuld bedøvelse*, 2005; Under general anaesthesia), Arne Dahl (*Europa Blues*, 2001; 2015), Stieg Larsson (*Män som hatar kvinnor*, 2005; *The Girl with the Dragon Tattoo*, 2008) and Jo Nesbø (*Rødstrupe*, 2000; *The Redbreast*, 2006), to mention just a few, have used these dark chapters from modern Scandinavian history to explore the complex and uncomfortable pasts of their nations and their resonance in present conflicts in novels that blend the genres of the social realist detective novel and the historical crime novel (Agger 2013: 137–72).

As Gunhild Agger observes, 'popular culture has always used, adapted and reformulated the histories, myths and stories of the past' (14), and her study of the genre-hybrid historical crime novel in the Scandinavian tradition demonstrates the great variety of ways in which past events (particularly the Second World War) are employed to construct thrilling crime plots for the present, to lend a documentary or authentic feel to the crime narrative and, Agger suggests, 'to function as a forum for the negotiation of national self-perceptions' (254).

Links to an uncomfortable past of not being wholly on the 'right side' in the Second World War was already present in Mankell's *Faceless Killers*. While the old couple found brutally killed in their farmhouse, 'in the heart of Scania', by 'foreigners' are 'innocent' victims of senseless violence, which to Wallander has come to characterize a new amoral age, the old man, Johannes Lövgren, turns out to having been less of a model citizen, less of a common, virtuous farmer. He, in fact, led a 'double-life'. He is described as 'a beast' who only thought about 'the German money' he had made from the war illegally selling meat to the Nazis, 'blood money' he later used secretly to pay out to a mistress and their illegitimate child. Lövgren's secret wealth offers the police a much-needed motive for the killings, and it provides a reference to an uncomfortable Swedish past where some, like Lövgren, 'pretended to be like everyone else' (Mankell 2011b: 74), but were in fact collaborating with the Nazis despite Swedish neutrality. In this way, the 'whitewashed' ('vitmenade') farmhouse, which in the novel is coded as an idyllic, peripheral and 'authentic' Swedish location brutally destroyed by 'foreigners', is itself shrouding an uncomfortable and brutal past, which only resurfaces when external events (contemporary border-crossing crimes) force the police to venture into the landscape and stir up the past. Again Mankell has inserted ambivalence into his text: the rural idyll that is invested in the old couple's farmhouse is 'whitewashed' in two senses: it inscribes racism, whiteness maintained through 'sanitation', into the crime scene while simultaneously suggesting that the idyll can only be maintained by 'whitewashing', forgetting and suppressing, the uncomfortable past of treason against the nation.

Detecting the relevance of past crimes to the corruption of a Swedish welfare idyll in the nineties is, however, wholly left to the readers as Wallander remains astonished and confused about the wider social and historical meaning of the crimes he is investigating: 'The murder of the Somali had been a new kind of murder. The double murder in Lunnarp, however, was an old-fashioned crime. Or was it really? He thought about the savagery, and the noose. He wasn't sure' (245). While the reader will necessarily sympathize with the confused 'everyman' police inspector who, in several ways, is unable to integrate his personal and collective pasts into the present, we are of course able to see that 'savagery' and 'nooses', an Eden disturbed by violent crimes, are not by any means new kinds of crime in the Sweden of the novel, and that the real 'systemic' crime Wallander is incapable of containing, as he is himself implicated as a perpetrator, is the present xenophobia and racism the novel asks us to view as the result of the welfare state's whitewashing of an uncomfortable criminal past.

In a perhaps more straightforward way, Jo Nesbø's *The Redbreast* evokes the eruption of an uncomfortable past in an uncertain and violent present in an extensive parallel narrative of Norwegian's fighting on the German side on the Eastern front and a contemporary Oslo around the year 2000 beset with millennial fears. Detective Harry Hole is investigating the mysterious presence of a rare, powerful sniper rifle in Norway. He traces it to South Africa and neo-Nazi arms smugglers and eventually to its planned use in an assassination plot against the royal family to take place on Independence Day, the national day of Norway on 17 May. What Hole and the readers learn about Norwegians fighting on the German side during the Second World War and contemporary neo-Nazi groups reads as a historiographical revision of the heroic national self-image of resistance and the systematic 'forgetting' of the thousands of Norwegians who fought on the German side – a self-image that helped keep the young nation state of Norway together in the aftermath of the war and cemented a subsequent image of Norway as a country that helps bring peace to the rest of the world. The latter image is challenged in the beginning of the novel by a radio interview with the visiting American president. The Norwegian reporters are ironically only interested in asking questions about Norway's international image as a harbinger of world peace ('what role have Oslo and Norway played in world peace, Mr. President?') and not at all in the actual results of the negotiations about peace in the Middle East, which leads Hole to wonder, much like Wallander, 'what is it with this country?' (Nesbø 2009: 5).

The assassin who suffers from multiple-personality disorder sets out to avenge what he perceives as a miscarriage of justice against those who fought against the Bolsheviks on the German side when they were prosecuted as traitors following the war. Though Hole in the end succeeds in thwarting the assassination, it is clear that the personality disorder of the killer represents a wider disorder in the Norwegian collective memory and identity; a disorder revealing itself in flag-waving nationalism (523) and a resurgence of racism, illustrated by neo-Nazis planning to make trouble at a mosque where the Muslim celebration of Eid is set to coincide with the national Independence Day celebration (167).

The detectives in the crime novels of the 1960s and 1970s inhabited a modern welfare state which, despite its promises of better times, social justice and well-functioning familial and national homes, was experienced as producing inauthentic lives, individualist and divisive modes of consumption. The novels are populated by individuals who share a deep sense of alienation and loneliness in the welfare state's engineered and sanitized urban spaces, who long for simpler times, more authentic lives and morally committed relationships (see Chapters 1 to 3). Post-1990 crime novels do not wholly abandon the genre's preoccupation with the urban, and their characters are certainly not less alienated or conflicted about the state of their families and society; however, as the harmonious and solid welfare state itself appeared to having become a hazy idea of the past following successive financial crises and weakened nation states in the wake of Europeanization and globalization, crime scenes are relocated to the rural peripheries where the landscapes themselves dramatize the loss in the present of a better past, even a better future.

The 'hyperlocations' in post-1990s crime fiction superficially function as 'authenticity effects' (Dussere 2014; see Chapter 1), stimulating a widespread nostalgia for particular social and national settings where the excess of specification engages the readers' exoticizing 'tourist gaze' and emphasizes the location itself as central to the crime novel's investigation and social critique – in the Scandinavian crime novel the crime scene is at least as important as the actual crime. Investigating such criminal peripheries as parables of disintegrating national imaginaries necessarily leads to the crime novels' preoccupation with the past and collective memories. In the crime novels discussed here, pasts are the source of traumatic individual and social memories, which have been suppressed or forgotten in the amnesic modernization of the welfare state, the utopian suburbia that colonized the countryside physically and culturally. The intimation is that memory wounds, veiled by heroic national narratives and welfare utopianism, reappear in the present as violent crimes, loss of morals and racism. In Nesbø's *The Redbreast*, as in Mankell's *Faceless Killers*, uncomfortable recollections of Nazi sympathies in the past are repeated in contemporary xenophobia and racism, revealing a collective incapacity to engineer the welfare state anew to be the purveyor of solidarity in a multicultural and multi-ethnic present.

6

Criminal peripheries: Peter Høeg's *Miss Smilla's Feeling for Snow* and Kerstin Ekman's *Blackwater*

In the 1990s, political and cultural divisions in Denmark widened as issues such as immigration, European integration and the multicultural society threw the country into a deep and persistent identity crisis. The decade would witness violent clashes between demonstrators and the police in connection with the ratification of the Maastricht Treaty in 1993, and the rise of the EU-sceptical Danish People's Party that branded itself as the defender of a monoethnic welfare state perceived to be under serious threat from mass immigration. A decade later, satiric drawings of the Prophet Mohammed published in the newspaper, *Jyllands-Posten*, led to the Cartoon Crisis that made headlines around the world and ignited violent protests and attacks on embassies in the Middle East. The international relations crisis deepened cultural and political divisions in Denmark that only got deeper with subsequent attacks on one of the cartoonists in 2010, a Danish critic of Islam in 2013 and the Copenhagen shootings in 2015, which targeted a public debate about satire and the freedom of expression and the Jewish synagogue in Copenhagen. While Denmark in the nineties was thrown into conflicts about its present and future multicultural and European welfare society, the increasing social and cultural

segregation of Danes from particularly Muslim citizens and immigrants shrouded Denmark's troubled colonial past in, for instance,
Greenland in a veil of forgetting, as refugees from distant parts of
the world replaced the stereotypical Inuit Other (Hauge 2004: 240),
yet new migrations also exposed memory wounds in the nation's
mono-ethnic and egalitarian self-image, rifts in its solid, modern
welfare state.

Identity crisis as a figure for wider social dysfunctions, as found
in Nesbø and in the heated debates about the multicultural society in Denmark, is at work in Peter Høeg's genre-hybrid and postcolonial crime thriller *Frøken Smillas fornemmelse for sne* (1992,
Miss Smilla's Feeling for Snow, 1993). In this novel, which became
a major international bestseller in the 1990s and was adapted for a
widely distributed English-language film in 1997, a contemporary
national identity crisis linked directly to colonial guilt is embodied
in the crime story's amateur detective Smilla Qaavigag Jaspersen.
She is a recognizable Scandinavian anti-authoritarian, alienated
heroine: a solitary professional estranged from most social and
familial relationships. She prefers the comforting logics of math-
ematics and geometry to messy human company and carries within
her the traumatic loss of her Greenlandic identity, the deaths of her
Greenlandic mother and brother. In many ways she is an early rela-
tive of iconic Scandinavian female sleuths such as Stieg Larsson's
Lisbeth Salander and later TV detectives such as Saga Norén (*The
Bridge*) and Sarah Lund (*The Killing*), all monomaniac investigators who sacrifice relationships and their own wellbeing for a
greater societal cause.

Smilla is a Greenlandic-Danish glaciologist who becomes
involved in the investigation of what she believes to be the murder of a Greenlandic boy, the neighbour's always dirty child Isaiah,
who had occasionally sought out Smilla's reluctant company when
his alcoholic mother was unable to care for him. When his lifeless
body is found on the snowy ground next to their block of flats in
Copenhagen, Smilla does not believe in the police's theory that he
had simply fallen from the roof by accident. Noticing subtle characteristics of his footprints in the snow, she believes that Isaiah had
been running away from someone he feared more than heights.

Smilla's investigation into Isaiah's mysterious death turns into an
intricate unravelling of colonial history, its effects on contemporary
Danish and Greenlandic societies and, not least, an investigation

into her own colonial family history, her conflicted sense of self and loss of cultural identity: 'I've lost my cultural identity for good, I usually tell myself. And after I have said this enough times, I wake up one morning, like today, with a solid sense of identity. Smilla Jaspersen – Greenlander de luxe' (Høeg 2005: 120). Smilla's most 'solid' sense of identity is, ironically, a 'fluid' and exclusive performance of her hybrid Danish–Greenlandic heritage, which she occasionally wears like her 'sealskin coat from Groenlandia, and a skirt from Scottish Corner' (69).

Apart from being able to deduct what happened to Isaiah from his movement over the snow-covered roof ('I have a feeling for snow'; 64), Smilla associates her ability to read snow and ice ('The text about ice'; 71) with a sense of the larger scale of social and colonial inequalities. Smilla realizes that the 'small catastrophe' of her innocent Greenlandic friend falling to his death is a small-scale version of the 'larger forces and catastrophes', a deadly 'avalanche', resulting from the incompatible and fraught relationship between the Danish welfare administration and Greenland:

> One of the great things you can learn from snow is the way great forces and catastrophes can always be found in miniature form in daily life. Not one day of my adult life has passed that I haven't been amazed at how poorly Danes and Greenlanders understand each other. It's worse for Greenlanders, of course. It's not healthy for the tightrope walker to be misunderstood by the person who's holding the rope. And in this century the Inuit's life has been a tightrope dance on a cord fastened at one end to the world's least hospitable land with the world's most severe and fluctuating climate, and fastened at the other end to the Danish colonial administration. (79)

Smilla's 'feeling for snow' is not only an aid to her as an amateur detective, but her well-trained sensibility also enables her (in contrast to the always anxious and aghast Wallander) to perceive the systemic violence (the precarious life of the Inuit tightrope dance under Danish rule) expressed in subjective violence (the haunted Isaiah falling to his death from the roof).

Smilla's fluid identity is the result of the colonial policies of the 1950s and 1960s with which Denmark turned Greenland into its northernmost county. Greenlandic society underwent a

'Danification' process that resulted in the decline of local traditions and languages, as Greenlandic was not used in the administration or in schools (105). Danification also involved the institutionalization and relocation of many Greenlanders including children to the Danish mainland, which had dramatic consequences for their cultural identity and familial relations. Another dark side to the Danish state's attempt at engineering modern, Greenlandic welfare citizens was that it created an ethnic-coded underclass – marginalized, physically and mentally segregated ethnic Others – represented in the novel by Juliane and her son Isaiah. While the Danish welfare state has been unable or unwilling to care for the victims of its own colonial practices, Smilla harbours deep sympathies for these social and ethnic outcasts, partly because she is herself inescapably viewed as an ethnic Other in Denmark despite her upperclass Danish parentage: 'I have a weakness for losers. Invalids, foreigners … Maybe because I've always known that in some way I will forever be one of them' (42). The portrait of Smilla suggests that because of her hybrid, peripheral or marginal position in society, she is in a unique position to react ethically and with empathy towards the alienated victims of a welfare state, whose nature it has been to forcibly harmonize and assimilate even the most obstinate of peripheries.

However, Smilla herself is also self-consciously a victim of assimilation as she has lost her own Greenlandic family, identity and language. Since, as she says, '[i]t's the language you think in, the way you remember your past' (105), the loss of her 'mother tongue' has exiled her from a part of her own heritage, which, throughout the novel, she attempts to piece together out of fragmented personal memories and colonial histories. Central to her sense of spatial and temporal dislocation was the death of her mother when Smilla was only six years old. She recalls her in nostalgic, at times exoticizing and mournful anecdotes as a larger-than-life Gaia figure and a gender-hybrid hunter, who eventually drowned in a canoeing accident. Smilla models herself on these fragmented memories of her mythical mother with longing and a deep sense of loss.

While *Miss Smilla's Feeling for Snow* is unique in Scandinavian crime fiction for its thematic exploration of an uncomfortable colonial past, it shares its preoccupation with the investigator's nostalgic longing for a more intimate, authentic 'elsewhere', with several of the crime novels discussed in this and preceding

chapters. Smilla's personal trauma, a trauma of violent uprooting and dislocation shared with the many fictional detectives, but
also with very real migrants, exiles and refugees, who are dis-
placed from their homelands and pasts, is deepened by her own
uncomfortable, colonial nostalgia for the uncorrupted, 'natural'
innocence of the now-colonized periphery. Her nostalgia is constantly oscillating between a deep sense of loss and a reflective,
ironic and self-critical perception of her longing as sentimental,
idealizing and possibly resulting from her own Westernized or
'Danified' guilt. Also she is a modern nostalgic simultaneously
homesick and 'sick of home'.

Smilla's home in Copenhagen is fittingly presented as a self-
conscious exile inhabited by an unsettled nomad:

> I have arranged my apartment like a hotel room – without get-
> ting rid of the impression that the person living here is in transit.
> Whenever I feel a need to explain it to myself, I think about the
> fact that my mother's family, and she herself, were to some extent
> nomads. In terms of an excuse it's a feeble explanation. (9)

Smilla is an exile, perpetually 'out-of-country and out-of-language',
who self-consciously creates, what Salman Rushdie has called,
'imaginary homelands' (Rushdie 1992: 10). This makes her state of
exile, her postcolonial nomadic identity, different from the nomadic
life associated, nostalgically, with her Greenlandic heritage. To
Smilla the past is emphatically 'a country from which we have all
emigrated' and her past Greenlandic home, as all essentialist mono-
ethnic constructions of home, will remain a distant, unapproach-
able 'elsewhere' (12). Her simultaneous reference to and deflation
of a 'sentimental' explanation of inheritance for her current state of
homelessness is a trait that exemplifies Smilla's reflective nostalgia,
which she employs in order to negotiate her ambivalent identity
made up, simultaneously, by the rich, scientific, white colonizer and
the poor, traditional, exploited Other. While the large colonial conflict is in this way exemplified in the struggles within Smilla's sense
of her own hybrid identity, her ability to perform and decentre both
'roles' is what makes her both a nuisance to the state representatives and a pertinent detective in a case where individual crises
merge not only with a local colonial history but also with a wider
world of global risks.

Whiteness

It is no coincidence that the tower block in which she lives is popularly known as 'Det hvide Snit' (Høeg 1992: 11; literally 'the white cut', which in Danish connotes lobotomy; translated in the US edition as 'the white palace' and in the UK edition as 'the white cells'). In Høeg's novel (particularly in the Danish and UK editions) the name refers to the welfare state's 'normalizing' subdual and marginalization of ethnic Others in segregated ghettos and the Danish colonisers' subjugation of the colonized Greenlanders:

> On a building site donated to them, the Housing Association has put up a number of prefabricated boxes of white concrete, for which it has been awarded a prize by the Association for the Beautification of the Capital. The whole thing, including the prize, makes a cheap and scant impression, but there's nothing mean about the rent, which is so high that the only people who can afford to live here are those like Juliane, whom the state is supporting; the mechanic, who had to take what he could get; and those living a more marginal existence, like myself. (Høeg 2005: 5)

By coding the 'prefabricated boxes' as 'white' and noting the ironic prize awarded by the Association for the Beautification of the Capital, which associates urban 'renewal' with a gruesome surgical intervention, the description of Smilla's home and the hyperlocalized crime scene becomes a comment on the general ghettoization of ethnic Others and those marginalized by the competition state of the 1990s. Yet, whiteness is an ambivalent figure in the novel much like Smilla herself. The whiteness and beautification of the building is the facade of the welfare state hiding the figurative and literal dirt of its marginalized inhabitants; whiteness is associated with the evil Danish scientist Tørk Hviid (White) and with generations of colonizers and ethnographers, who projected onto the white expanse of the Greenlandic landscape a colonial discourse of 'emptiness' and 'innocence' (68), which made the country an always 'hospitable land' to 'scientific experiments' (32); but white is also the snow that falls heavily on Copenhagen at the novel's beginning and lays glittering on the roof of the tower block; and the white milk of Smilla's mother's white breast ('I go to her breast, which is brilliantly white, with a big, delicate rose areola. There I drink *immuk*, my mother's milk'; 30).

Smilla has learned to read not only the morphology of snow, but, more importantly, the fluid and contradictory personal and cultural meanings of its 'whiteness' that will enable her to understand its hidden 'truths' – another term Smilla associates with whiteness (64). Whiteness, in other words, is associated with the colonizer and the colonized; with parasitical, violent science and a hospitable, innocent host; with concealment and revelation; and with Smilla's lost childhood, its longed for comforts and intimacy.

Smilla carries within herself this ambivalence. She identifies with the peripheral and the marginalized in the Danish welfare state but is also shaped by the cultural and epistemological system of the white colonizer. Smilla's wealthy Danish father is a scientist who met her mother in Greenland where he went to undertake medical experiments. He abandoned them when Smilla was a child, and as an adult she exploits his parental and colonial guilt in the same way as she is aided by the scientific tools of the colonizer in her own investigation – tools that will in the end shed light on the crimes that have been perpetrated against Isaiah and Greenland in the name of science and welfare administration.

Science and numbers have become Smilla's refuge in her inability to recapture her Greenlandic past, her sense of belonging, through language. When as a child Smilla went fishing with her mother and experienced sea-sickness, she understood that she harboured a 'feeling of alienation towards nature', a feeling of both spatial and temporal dislocation from her Greenlandic identity, which instilled in her a desire to understand ice: 'To want to understand is an attempt to recapture something we have lost' (27). To achieve a scientific understanding of the landscape from which she has been emotionally and physically exiled, to gain a feeling for snow, is Smilla's substitute for her lost authentic connection with the past, her traditions and lost 'nature' – losses, as Giddens has pointed out in a wider context, comparable to those ensuing from the processes of globalization. Wanting to understand what happened to Isaiah is, therefore, also a way for Smilla to recapture something lost beyond his young life and beyond her own personal experience, even beyond the specific local conflicts arising from colonial subjugation. Smilla's investigation leads her into a heart of whiteness, which suggests more universal uncertainties and homelessness in an age of globalization and impending natural catastrophe, fears of a loss of reckoning in a landscape without clearly defined signposts and solid borders between identities, traditions and nations. At the same time, Smilla is guilty of using science to understand and recapture a lost 'elsewhere' from which she has been personally exiled by her 'Danishness', embodied in her scientist father, who figures as a more benevolent specimen of the sinister, colonialist and reckless scientists, who are exploiting, 'mining' and have the rights to the figurative and literal 'underground' of the Greenlanders, their culture and landscape.

Smilla's internal exile mirrors the 'exiled' and suppressed colonial guilt in the Danish collective memory – a forgotten uncomfortable past (and present), which has left the country incapable of adjusting to a globalized world where the fluid, mobile and eccentric periphery has become the new normal; as Smilla says of Danes: they 'always choose the comfort of suppressed information rather than the burdensome truth' (374). Smilla, who has a feeling for snow, also has a troubled yet unquestionably valuable feeling for the homelessness and disappearing borders that characterize a globalized 'runaway world' (Giddens 2002).

As Judie Newman has argued, Smilla is perceived as a dangerous figure by the authorities because of her marginal, nomadic and placeless nature (Newman 2004: 16). She challenges official social structures by her ethnic hybridity, and 'contaminates' the clearly defined boundaries and borders of the nation with her antiauthoritarian behaviour, which has resulted in her being thrown out of any institution that has ever tried to contain her (Høeg 2005: 89). 'In a small country like ours', the police investigator Ravn tells her, 'you are a sensitive issue, Miss Jaspersen' (90). Refusing to stay in her place, she is constantly threatening to expose the colonial guilt that the welfare state has done its best to subdue. She is one who has always stirred up conflict (90), and by meddling in the case of Isaiah's death, she is posing a direct threat to the state. To stop her investigation and contain her menacing presence, Ravn threatens her with a punishment reminiscent of the white blocks of flats provided by the welfare state: 'Imprisonment ... in a little soundproof room with no windows'. He knows this would be 'particularly uncomfortable for somebody who grew up in Greenland' (91), and Smilla confirms that 'the Greenlandic hell is not the European rocky landscape with pools of sulphur. The Greenlandic hell is the locked room.' In this way colonial practices are being reproduced in the contemporary state's method of bringing the unruly margins and Smilla into the system reminiscent of the relocation of the 'primitive' and not-yet-Danish Greenlandic children to Denmark.

Global risks

Smilla's scientific knowledge of ice is instrumental in her investigation into Isaiah's death where, particularly in the first part of the novel entitled 'The City', she performs as a classical urban, rational or forensic detective. However, her scientific sensibility also extends to a talent for navigating the indistinguishable whiteness of the arctic (she 'only ha[s] to look at a map once and the landscape rises up from the paper'[68]), and by extension a globalized borderless world where '[t]here's nothing "local" left anymore ... If something happens in Greenland, it's connected to something else in Singapore' (218). The connection between the Arctic *locus criminis*, towards which Smilla travels on board the ship Kronos (the Greek god who devoured his own children) in the novel's second part, 'The Sea', and the wider world is central to understanding the original 'avalanche' that set in motion the events, which led to Isaiah's death.

Smilla's investigation uncovers a scientific conspiracy to conceal the presence of a meteor and a deadly parasite deep in the Greenlandic tundra. It was this 'prehistoric' parasite, a deadly 'arctic worm', which caused the death of Isaiah's father when he was working for a previous scientific expedition to the meteor as a diver in the infested melting water. Isaiah had also become infested with the parasite as he was present in the ice cave at the time and had jumped into the water where the body of his lifeless father was floating near the surface. Smilla considers the parasite, which 'can live anywhere' (399), as posing a catastrophic risk to humanity and the environment if the Danish scientists succeed in bringing the meteor aboard the ship as they intend. It swiftly spreads between humans, and, unlike the common arctic worm, the 'primordial parasite' usually kills its host. In this Gothic figure a deep past is truly haunting the present.

Tørk Hviid is the latest of Danish scientists, who for three decades has succeeded in keeping the meteor and the parasite a secret in order to promote his own career with a Nobel Prize in sight despite the local and global risks posed by their discovery. Hviid is the one who has taken regular biopsies from Isaiah to monitor the parasite and from whom Isaiah tries to flee. As the stereotypical 'white' egocentric and 'evil scientist', he is portrayed as a parasite himself penetrating the skin of the innocent Greenlandic child, representing the Danish colonial and scientific exploitation of ethnic and cultural Others (Newman 2004: 16).

The novel is in its postcolonial exploration of 'the Danish burden' and the loss of cultural identity to colonialism and modernization also a more universal critique of modern civilization and blind trust in science and technology; as Smilla says, 'We are all proselytes of science' (375). According to Kirsten Thisted, the figure of the apocalyptic parasite and the meteor must be seen as alluding to 'nuclear explosions, gene technology, biological warfare' and other global 'risks' central to widespread anxieties in the nineties and beyond (Thisted 2002: 316).

Miss Smilla's Feeling for Snow is at first a crime novel wherein traces of violence in a hyperlocalized crime scene (the death of a Greenlandic child in an overdetermined geographical and social setting) set off Smilla's investigation into a personal and societal colonial past. Her investigation reveals that this uncomfortable past is still very much unresolved both in her own mind and in the wider society. As Smilla begins her perilous journey 'home' on board the mythical ship toward the original *locus criminis* deep in the Greenlandic landscape, the novel shifts in mode from a novel of detection to a claustrophobic science-fiction eco-thriller. With this shift the social-realistic detective's investigation of a familial and local condition is also revealed to implicate wider civilizational conflicts and global crises. If the small catastrophe of Isaiah' death opens up wounds in a personal and national colonial history in the detective narrative, the science-fiction thriller investigates the more abstract crimes of Western scientific hubris and global drugs trafficking. However, the local and the global, the periphery and the centre, are intimately linked in Høeg's novel. The Arctic periphery and its fragile ecosystem epitomizes border-crossing environmental risks, like the polar bears Smilla uses as an excuse for why she had been illegally transgressing national borders in the past: 'Bears can't read maps, so they don't respect national boundaries' (Høeg 2005: 87).

Smilla's own boundless hybridity and her sense of the borderless Arctic enable her to understand the grave dangers posed by the deadly parasite, which is at home everywhere, in the hands of ego-centric scientists embedded in an outdated world view. The systemic colonial violence against the Inuit is intimately related to the border-crossing violence of drugs trafficking and environmental degrad-ation in the novel's globalized world. Behind both paradigms stand antisocial scientists who, unlike Smilla, unchecked by societies that 'choose the comfort of suppressed information' over confronting 'burdensome truths', have abandoned 'reason' and 'sensibility' for solipsism and invasive exploitation of innocent children, the mar-ginalized ethnic Others and the environment.

Hviid is not only a colonial parasite about to commit an envir-onmental crime against humanity, but is also already connected to global crimes and the 'world trade in heroin' through his past work refining drugs in a laboratory in the jungles on the border between Cambodia and Laos (200). When Smilla mentions that events in Greenland are connected to events in Singapore, she is not only rehashing a cliché of global connectivity, but is also describing actual connections in the narrated world between crimes originat-ing in different locations and at different points in time. Figuratively, the borderless whiteness of the Arctic associates the border-crossing white powder of heroin originating in another border zone far from Greenland and Denmark. However, Smilla realizes that Kronos is also used for smuggling this heroin to fund the expedition, and in this way global trajectories converge in the heterotopic Kronos, this dystopian vessel of global risks.

Kronos is an apt figure for globalization and divine punishment for human scientific hubris. It embodies an 'after-babel' world in miniature carrying a motley crew, who are, like Smilla, exiles, root-less victims of neocolonialism with disintegrating identities and languages:

The crew's mess on board the Kronos is a Tower of Babel of English, French, Fillipino, Danish, and German. Urs drifts help-lessly among fragments of languages he has never learned to speak. I sympathize with him. I can hear that his mother tongue is disintegrating. (Høeg 2005: 281)

Kronos, then, lives up to its mythological name as the devourer of its own children; yet, not only in an abstract sense. The police investigator Ravn, who eventually helps Smilla, even though he has been tasked with investigating her, lost his own daughter in Singapore, where she was working as a consular secretary. Her death was covered up as a suicide (218), much like the authorities' attempt to conceal the real reason for Isaiah's death. However, it turns out that it was Tørk Hviid who had pushed her from a balcony, because she was working for the police and was the sole survivor after a raid on his heroin lab. As Ravn is also in a state of mourning for a lost child, he sympathizes with Smilla and her will to understand the truth about Isaiah's death. As he explains: 'I don't care for the insufficiently explained deaths of little children' (201).

As the global trade of heroin was Hviid's reason for killing Ravn's daughter, so a border-crossing Arctic parasite became the reason for chasing Isaiah to his death. Smilla's own story, of course, is also a narrative of lost childhood and absent parents. In this way, *Miss Smilla's Feeling for Snow* has progressed from the local particulars of a crime story about the death of a child, through an investigation into a regional colonial history, to a global environmental science-fiction thriller preoccupied with a critique of science and Western civilization to become, again, in the words of Mary Kay Norseng, 'really a novel of nothing but children', a novel of lost, wounded and dead children and parents in mourning (Norseng 1997: 59).

Høeg's novel is reminiscent of Mankell's Wallander novels. Like Wallander, but for very different reasons, Smilla is in the first part of the novel a self-diagnosed melancholic depressive. Wallander conforms to what Smilla thinks of as a European method of coping by listening to mournful music, engaging in activities that may distract momentarily and through substance abuse short of 'a line of good cheer in powder form on a pocket mirror with a razor blade and ingest it with a straw' (Høeg 2005: 95) – Wallander, as many of his fictional male colleagues, prefers alcohol and junk food. Smilla's 'Greenlandic way' of dealing with depression consists of 'walking into yourself in the dark mood. Putting your defeat under a microscope and dwelling on the sight.' They are both in mourning for a lost idealized past, both battling with lost parents, and are both homeless in an age and a social landscape where they appear as foreign bodies.

However, while Wallander's physical wound represents a trauma that keeps his anxious mind from engaging with and understanding the social and cultural transformations of a changing and globalized Sweden, Smilla's 'wound' sets in motion a series of events that allows her to explore, however fragmentarily, her own precarious location, to confront her own lost childhood through her investigation into Isaiah's:

> I think about what has happened to me since Isaiah's death. I see Denmark before me like a spit of ice. It's drifting, but it holds us frozen solid inside the ice masses, each in a fixed position in relation to everyone else. Isaiah's death is an irregularity, an eruption that produced a fissure. That fissure has set me free. For a brief time, and I can't explain how, I have been set in motion, I have become a foreign body skating on top of the ice. (Høeg 2005: 205)

Instead of leading to her further imprisonment in 'the locked room' of the 'drifting' and cold-hearted Danish welfare state, Smilla's mourning for Isaiah and her confrontation with her own past have set her in motion as a foreign body that cannot be contained by the 'white cells' of the colonial state. Isaiah's death becomes a fissure through which Smilla is reborn in his image to fulfil his prophetic name: the God in Isaiah's prophesy who calls out the sinners and gives the world to 'a little one' who 'shall become a thousand, and a small one a strong nation' (Isaiah 60:22). Smilla becomes the tool with which Isaiah and the other children, 'the little ones', may avenge themselves at the novel's end where Tørk Hviid scrambles to his demise on the thin ice. Here Smilla and Isaiah finally melt together in a symbolic gesture of birth or rebirth:

> [T]he current has hollowed out the ice so it's as thin as a foetal membrane, and under it the sea is dark and salty like blood, and a face is pressing up against the icy membrane from below; it's Isaiah's face, the as yet unborn Isaiah. He's calling Tørk. Is it Isaiah who is pulling him along, or am I the one who is trying to head him off and to force him towards the thin ice? (Høeg 2005: 410)

In the end, the scientist killer has lost his bearing on the ice, where he might eventually 'fall as Isaiah fell' and become 'one with the landscape' because '[y]ou can't win against the ice' (410). *Miss Smilla's Feeling for Snow* ends in a fog of indistinguishable figures and whiteness. The end is left open ('there will be no conclusion'; 410) evoking the final scenes of the foundational Arctic Gothic science-fiction thriller, *Frankenstein; or, The Modern Prometheus* (1818). The homeless and nomadic monster in Shelley's Gothic novel, built to survive in harsh environments, is akin to Høeg's 'monstrous', hybrid detective. Both 'monsters' indict scientists, who are guilty of delivering them into a world of permanent exile and identity crises, of colonizing and abusing innocent bodies for personal gain and being oblivious and non-sympathetic to the personal and ecological consequences of their actions.

Høeg's novel is another example of the use of Gothic elements in contemporary crime fiction dramatizing the perilous suppression of the past and the peripheral in an age of urban modernity and globalization. However, the novel does not pose an 'innocent' or 'unspoilt' idyllic periphery against the dramatic and violent uprootings of colonial exploitation and the degradation of the environment associated with the progress of industrialized and globalized 'civilization'. The Arctic periphery is not an idyllic, 'solid' landscape or a past idyllic 'elsewhere' into which the primitive Other will merge – it is not a lost home preferable over a mobile and fluid present, at least in Smilla's bifocal perspective.

On Kronos, Smilla harangues against the black telephones that are installed in every room allowing the person on watch to interrupt at any moment with orders. The phones represent to Smilla 'the result of the past forty years' ingenious, pettily terroristic, sophisticated and abnormally superficial technological development' (274). The implied authoritarian surveillance that characterizes life on board the ship reminds Smilla of her aversion towards 'the whole rotten monstrosity of government controls and demands that fall on your head when you come to Denmark' including passport controls and birth certificates. However, what bothers her most and installs in her an uncomfortable sense of guilt is that this 'Western mania for control and archives and cataloguing' characterizing a colonial administration, can also be seen as a 'back-handed' blessing as it provides at least material protection of an existence 'that was one of the most difficult in the world' (274–5). The implicit reference in this passage to a contemporary age of mass migration, with oppressive identification processes and surveillance as conditions for the safety of exile, becomes more explicit in the anecdote Smilla immediately recalls about Ittussaarsuaq, who as a child had migrated with her family and tribe to Greenland 'during the migration when Canadian Eskimos had their first contact in 700 years with the Inuit of North Greenland'. When they asked her as an eighty-five-year-old woman, who had 'experienced the entire modern colonization process, moving from the Stone Age to the radio', 'how life was now, compared to the past, she said without hesitation, "Better – the Inuit rarely die of hunger nowadays"' (274). Apart from suggesting that Smilla's otherwise overt anti-colonialism, anti-authoritarianism and iconoclasm are at times tempered by her own Westernized half, this passage also points to the fact that the Greenlandic periphery, as seen from Denmark and the West, has a deep and more recent history of migration and modernization that has made it irreversibly like 'anywhere else' in our globalized world.

Smilla's constantly oscillating hybridity, her reflective nostalgia for a lost idyllic home and past that perhaps never was, and her sense of the systemic and universal expressed in the subjective and particular, are combined personal and intellectual traits that mobilize her, or defreeze her, from the 'solid' ice that marks the clearly circumscribed boundaries of life in the modern Danish welfare state. As the nation continues to suppress anything that might challenge those boundaries, it will continue to reproduce the violence of colonial subjugation against Greenlanders and refugees and remain in ignorant bliss about the global consequences of local actions. The Gothic wilderness of the Arctic landscape is also in Høeg's novel an uncontrollable and avenging force, but it is no longer a peripheral space of radical, exoticized Otherness – instead the Arctic reflects the global risks that began to impress themselves on lives around the world in the 1990s, a criminal and violent periphery as anywhere else, whose 'text' we refuse to understand and draw sympathies from at our peril.

Yet, what does it mean to understand 'the text of the ice' (in a true postmodern fashion this description also points to the novel itself) in a crime novel that ends with the mysterious words: 'Tell us, they'll come and say to me. So we may understand and close the case. They're wrong. It's only what you do not understand that you can come to a conclusion about. There will be no conclusion' (410).

The prophetic tone in which Smilla allows herself to 'speak' in the place of 'the real prophet' Isaiah is uncanny. Of course it plays with the detective novel's penchant for explanations, the final disclosure of causal events and placement of guilt. The novel's refusal to end in this way is a trait that Høeg's novel shares with other international postmodern crime novels. Yet, there is more at stake in the survivor testimony Smilla imagines she will be required to give by the collective 'they' upon her return. She could, as the novel seems to insist on pointing out, bear witness to the fact that we have all been guilty of colonial and environmental violence, that 'we are all proselytes of science', which has had fatal consequences for those marginalized by the colonial welfare administration and will eventually lead to the annihilation of human life by primordial parasites unleashed from their eternal slumber under the ice by, if not divine, then at least cosmic intervention in the shape of a meteor and banking on our will to knowledge and scientific egotism. This particular kind of guilt, which Smilla could have chosen to expose, and 'with which ecological awareness is associated', according to Timothy Morton, 'strongly resembles the realization at the heart of a *noir* detective story: *the detective himself is the guilty party*. The person who is looking is the one who is ultimately seen' (Morton 2012: 16). This is the paradox of Smilla's own will to knowledge and eventually the source of her depression, melancholia or lingering sadness. She knows that her attempts to restore links to her lost past, to an imagined cohabitation with nature (without 'seasickness' or 'sickness of home'), through her scientific understanding of numbers and snow will only widen her distance from the longed-for elsewhere. Similarly, by testifying that the violence against nature, against the Inuit and herself can be ultimately understood from a solid point outside of the experience itself, Smilla would have been disingenuous to her own painful attempt at living through her guilt as both victim and perpetrator. What is needed in order to grasp and relate to the interconnectedness of diverse particulars, locations and temporalities that thicken the space around our global experience, Høeg's novel seems to be suggesting, is not colonial guilt, more knowledge about anthropogenic climate change or maps of global exploitations, but instead an aesthetic experience of what Morton calls 'primordial sadness, the feeling of vulnerability and the courage to face it' (18). It is exactly Smilla's courageous, at times performative or evasive, confrontation with her own vulnerability throughout the novel that has attracted a global audience. It is not her feeling for snow that makes it possible for her to coexist with her divided self or to develop sympathies with the most unlikely, eccentric strangers she encounters in her quest to honour the friendship she had developed with the most unlikely and dirtiest of prophets, Isaiah, instead it is her courage to take on her own fears of administrative archives, of seasickness and enclosed spaces that allows her to develop sympathies and trust with strangers, with Isaiah, the Mechanic, Ravn and Urs. This is at least what Smilla comes to think of following her realization that the eruption of Isaiah's death has opened a fissure in her life, mobilized her and momentarily set her free to skate across Copenhagen Harbour, 'dressed in a clown hat and borrowed shoes':

> From this angle a new Denmark comes into view. A Denmark that consists of those who have partially wrested themselves free of the ice. Loyen and Andreas Fine Licht, driven by different forms of greed. Elsa Lübing, Lagermann, Ravn, bureaucrats whose strength and dilemma is their faith in a corporation, in the medical profession, in a government apparatus. But who, out of sympathy, eccentricity, or for some incomprehensible reason, have circumvented their loyalty to help me ... This is the beginning of a social cross-section of Denmark. The mechanic is the skilled worker, the labourer. Juliane is the dregs. And I – who am I? Am I the scientist, the observer? Am I the one who has been given the chance to get a glimpse of life from the outside? From a point of view made up of equal parts of loneliness and objectivity? Or am I only pathetic? (Høeg 2005: 205)

Perhaps pathetic or sentimental, as the novel's title also seems to be suggesting, if we agree with Cassuto's understanding of the centrality of sentimentalism to the hardboiled detective as one who 'relies on reason only in concert with intuition – that is, feeling' (Cassuto 2009: 13). Smilla's 'feeling for snow' depends not solely on her scientific reasoning but more importantly on her ability to create emotional bonds and sympathies with unlikely others. Smilla finds courage in Isaiah's death to confront her guilt and uncomfortable past. Her courage also spreads like a parasite to those eccentric Others, to strangers, who are wresting themselves free from the ice that has had its firm grip on life in the Danish welfare state. This ability is why Smilla's hybridity is not only a 'sensitive issue' in a small society like the Danish, but also a sensible reminder of the need for courage to explore the discomforts of guilt, confront the abuse of the most vulnerable and create affective bonds in order to be able to commit ethically to the strangers of a globalized world.

Guilty landscapes

While environmentalists had been warning about the local and global consequences of pollution and other human interventions to the environment for decades, by the end of the 1980s it became evident that modernity, in Giddens' terms, had put 'an end to nature', in the sense that a common anxiety in the postindustrial 'risk society' was borne out of the realization that environmental disasters, threatening to make the planet uninhabitable, were in fact anthropogenic phenomena (Giddens 2002: 43). Particularly one environmental disaster had a profound impact on Scandinavia in this period, when the accident that occurred at the Chernobyl nuclear power plant in Ukraine in 1986 sent radioactive clouds towards Sweden and Norway leaving deposits of radioactive fall out (Hedenborg and Kvarnström 2004: 324).

Kerstin Ekman's crime novel *Händelser vid vatten* (1993, *Blackwater*, 1995) is saturated with the decade's anxieties about an already ongoing ecological disaster linking a contemporary critique of civilization with flashbacks to demonstrations against uranium mining in the Swedish mountains in the 1970s. In Ekman's novel, acid rain, deforestation and drained wetlands have turned the wild landscapes of North-Western Jämtland in central Sweden into an environmental crime scene. She describes the slow death of the local environment with its wider social effects on the small, rural community in an elegiac mood that matches the horror of the bestial murder of two tourists in a tent by the river Lubber in the early 1970s – one of them on his way to join a utopian eco-socialist commune on Starhill Mountain.

In the novel these killings are, despite their gruesome particularity and direct impact on subsequent events and the lives of a large gallery of characters, symptoms of a less visible systemic violence involving 'crimes' committed against the national periphery involving depopulation, industrialization, pollution and deforestation. While the killer will eventually be identified two decades later, the initial absence of a perpetrator, a motive for the killings and an effective investigation opens up for an epidemic spread of misplaced guilt throughout the community and suggests that the murders and the fallen idyll of the peripheral community are all part of violent historical processes for which an unequivocal guilt will never be placed.

The violent killings of the past flow into the investigation in the narrative present of the novel, where another body is found in the water of the same river. These are the 'events by water' (the literal translation of the Swedish title) that frame the temporal span of the novel from the early seventies to the early nineties; events that destabilize the identities, memories and relationships of those inhabiting the landscape of the criminal periphery.

The dominant narrative mode of *Blackwater* is recollection. Most of its storyline contains a narrative analepsis spanning eighteen years, which is initially sparked by Annie Raft's fragmented memory ('Clear and irrefutable memories were actually very few' [Ekman 1996: 9]) of seeing a not-quite-human stranger, she believed to be the killer, passing her on that fatal Midsommer's Eve. She recalls that he looked Vietnamese, but he will later turn out to be the innocent half-Sami boy Johan Brandberg. In the opening of the novel eighteen years later, Annie is terror-stricken when she recognizes the same stranger in a relationship with her now grown-up and pregnant daughter Mia. Before she can reach for the shotgun she keeps by her bed 'a wound open[s] itself in time' (4). What she has seen, what opens the wound in time and facilitates the retelling of the past, is something 'primaeval', which signifies both a non-human temporality belonging to the wild natural world of Blackwater, to its ancient forests, and the traumatic eradication of temporality between the past events and their haunting memories in the present.

Annie's initial traumatic experience of finding the victims in the collapsed tent by the river, the for many years unsolved murder case, and her accounts of the violence committed against the forests (the clear-felling on the mountain), are all part of the traumatic memory wound that cannot heal, which expresses itself in the shotgun Annie keeps within easy reach and her visions of an unfolding environmental catastrophe. The narrative present of the novel is marked by a pervasive ecology of fear, a recognition of human precariousness and contingency, which will in the end have fatal consequences for Annie.

Throughout the novel it is unclear as to what extent violence, trauma and anxieties should be considered as having been brought to the place from the outside or instead be understood as a condition of the eccentric place itself, its wilderness and liminality. After finding the remains of the two tourists, the horror of the crime scene makes Annie uncertain about the very nature of the landscape into which she has arrived. She is 'no longer sure of the place. It was not marked, had no boundaries. It wandered like a sunspot between shadows of clouds. It was an event, an event by water. As everything is' (Ekman 1996: 59). Helena Forsås-Scott has pointed out that the Swedish original literally reads 'Like everything here' (Forsås-Scott 1995: 78). Ekman's formulation stresses the site-specific condition: it is precisely 'out here' in this ever-changing border landscape that any solid sense of place disappears in a contingent and overpowering series of events tied intimately to the 'black water', which is an ambivalent figure for the primordial, mythical forces of nature and the pollution of wetlands that signify two ways in which humans and nature are intricately enjoined. The name Blackwater can be seen to stand for Ekman's central exploration of what it means to live in the Anthropocene, according to Anne-Marie Mai, 'where in nature humanity everywhere meets traces of itself and its own activities' (Mai 2015). The central figure of water, as also Lars Wendelius has pointed out, is ambiguous in Ekman's novel (Agger 2013: 163; Wendelius 1999b: 27), similar to the ambiguity of snow or whiteness in Høeg's *Miss Smilla's Feeling for Snow*.

The crime novel itself is as shape-shifting as the landscape it describes, not only in its generic hybridity, but also in its blend of the police and detective novel with mainstream fiction, family history, dystopian fiction and myth. The forking paths of Ekman's narrative criss-cross temporal planes and follow several characters, whose paths will cross in various and at times fatal ways; for instance, the disintegrating Brandberg family whose youngest son Johan flees from his violent stepfather and overprotective mother immediately after the killings and after having been thrown into a well by his half-brothers. We learn about his erotic encounter with the mystical Ylja and his life in exile across the Norwegian border with his mother's Sami family. Here he attends university to become a meteorologist, with funds from the Brandberg family's forestry activities.

We also meet the district doctor Birger, who will later work with Johan as an amateur detective investigating the killings, and we learn about his crumbling marriage to Barbro. She is a mostly absent environmental activist, preoccupied with demonstrations against uranium mining in the Swedish mountains, and overcome with grief at the disappearance of the forest and a miscarriage she recently suffered, which she believes happened because she had been picking berries under the power lines. Barbro eventually leaves Birger to become a weaver and lover of Dan Ulander in the counter-culture Starhill commune.

The first part of the novel mostly follows Annie and her life at Starhill in the early 1970s. She is on her way to the commune, when she encounters the murdered tourists and the 'foreigner' crossing her path. Her life on the mountain is marked by hardship, poverty – they simply do not know how to coexist with nature – and the deceit Annie suffers believing Dan is in love with her, which is the reason why she decides to leave Stockholm in the first place. It turns out she is only one of many in this 1970s dysfunctional hippie-utopia of open relationships. When she gets pregnant, she decides to leave the precarious life of the commune as winter sets in. On her way down from the mountain, she encounters the 'incomprehensible violence' of the clear-felling of the forest at close hand, but to her own surprise she finds sympathy in the driver of the machine Björne Brandberg, who helps her escape from the mountain and settle in the town. Over the years, Björne, whose name recalls the primordial and dangerous wilderness of the periphery (Björn means bear in Swedish), becomes a recluse, a cabin loner on disability welfare, after having been accused of rape, yet he continues to help Annie with various manual work over the years.

Annie will also suffer a miscarriage following her stay at Starhill, and with this list of characters, their shared experiences of dramatic change and coincidental encounters, Ekman is creating a network of intertwining themes including the violent death of the landscape, the dissolution of families and relationships, fallen utopias, barrenness and miscarriages, and, as Wendelius has pointed out, 'violations against nature and violations against women appear here as parallel phenomena' (Wendelius 1999b: 31).

Similar to several of the more urban Scandinavian crime novels, *Blackwater* is a narrative about broken illusions, about the personal and social consequences of progress and industrialization from the golden age of the welfare state through its twilight years to its final dissolution. As in Høeg's novel published the year before, Ekman's is preoccupied with the local consequences of wider civilizational or global processes, the vulnerability of individuals and communities on the porous borders of the welfare state, in an investigation into the darker sides of progress as seen from the perspective of the gradually disappearing rural periphery.

Blackwater reads much like Mankell's Wallander novels as a parable of the demise of the modern Swedish welfare state. The village and landscapes around Blackwater flourished during the war and well into the fifties (Ekman 1996: 334). Later the grasslands dried out and industrial forestry transformed the primaeval forests into exposed barren land and plantations. The 1970s witnessed a growing conflict in the relationship between humans and nature, which in Sweden, according to Ann-Sofi Andersdotter, can be traced to farming and forestry policies from the 1950s to the 1970s. At the same time as the urban centres of the welfare state underwent radical transformations and expansion, in the countryside forestry was rationalized and the need for fewer hands drove the excess workforce away from the small villages and into the cities. Those who remained in the rural areas took to modernizing farming and forestry techniques to further increase productivity and profitability at the expense of the natural environment and the traditional rural communities (Andersdotter 1999: 282). To the latter group belong the Brandbergs, a family with strong ties to Blackwater and its forests, who, true to Ekman's pervasive use of ambivalence, also invest in machines used in the clear-felling of the ancient forests.

Crime tourism

The flawed relationship between the modern age and the natural environment is furthermore illustrated in Blackwater's reliance on tourism for sustenance, which, as previously mentioned, had replaced the more 'authentic' or dependent relationship between humans and the countryside they used to inhabit and of which they lived:

> Then finally the tourists came. They wanted to see the river Lobber. A society that absorbs its life force out of fatal violence has to pay tribute to the village and its mystery – because it is unsolved. There the force is unfettered ... If you solve the mystery, the force runs out and the village becomes a dying village among many others. A place no one sees and no one knows about. (Ekman 1996: 334)

An increase in tourism following the media interest in the double murder illustrates what Mark Seltzer has called a contemporary 'wound culture: the public fascination with torn and open bodies and torn and open persons, a collective gathering around shock, trauma, and the wound' (Seltzer 1998: 1). With her narrative of the demise of the natural environment, Ekman is suggesting that the dissolution of once-thriving communities, who used to live in balance with the landscape and its dark forests, have in the modern, industrialized Sweden become the object of collective fascination. The urban desire for the mystery of inexplicable violence and crime is paralleled in a modern nostalgic attraction to the spectacle of the fallen idyll of the countryside. It is furthermore suggested that the inability to solve the crime over eighteen years has been a dubious benefit to the village itself, as the still-open wound has become a 'black jewel' (8) to the village, at the same time as the unsolved murder infests the community with anxieties that will lead to a new murder eighteen years later.

It is hard to overlook the meta-commentary in Ekman's portrayal of this touristic wound culture, where a violent urban society projects itself into the fallen idyll of the rural landscape, thereby creating an entertaining spectacle of self-affirmation against the peripheral Other. Such 'crime tourism' is attached to the very phenomenon of reading hyperlocal Scandinavian crime fiction itself, as this genre is at times read and marketed as nostalgic guides to idyllic and nondescript rural regions that only become interesting and meaningful to tourists when turned into violent crime scenes. More recently, and in the wake of internationally distributed TV series and film adaptations of Scandinavian crime fiction, the tourism industry has been cashing in on, what critics such as Stijn Reijnders and

Ingrid Stigsdotter have called, 'guilty landscapes' (Waade: 2013). The term captures the topophilic desire of crime novels, literary tourists, readers and TV viewers for Nordic criminal peripheries, where a 'pastoral setting, presented as idyllic, inviting and peaceful, becomes the scene of a horrible crime and in the process loses its innocence' (Reijnders 2009; Stigsdotter 2010: 248).

The Nordic welfare idyll disrupted by violence provides a fitting figure with which to explain why it is that comparatively non-violent, peaceful harmonious welfare states are producing what appears to be an unsustainable surplus of violent crime fiction, and why this genre has had such an appeal in a wider Western 'wound culture'. The desire for guilty landscapes in crime fiction and crime tourism both relies on an ingrained nostalgic sense of the once harmonious welfare state as a bucolic landscape and the projection of anxieties arising from a violent global world into the landscape, where they may be contained in their radical foreignness.

Annie Raft's early experiences of the natural environment around Blackwater are related as a similar experience of a radically foreign place, a sense deepened by the spectacle of violent crime. She is one of the many original city-dwellers of the novel, who, like the eco-socialists of Sjöwall and Wahlöö's police procedurals from the 1970s, sought refuge in the 'new' utopias of coexistence and self-realization outside of the alienating, rationalized urban environments. However, the violent 'event by water', Annie encounters when she arrives with her daughter in the early 1970s, becomes an unresolved traumatic memory, which will have fatal consequences for her in the novel's present.

The violence committed in this, to her, foreign landscape dramatizes the novel's ambivalent expression of the encounter between the modern individual and the wilderness. As a stranger to this environment, she represents the modern, urbanized Swede and the cause of the disappearance of the forest, yet she is at the same time a victim of the landscape's own foreignness, its visceral, constantly mutating and violent natural environment. When Annie and Mia first make their way on the bus to Blackwater, she is struck by the foreignness of the place, as if she has just arrived at a crime scene and she is looking at the dead 'body' of the landscape:

They were travelling in a foreign country. When a large, cold lake was glimpsed between the trees, that was the only break in the monotony that would soon disappear and be replaced by another ... In the felled clearings the great network of water had been cut off and the ground had dried to dead flesh in the body of the landscape ... Nor did she know that the felled clearings they could see from the road were only the small ones, that larger and larger areas had been cut off from their links with the clouds, making them incapable of giving anything back when the acid rain trickled through them. (Ekman 1996: 10–11)

Annie's first glimpses of the foreign landscape from the safety and perceptive framework of the bus are of a gradually revealed corpse. Through this anthropomorphism, Ekman points out the already visible consequences of the disappearing forests for human life and the environment alike in the form of acid rain, radiation and the ensuing loss of non-human or ecological memory. When Annie and Mia finally leave the safety of the bus, only to find that Dan is not there to drive them to Starhill, they have to make their way through the 'foreign' landscape on foot by themselves. Their hike gives a new perspective on nature, which is far from the benign, idyllic, always sunny and hearty periphery of human existence, at times dreamt up by environmentalists – of whom there are quite a few in the novel.

Nature is also guilty in *Blackwater* as a dark, violent force inseparable from the human world. Separated and protected only by a thin layer of canvas from the outside world, the tourists in their tent are frail and exposed in the landscape; nature and time are persistently in the process of obliterating human places and memories, as in the gradual erasure of letters in the name of the village on the official signpost: 'BLA KW TER' (Ekman 1996: 194) – now eighteen years later it reads 'BL KW E' (409). Nature is constantly threatening and in the process of rewriting the landscape, which is figured throughout the novel both as extra-human and as metonymically related to the human body or a figure for memory itself – as in one description of paths in the landscape: 'A network of paths, walking veins, memory vessels' (413). The flow of water, seasons, human habitats and the movements of animals constantly change the landscape, so that the map they have been given to guide them through the landscape towards Starhill bears little resemblance to the actual experience of walking through it: 'Annie was uncertain. The map told her nothing about the network of paths across the pasture, nor about the numerous small wooden buildings gleaming in the night light' (47). The forest wilderness through which they also have to find their way is dark, decomposing, sick and Gothic: 'They came into forest consisting almost entirely of twisted birches hung with lichen. Some had fallen and were slowly rotting; grey fungus grew like tumours out of them' (48); Annie loses her bearing, must change direction and have another look at the map, which is hard to read in the grey light under the trees. Annie is ill-prepared for the unmappable place in which she finds herself, a place of constant and menacing change produced by the living and dying environment itself and human habitation.

> [W]hen they had left Ola's car, she had had no idea the landscape was so full of paths branching off and dissolving into long wet streaks of marshland, diffuse grey buildings and human installations where there should have been wilderness, heights and hollows she had not expected. Not even the names matched those on the map. (Ekman 1996: 48)

These topographical conditions are complementary to Annie's traumatic loss of bearing following her discovery of the crime scene as expressed in the previously quoted passage: 'she was no longer sure of the place. It was not marked, had no boundaries'. The landscape Annie encounters in this northern periphery is a guilty landscape, not because of its indifference to the memory of violent acts committed by humans, nor because of its radical otherness, but exactly because it corroborates the precarious nature of human memory and existence. The final 'event by water' of the novel, the second killing eighteen years after the first, illustrates this conflation of landscape and memory, nature and the human.

First of all, Birger and Johan's investigation reveals that the double murder was as coincidental and unpredictable as the liquid landscape in which it took place. While Annie was convinced the perpetrator looked stereotypically foreign and identical to Johan, and Johan's own mother Gudrun also feared this to be the case, he and Birger are able to show that it was in fact Björne, who had killed the tourists. He had believed, wrongly, they were taking the wild buzzards he had taken it upon himself to guard. Suspecting, now eighteen years later, that Annie had recognized Johan, Gudrun takes the ultimate step to protect her son by shooting Annie by the banks of the very same river. It is finally Johan who finds her floating in the water after a lengthy search. In the end, Annie's anxieties about the 'stranger', about a more abstract impending violent attack, prove to be what eventually confines her to the very same violent river and criminal landscape, which eighteen years before had traumatized her experience of the place.

In a state of mourning and frustrated by the inexplicable paths that led to Annie's death, Birger who had become Annie's partner, recalls an expression she had used: 'how unpleasant and vile everything is! Living and struggling and then falling apart because of an anomaly in cell formation, or a bunch of bacteria, or shotgun pellets – or water! *Enjoined through water*. Why had she said that? "I am enjoined through water"' (332). Birger senses with Annie the shared precariousness and vulnerability of nature and human life in the periphery, where all that is solid dissolves into water, where the biological processes are as unpleasant and murderous as a shotgun, but also where the interdependence of human life and the natural environment is most apparent from the scale of the cell to smaller or larger catastrophes that condition the enjoined life world.

Annie appears to having been able to predict the circumstances of her own death; or perhaps we should see her floating body as an accidental premonition of her own utopian 'nature doctrine'. She maintained that the forest would eventually rise again out of the felled and barren landscape, that nature will survive man and submit the civilization we have built to fend off the uncertainties and dangers of the natural environment to eternal oblivion: 'there's nothing that is not nature. We are all nature. Even the big cities will be broken down into quarries where eagles nest and lizards sun themselves on the walls. Into jungles or secretive formations of spruce forest' (317). This post-apocalyptic doctrine of Annie's – reminiscent of the rampaging natural environment in J. G. Ballard's *The Drowned World* (1962) – suggests that her submerged and traumatized body has finally joined and found release in the deep time of this Swedish river of forgetfulness, in the primordial natural environment, while those in mourning are left to keep open their memory wounds, as Annie once did, in attempts to keep nature at bay. Mourning Annie's death, Birger wonders how often he will have to return to Annie's house 'to keep back the ravages of time; the grass, the snow, trees felled by storms, the undergrowth creeping in and mice gnawing. He would have to keep time at bay so that her house could remain untouched and still' (406). What the future has in stall for Johan and Mia, who will have to live with the memory of one mother having killed the other, is left open at the end of the novel; however, there is hope in Johan's determination that even if their child will be condemned to 'such knowledge' of an 'uncomfortable past': 'it'll have to be possible' (440).

In its wider critique of modernity, an age beset with global anxieties of environmental cataclysm and war, Ekman's novel may be seen to suggest that there is hope for the children if they do not fall prey to their overprotective parents – including the two mothers in the novel who are prepared to kill to protect their children. These parents also include those who oppose Annie's unorthodox teaching methods that were meant to enable the children to confront their fears through mnemonic techniques, to 'memorize knowledge' like the ancient orators of the Gilgamesh epic (363). She had discovered that her pupils harboured suppressed fears of how to survive in nature 'if everything runs out ... The electricity. If the cables fall down. If there's a war and a nuclear bomb' (360); and fears produced by having seen on TV 'a girl running along the road with her burning skin crackling into a white map pattern' (the iconic footage of nine-year-old Kim Phúc after a napalm attack in Vietnam 1972). As a pedagogical tool, Annie offers them practice in the old ways (brewing, weaving and tanning) and mnemonic tools with which they can create their own 'Memory Lanes' (364), reminiscent of the winding paths in the landscape, to connect and individualize remnants of a local almost forgotten ancient culture better attuned to the environment and their experiences of a wider global world. Alleviating present anxieties about the eruption of violence in the far away and near, through a memory culture that actively seeks to maintain well-tested practices proven to facilitate resilience and survival in nature as well as in culture over time is what the symbolic gesture of Annie's final submersion in the landscape may suggest.

A degenerate society

In a speech delivered in 1995, Kerstin Ekman talks about 'the degeneration of my society and my civilization and its route to this downfall' in her father's dreams of technological progress, industrialism and the welfare institutions that seemed to 'rise straight out of the forest with its marshy land where nothing but elk roamed, and out of the quiet of farms smelling of manure':

> When my father said they were building a society around me, he was not, first and foremost, thinking of the political construction which came to be called The People's Home and was to distribute security and material prosperity as evenly as possible. Instead, with all his heart and talent for construction, he was thinking about what he was involved in: the dream of technological progress. He was about to build a clean, comfortable, rapid and sensible society. (Ekman 1995: 81–2)

This is the image of a modern, rational Sweden emerging 'from a peasant past' without history and without memories that Ekman has submitted to critique in several novels over the years, and also the story of the welfare state we have found recounted in several crime novels across Scandinavia since the late sixties forming a common thematic preoccupation in novels by, for instance, Staalesen, Mankell, Larsson, Dahl and Høeg. In Ekman's eco-crime fiction, the linear time of modern progress stands in stark opposition to the cyclical time of the natural environment. The new time of the welfare state demanded 'a new kind of human being, quick, mobile, with no roots and preferably no memory' (84). In such a society, Ekman says, 'that is in a violent and rapidly continuing process of change, human beings become in more than one sense obsessed by it' (84). Ekman's is a critique of civilization from an elegiac eco-critical point of view. However, while Ekman's 'nature' is fashioned in the language of loss and perhaps even nostalgia, her landscapes and the criminal periphery in which a crime novel such as *Blackwater* 'takes place' are exploring the Anthropocene, insisting that the natural environment is not separated from the humans inhabiting it – and it is rarely a peaceful, idyllic or nonviolent existence or coexistence. 'What I have done' in *Blackwater*, she says

> is only to shift the focus out to the fringe, to a mountain world where the vulnerability of the landscape and the people is still distinguishable. The shadow that follows those who are active, the financially successful in this society, is called there, as here,

violence. Deadly violence. Though it only becomes truly apparent when you move far out on the borders of the built-up areas. Out into the forest. The forest with its paths was once a great memory which people who lived there had in common. Feet memories. Leg memories. A network of paths, walking arteries, ducts of memory – finer and finer right out to the tips of the spruce forests towards the marshes and mountain heaths. All that has gone. The space of the forest has been cut down, the ground churned up and ploughed by great earth-moving machines. Just as the Sami's memory lanes in the mountains have disappeared as the ground has been criss-crossed by terrain vehicles, scooters and moto-cross bikes. The forest growing up now in the felling areas will not become a source of memory and knowledge for the people of today. That time has passed. (Ekman 1995: 88)

Kerstin Ekman's is a dark ecology, to use a term fashioned by Timothy Morton, a noir ecology, where the roots of the criminal centre, our violent society, are only truly apparent in the criminal periphery (Morton 2010). For Ekman the disappearance of the ancient forest and threats to the environment are violent attacks on our collective and individual memory without which we are unable to understand our shared vulnerability:

Anyone seriously asking himself or herself what it is to be a human being, must occasionally stay on the borders of what is human and on the outskirts of what is society. This diffuse region, where the shadow is active, where the darkness takes shape and where fragmented and suppressed emotions and ideas gather and become possible to grasp – for me that region is the forest. (Ekman 1995: 86–7)

In Høeg's novel, this region on the outskirts of society is the borderless wilderness of Arctic Greenland. As we have lost the forest, according to Ekman, which was once the 'the screen on which people projected their ideas about what was different. About what was evil', in an age that has 'incorporated [the forest] into modern technological and economic thinking (87), we have become unable to deal sensibly with the strange and violent change. This notion coincides with Yi-fu Tuan's claim that the sprawling and primeval forests used to function as 'landscapes of fear', defined as those mental or material human constructions that exist 'to contain chaos'. We should include crime novels among those mental constructions, along with 'children's fairy tales as well as adults' legends, cosmological myths, and indeed philosophical systems' including the welfare state, which provide 'shelters built by the mind in which human beings can rest, at least temporarily, from the siege of inchoate experience and of doubt' (Tuan 1979). Perhaps this realization is why Ekman returned to the crime genre, or at least to her new version of a hybrid crime novel, after having taken a hiatus from the genre over several decades. Crime novels are narrative landscapes of fear much like the old legends and tales, 'shelters built by the mind', to withstand the pressures of violent social upheavals and the anxieties they produce. Ekman's *Blackwater* is a 'landscape of fear' not dissimilar to Walter Benjamin's experience of reading crime fiction as replacing, momentarily, fears of the mode of travel by train as a synecdoche for the wider spatiotemporal pressures of modernity.

Crime novels by Høeg and Ekman or, indeed, Mankell from the early 1990s, crime fiction that both sold massively in the Scandinavian countries and abroad, appeared at the cusp of an age of crises beset with fears of dramatic change and insecurity, yet they do not merely pretend to distract or to impose an artificial order on human experience, neither do they relocate us to a better and safer utopian past. They do, however, offer landscapes of fear into which we might project our anxieties without necessarily confirming them, instilling in us a sense of possibility for critical reflection and encouragement for adventure and courage. Høeg and Ekman's novels demonstrate a common preoccupation in Scandinavian 'welfare crime novels' with a Scandinavian anxiety, which is less about providing a false sense of security in a turbulent, runaway world, and more about seeking adventure and stimulating curiosity. In the words of Yi-fu Tuan, such studies of contemporary fears are 'not limited to the study of withdrawal and retrenchment; at least implicitly, [they also seek] to understand growth, daring, and adventure' (Tuan 1979).

7

Investigating the family in the welfare state

Crime fiction has recorded the effects of rapid modernization, urbanization and globalization on Scandinavians as they have attempted to navigate the increasingly more oblique social and national landscapes of their welfare states. As the previous chapters have demonstrated, even the most dystopian and melancholic of crime novels have been preoccupied with representing how trusting interpersonal relationships may be mended in an age where crises and conflicts have shattered the utopian dream of 'the good', harmonious welfare state, pictured as a happy nation family gathered around an 'utopian realism' of progress, solidarity and moral responsibility, inherent to the symbolic realm of the welfare state. It is, however, notable that few if indeed any of the Scandinavian detectives we have encountered so far find themselves in a familial setting reminiscent of the happy family pictured in the Social–Democratic election poster at the height of the golden age of the welfare state in 1960 (see Chapter 1; Agger 2011: 118; Tapper 2010). It is, nevertheless, an equally common trait in Scandinavian crime fiction that although the detectives' families and bodies are as broken as the failed and corrupted welfare states they attempt to navigate, the sentimental horizon of good homes, trusting relationships and love are still dominant expectations, which are, if not fully met then at least partially realized through their winding and troubling encounters and resilience in the face of violence, social injustice, uncomfortable pasts and moral decay. It has become a cliché of the genre

that at first male and more recently female investigators need to
struggle with and refract their conflict-ridden private lives through
their investigation of violent crimes and failed institutions in the
public sphere. Beck, Veum, Wallander, Blomkvist, Holm, Arnaldur
Indridason's Erlendur, Håkan Nesser's Van Veeteren and Unni
Lindell's Cato Isaksen, to mention a few, are all male detectives who
must cope with strained family relations. Since the 1990s this male
dominated 'ulcer school' has been matched by the dramatic rise of
narratives featuring female sleuths, such as Liza Marklund's Annika
Bengtzon, Elsebeth Egholm's Dicte Svendsen, *The Killing*'s Sarah
Lund and *The Bridge*'s Saga Norén, whose inability to maintain a
balanced family life and troubled interpersonal relations stand in
stark contrast to their investigative abilities. However, in their different ways these detectives are searching for meaningful interpersonal ties, homes and relationships at the same time as the crimes
they investigate expose such ties, social norms and institutions as at
best fragile if not outright dangerous.

The millennial feminist crime novel

Crime fiction has traditionally been dominated by male authors,
hardboiled male sleuths and disillusioned policemen, lone wolfs
whose physique, rational thinking and traditional morals contrast
with the corrupt powers governing the modern cities and state
bureaucracies. For Raymond Chandler there was no doubt: The
hardboiled detective must be a man with a capital M (Chandler
1988: 18). Women represented in the hardboiled detective story
either played the part of the submissive housewife, the sweet
secretary or a dead body, or she was cast as the femme fatale
seductress. Though female detectives have appeared throughout
the history of the genre, crime fiction has been 'resistant to a
female protagonist', as gender transgressions of hegemonic mas-
culinity and 'normative sexuality' have conventionally been seen
as incriminating traits in the genre (Plain 2001: 6; Worthington
2011: 41). It was only towards the end of the twentieth century that the stereotypical gender images in crime fiction were
challenged following the struggles and cultural impact of 1970s
feminist social and political movements. It was predominantly,
yet not exclusively, women writers, who infused the genre with

much-needed feminist perspectives into new environments and life worlds. Feminist crime fiction appeared in the United States in the 1980s with writers such as Sara Paretsky, Marcia Muller and Sue Grafton, who broke through to the mainstream and the best-seller lists around 1990 with their 'female "tough gal" outgrowth of the male hard-boiled novel' (Walton and Jones 1999: 11). Peter Høeg's success with his hardboiled Danish-Greenlandic scientist Smilla Jaspersen on the American bestseller lists in 1993 needs to be seen as part of this new domestic wave of female investigators in the mainstream of American popular culture.

According to Karl Berglund, the number of Swedish women crime writers rose dramatically around the turn of the millennium. A similar tendency was noticeable in Denmark and Norway, where especially Norwegian writers such as Anne Holt and Karin Fossum had already gained a wide Nordic readership by the mid-1990s (Berglund 2012: 59–60). The first Swedish and Danish bestseller writers were found through competitions such as the Poloni Prize in Sweden, which in 1998 was won by Liza Marklund. A similar prize in Denmark was won by Gretelise Holm for her debut novel *Mercedes-Benz syndromet* (1998, The Mercedes-Benz Syndrome). Both authors would become exponents for Scandinavian feminist crime writing. The rise of these new voices in a now less male-dominated literary field helped expand the conventional Scandinavian socio-critical crime novel with an emphasis on the gender-specific structures that underwrite the violent and fundamentally unjust and unequal society. In the feminist crime novel, gender roles are often represented as (positively) ambivalent, and themes such as men's violence against women, rape, child abuse, prostitution, international trafficking, the still existing glass ceilings and vulnerable families have become common themes and have also been adopted by male writers, most famously, of course, by Stieg Larsson.

The family detective: Marklund, Läckberg, Gazan

The protagonist in Liza Marklund's first novel in a series of, so far, eleven books, *Sprängaren* (1998, *The Bomber*, 2000), is the successful, hard-working journalist, wife and mother to young children, Annika Bengtzon. When we first encounter her, she has recently been made editor of the crime-news section of the tabloid newspaper *Kvällspressen* (*The Evening Post*). Complementing the crime plot of the novel, we witness her repeated conflicts with both male and female colleagues, who try to undermine her authority. As the novel progresses it becomes clear that in Bengtzon's Sweden, women have not achieved equality on the labour market; to be a woman in an executive position, it is emphasized, is still a disadvantage.

In *The Bomber*, Annika Bengtzon is reporting on what at first appears to be a terrorist attack on the Olympic stadium in Stockholm. However, it becomes clear that the spectacular bombings are personally motivated, and both the first victim and the terrorist turn out to be women. As a consequence of her professional success, in her private life Annika feels incapable of living up to the demands of being an equally successful wife and mother. As Per Svensson has rightly observed, she is, unlike her melancholic and nostalgic male counterparts, an investigator who is, at least in the first novel of the series, happily married. She is an upper-middle-class 'insider', who finds herself 'in the middle of Sweden – and loving it' (Svensson 1999: 181). While she does indeed appear to be mostly satisfied with her stressful life, 'with her mobile phone', her girlfriends and family, she does find it difficult to live up to the image of the 'ideal mother', who effortlessly enjoys Christmas baking with her children while at the same time managing and advancing in a demanding career. At the newspaper, however, she has a 'short fuse' when a female colleague prioritizes her family over work when a story needs immediate attention. Annika Bengtzon is as much a victim of persistent gender inequalities as she is guilty of their conservation.

Annika Bengtzon is a new kind of heroine in Scandinavian crime fiction. There are still inequalities for women in the work place, but her Sweden is not a 'lost paradise', a welfare utopia, as Svensson also observes, but one in which individual idealism and progress may lead to a brighter future, if not for the benefit of the wider society then at least for a woman, who is not afraid to take on the patriarchal society even if it means to live with the anxiety of not quite living up to the ideals and persistent social norms of motherhood. In this way, Marklund's Annika Bengtzon series may be read as an example of a post-welfare crime novel as it accepts that the big collective project of the 'people's home' has shattered into 'countless small and individual' projects (182).

A similar critique has been levelled against Stieg Larsson's hyper-individualist heroine, Lisbeth Salander, whose private vendetta could appear to be merely reproducing the symbolic violence of the neoliberal and competitive society, which she is seemingly called upon to destroy (Stenport and Alm 2009). According to such a view, the dystopian social criticism we have come to expect of Scandinavian crime fiction since Sjöwall and Wahlöö, even the mere nostalgic longing for a past welfare society and its harmonious collectivism, which tended to dominate the police novels of the 1990s, has dissipated in the hands of crime writers in the twenty-first century, where collective social responsibility, even collective guilt, is subordinated the aspirations of the individual, who has learned to 'perform' successfully on the stage of the narcissistic, neoliberal state. There is, of course, something to this diagnosis, though I do not believe it is the whole story, as I attempted to demonstrate in my discussion of Larsson's *The Girl with the Dragon Tattoo*. Marklund's *The Bomber* is also, I believe, a more complicated narrative about female agency in the post-welfare state than the 'little story' about Annika Bengtzon's private aspirations may suggest.

The novel has a parallel storyline that consists of a personal record written by the murdered director of the Olympic organization, Christina Furhage. In these, she reflects philosophically on the banality of love and her 'true love' for her work. She presents herself as a defeminized woman. Uncertain about her own sex, she did not conform to the heteronormative society and had a relationship with a militant lesbian colleague. The only thing Furhage knew for certain was that she was an individual, a human being, which, incidentally, is also the first definition Annika offers of herself, followed by her other identities as a mother and a wife – a theme which is closely connected to Henrik Ibsen's feminist heroine Nora, who in *A Doll's House* (1879) slammed the famous door on her family to embark on her own self-discovery as an independent woman.

Furhage's personal record functions as a radical (feminist) reflection on Annika's own life experiences and conflicting self-images. Annika and Furhage also share the fate the killer, Beate Ekesjö, has planned for them both. She is bent upon killing them as revenge for their suppression of her career ambitions and need for visibility in a competitive world, where she has become an outsider and now a near serial killer. The professional and private life of Annika is reflected in and approximates both the victim and the criminal; the small conflicts of everyday life are expanded into the crime narrative's larger, more violent world, and it is through the crime story that readers gain access to Annika's equally explosive emotional inner life, which constantly flows between the residue of the incompatible gender roles she needs to perform to stay afloat in her pond of our liquid modernity.

Where Marklund's version of the feminist crime novel emphasizes the necessity to empathize with the social pressures on women related to the demands of a competitive, masculine professional life and the resistant social norms associated with motherhood and femininity, Annika has not entirely escaped the demons (many of them her own) modern women must fight to become an individual first. As a 'narrative of proximity', to use a term coined by Gill Plain, 'a discourse in which the other proves uncomfortably similar to the bourgeois individual self', Annika Bengtzon's comfortable life 'in the middle of Sweden' is revealed to be predicated upon a deeper systemic violence in which female agency, her own included, is uncomfortably tied to an imitation of male violence and an oppressive individual guilt about wanting to be an individual in her own right (Plain 2001: 223).

Camilla Läckberg's amateur investigator and a biographer of prominent Swedish women writers, Erica Falck, has fewer demons to battle than Bengtzon though there is enough to worry about in her near family and in the small, idyllic, yet surprisingly violent town of Fjällbacka on the west coast of Sweden. A former fishing community, Fjällbacka conforms to a Scandinavian 'criminal periphery', as discussed in Chapter 5. It is an idyllic small town, haunted by a suppressed criminal past that reaches violently into the present: a morally wayward community suffering from postindustrial depopulation and the transformation into a mass-tourism monoculture. In Läckberg's first novel of the series about Falck, *Isprinsessan* (2003, *The Ice Princess*, 2007), she has returned to her rural hometown to sort out the estate after the death of her parents. While her personal life is soon filled with worries about her sister, who exhibits clear signs of living in a violent relationship, Falck is confronted with the suspected suicide of her childhood friend, 'the ice princess' found frozen in her bathtub. Together with the police detective Patrik, with whom she initiates a relationship that develops over the next volumes in the series, she begins her own investigation into what she soon suspects to be a murder case. In the end, the death of her childhood friend turns out to be related to a wealthy family's attempt to cover up an old story involving paedophilia and a chain of related attempts in the community to keep the misdeeds of the past hidden.

While relationships and conflicts related to gender are treated more stereotypically in Läckberg's novels, her treatment of the family as an often troubled and guilty collective is more complex. In *The Ice Princess*, the family unit and especially the mother figure is described as treading a fine line between providing comfort and suffocating overprotection – and here, as in Kerstin Ekman's *Blackwater*, the crime centres on a mother who kills to protect her son against the judgement of the rest of the community.

Where gender roles in the wake of women's struggle for equality in the work place and at home has been treated extensively in the feminist crime novel as representative microcosms of the gender-based inequalities, conflicts and violence in the wider society, it is also the family and its suppressed lies that are targeted in Sissel-Jo Gazan's scientific crime novel *Dinosaurens fjer* (2008, *The Dinosaur Feather*, 2011). The hardboiled student and single mother Anna Bella is not only excavating an old scientific feud about whether dinosaurs are related to birds, the macabre murders of her academic supervisor and a fellow university student, but also her own buried childhood history of betrayal and deceit. Her motive for uncovering what happened in the past is to enable a reconciliation with her new role as a single mother and with the man, who had recently abandoned her and their child, figured as a compulsive repetition of Anna Bella's own traumatic past. In several other family crises portrayed in the novel, it is love affairs, homosexuality and alternative lifestyles that are demonized and suppressed by family members with violence and death as the ultimate consequence. Just as the dinosaur bones must be dug out of the ground to enable a scientific determination of their evolution, also the families' skeletons must come out of their closets to enable forgiveness and reconciliation between the individuals, their families and traumatic pasts; the traditional family, in other words, needs to be exposed for its oppressive stranglehold on individuals' ability to live independent lives in more equal and intimate relationships. This repeated portrayal and investigation of family crises can of course be understood as a symptom of a wider denigration of the traditional family structures and values in the Western world. However, in Scandinavian crime fiction the conflictual relationship between individuals and their families may be considered as intricately tied to deep-seated sociocultural norms related to the welfare state rather than simply an expression of anxieties related to social change.

Pippi and other Scandinavian 'statist individualists'

In their article 'Pippi Longstocking: The Autonomous Child and the Moral Logic of the Swedish Welfare State', Henrik Berggren and Lars Trägårdh uses Astrid Lindgren's Pippi Longstocking stories as an allegory for Swedish culture during the golden age of the welfare state in the 1940s and the 1950s (Berggren and Trägårdh 2010: 50). The stories present in the superhuman and self-sufficient Pippi figure and the 'reassuring' nuclear family of her friends and neighbours Tommy and Annika two seemingly conflicting positions and aspirations at the heart of the Swedish and Scandinavian welfare societies: 'total individual sovereignty' and 'the absolute necessity of a stable social order' (52). Lindgren's 'welfare narrative' (Hansen 2010; Simonsen and Stougaard-Nielsen 2012), according to Berggren and Trägårdh, culturally embeds the tension between individual freedom and the social state, which they perceive as central, perhaps even exclusive, to the Swedish welfare state and to a lesser degree to the other Scandinavian countries. The overarching ambition of the welfare state in the twentieth century was to 'liberate the individual citizen from all forms of subordination and dependency in civil society: the poor from charity, the workers from their employers, wives from their husbands, children from parents' (53). This reliance on state intervention in roles and functions traditionally held by the family to ensure individual freedoms suggests that in Sweden 'the key alliance is between state and individual, rather than family and state' or, indeed, between individual and family (53).

A central preoccupation of the welfare state, therefore, was to target gender inequality with the adoption of new social policies such as state-run childcare and maternity benefits initially meant to enable women to care for their young children while participating in the workforce. 'By the 1990s', according to Mary Hilson, 'the Nordic labour markets demonstrated some of the highest female labour force participation rates in the world, a characteristic that was described by many scholars as a further distinctive feature of the Nordic welfare model' (Hilson 2008: 107). However, a consequence of this circumvention of the family by the direct relationship between the individual and the state may also suggest that the Scandinavian welfare state actively weakened the status of the family, which may have resulted in 'cold' societies devoid of meaningful interpersonal relationships and true intimacy: 'High divorce numbers, loneliness, psychological illness are often emphasized as consequences of the alliance between the state and the individual against the family' (Berggren and Trägårdh: 75). Critical views of the social state as the harbinger of alienation, loss of morals, conspicuous consumption and egocentrism – a fear that the bonds of trust which guaranteed the welfare state in the first place become undone by its very success – are also related to this perceived weakening of the family by an intrusive and ubiquitous welfare state.

Against the commonly held belief that the universal welfare state inevitably undermines individual autonomy and freedoms, the Scandinavian welfare state, in fact, helped to strengthen individual autonomy 'by freeing citizens from their family obligations as well as from the constraints of the market' (Hilson: 107–8). According to Trägårdh, apart from social trust, which has not waned with the expansion of the state, it is 'statist individualism', 'a concept that captures the seeming paradox of an ethos that is based on a strong alliance between the state and the individual aiming at making each citizen as independent of his or her fellow citizens as possible', that sets Scandinavian welfare states apart from other societies (Berggren and Trägårdh: 56; Trägårdh 2012: 41).

The Scandinavian countries are 'different countries' when it comes to the place and function of the family. In comparative surveys, Swedes appear 'radically less inclined to let themselves be governed by an ethics and ethos that makes the individual subservient to the traditional family, the clan, the religious community and other "tight-knit" institutions of the civil society' (Trägårdh 2012: 41). According to Trägårdh, this has made the Scandinavian countries the least family dependent and most individualized in the world. However, although life-long marriages are waning in Scandinavia as in the rest of the Western world, Scandinavians are still family centred, with comparatively high birth rates and time spent with children as confirmed by the World Values Survey (43).

Statist individualism may be what we find represented and confirmed in these crime narratives where male and female detectives negotiate their professional and gendered identities in their confrontation with familial strictures and inherited traumas. To be independent and free as an individual does not mean the end to the family – independence is the family's very precondition in modern Scandinavia, a much-desired 'horizon of expectation' and a central preoccupation for the detectives in Scandinavian crime novels. The ideal family, as suggested both by Trägårdh's 'statist individualism' and several of the contemporary crime narratives, is one that enables equal and intimate relationships without the bonds of traditional notions of femininity and motherhood, and without the social and physical violence that comes with the patriarchal family form.

Related in a genre with an in-built resistance to gender transgressions and an historical obsession with maintaining the integrity of homes and families against outside evils, Scandinavian crime fiction, especially on TV, has developed a particular set of female detectives who bend the gender positions of the traditional police novel and explore the sacrifices needed to maintain a state that can guarantee justice, equality and social trust in the post-welfare society. These TV series deal explicitly with the triangulation of individuals, families and the state; they present particular views on the modern family and were themselves made for 'family viewing' (except for young children!) on prime-time public broadcasting TV.

Family viewing: *The Killing* and *The Bridge*

Women crime writers not only rival their male colleagues on the bestseller lists across Scandinavia, but they have also bestowed their female detectives with conventional masculine traits such as the hardboiled monomaniac professional sleuth, familiar with every corner of the cities' underground and mean streets. Especially the new Scandinavian hardboiled female detectives have achieved a cult-like following outside of Scandinavia through TV series such as *Forbrydelsen* (2007, 2009, 2012, *The Killing*) and *Broen/Bron* (2011, 2013, 2015, *The Bridge*). The regional and international success of these TV series has to a large extent depended on what is generally perceived to be their refreshingly 'new', mysteriously unsociable and unsentimental female heroines, the police detectives Sarah Lund and Saga Norén. They share their ambiguous gender positions, hardboiled manners, troubled family relations and an all-consuming devotion to their work with their literary counterparts. Sarah Lund shares stereotypically gendered conflicts with Marklund's Annika Bengtzon and Läckberg's Erica Falck: 'to learn how to administer their gender and role as a mother professionally when working' (Agger 2011: 117; Povlsen 2010: 44). Lund is divorced with a teenage son, and her relationships with her son and mother become increasingly strained as the serial progresses. Saga Norén notoriously and at times to great comic effect struggles to engage empathetically with other people. It is suggested that she suffers from Asperger's syndrome and that her condition may be related to a traumatic childhood, the suicide of her twin sister and her subsequent estrangement from her parents. They eventually reappear in the third season placing Saga's career as a detective at risk, thereby threatening to rob her of her only real purpose in life and the only 'family' she knows.

Both Sarah Lund and Saga Norén struggle with expectations related to their gender as empathizing and nurturing women – roles they either cannot or will not fulfil as it would inhibit their ability to perform as detectives. They are presented as 'gender transgressors', imbued with traits that generically belong to male detectives, which is further amplified by their contrasting feminized male colleagues, who are emotionally intelligent and primarily devoted to their equally fragile nuclear families. The 'family crisis' explored in these TV series through ambivalently gendered detectives must be understood in light of Sarah Lund and Saga Norén's function as representatives of the state, as Scandinavian statist individualists.

In the socially engaged tradition of Scandinavian crime fiction, *The Killing* is, over its three seasons, set in a contemporary globalized, post-welfare state Denmark with storylines that explore political corruption and racism (season one), Denmark's involvement in the war in Afghanistan (season two) and the effects of the global financial crisis (season three). At the centre of this turbulent world stands Sarah Lund in her worn jeans and famous, yet even for a TV cop rather informal, gender-neutral and an unthreatening Faroese jumper. Her dedication to solving the murder of Nanna Birk Larsen in the first season of the series leads her to constantly postpone her departure from the Copenhagen police force to join her Swedish fiancé with her son in their future home in Sweden. Gunhild Agger views this compulsive behaviour as part of a larger pattern explored in the series, which she terms the 'invalidation of home' (Agger 2011: 120). Belonging to this pattern are also the present and future homes of the victim's family: the present home has been infiltrated by the killer. His murder of the daughter will eventually result in the father's violent revenge and the eventual dissolution of the family, symbolized in the future home, which has been left in a state of repair, unfinished, as a ruined idyll slowly rotting away.

Lund's inability to care for her own family and engage empathetically with her son and mother is in stark contrast to her compassion for the victims of the crime, Nanna and her grieving family, a contrast which emphasizes her devotion to her role as a police detective (118). In fact, it could hardly be otherwise in a crime story where the 'protection' of the family's own integrity, without the interference of the state, will have such violent consequences.

While we are at first led to believe that the killer should be found within the corrupt political system, it is finally revealed that a close friend of the family, an employee in the family business, killed Nanna to protect the family from the shame of her relationship with a foreigner. Consequently, due to emotional stress and his loss of trust in the state's ability to provide justice, the father takes the law into his own hands. The fact that the grieving family had the killer in their midst all along and in the end responded with vigilante vengeance renders the family suspect, according to Bruce Robbins:

> They are suspects in a crime that has not yet happened, but toward which much of the series nevertheless points: the crime of revenge for their daughter's murder ... This temptation to rescind the state's monopoly of the legitimate use of violence makes the

grieving family the main onscreen bearer of lack of trust in the state. The family is anti-statist. This anti-statism turns out to be a terrible mistake, almost a fatal mistake. (Robbins 2015)

To Robbins, *The Killing*'s central family crisis is presented as an allegory of the need for trust in the state against the latent violence of the bereaved family. While the family blames foreigners for all evils, it equally distrusts the state's ability to provide justice for their loss – the solution is, however, not just any kind of state. Sarah Lund is the 'outsider', 'the cold, inexpressive, unlikely representative of the state', whose 'sacrifice' of her own family and career resulted in at least a successful solution to the case. She is the statist individualist who, at least in the first season, presents an alternative to the corrupt and amoral political system and who serves the state and justice first before her own family.

However, Lund is a complicated figure for the state. She both suggests an 'ideal', incorruptible, if not heroic image of the state as the protector of individual freedom, and an outsider, who is constantly under threat of being suspended. As a hardboiled lone wolf, she frequently acts on her own outside of the police collective, which makes her a figure for all that is wrong with the present state and political system, where every institution seems as morally wayward as the family in crisis.

It may seem paradoxical that the last bastion of the state in *The Killing* is a female detective who appears to be a failure of socialization. In this Sarah Lund has a twin sister in *The Bridge*'s Saga Norén. On top of being a hardboiled female detective whose behaviour transcends any norm traditionally associated with her gender, she too is a social outsider who 'suffers' from an inability to respond empathetically to anyone she comes in contact with: she asks inappropriate questions, shows no concern for other people's feelings and is neurotically following rules and regulations to the dismay of her laidback and sociable Danish colleague Martin Rohde.

Her lack of empathy and antisocial behaviour emphasizes her deviance from the norm, but a deviance necessary for protecting societies against border-crossing crimes, which effortlessly crisscross the Öresund Bridge connecting Denmark and Sweden, crimes that constantly blur the borders between the social and the individual, the far and the near: What at first appears to be a case of a serial 'truth terrorist' on a mission to avenge social injustices turns out to be a disturbed former friend's personal vendetta against Rohde for ruining his family (season one); a case of serial eco-terrorism (season two) and what at first appears to be serial killings of civil-rights activists motivated by a right-wing commentator turns out to be a young man's carefully planned revenge against his biological father and those who had wronged him as a child growing up in foster homes (season three). The larger world of social insecurities linked to the globalized, neoliberal state (social change, inequalities and climate change) is the smokescreen behind which ancient crime themes of revenge and jealousy leave a wake of broken families. It is central to the series that the investigations' revelation of the personal and familial motives behind the crimes are 'proximate' to the detectives' personal conflicts. As the serial progresses, Saga appears increasingly implicated in her own traumatic family history, and her two Danish partners, both of whom are family men, are either failing to keep their families together or are living in a drugs-infused limbo with the ghosts of a wife and young children, who had mysteriously disappeared.

Like Lund, Saga Norén is a borderline character. Her story is a 'narrative of proximity' wherein the protector of the state comes uncomfortably close to its threatening other. According to Suzanne Keen, 'in the popular cultural view, lack of empathy spells social problems, danger to others, criminality, and inhumanity' and 'lacking empathy often correlates with sociopathic behaviour, with the profiles of serial killers' (Keen 2007: 10). By the end of season three, we are still unsure about Saga's possible involvement in the death of her sister, but her personality disorder, which makes interpersonal relationships if not impossible then at least difficult, effectively contradicts this 'popular cultural view' of deviance. Conversely, it may be suggested that in order to deal with criminals in a post-welfare state, its representative has to be proximate to the deviant, antisocial criminals: the borders are becoming increasingly blurred between the serial detective and the serial killer. Saga Norén's abnormal inability to set personal and familial motives above the state is, however, according to Robbins, 'a refusal of that kind of "normal" social relationship that would ordinarily permit and even encourage state corruption: favoritism, cronyism, collusion with private economic interests, and so on. These are exactly the charges that Nordic noir is usually taken to be levelling at the welfare state'.

As such, the antisocial detective can be viewed as a statist hero, as she effectively dispels her own bonds of dependence associated with the family, which both in *The Killing* and *The Bridge* is presented as a source of violence and vengeance. On the other hand, at the end of three seasons of both crime serials, their statist morals are arguably compromised or near compromised when faced with the stereotypically deviant postmodern serial killer. Lund has in the end lost all faith in the justice system and sacrifices herself and her dreams of a future extended-family home when she takes the law into her own hands and executes the serial child molester. Saga Norén struggled in the end of season three with her professional obligation to save the life of the serial killer, who had staged his own execution accompanied by his biological father and his new-born baby. Norén was 'saved' by her partner, as she had in season one saved her then partner Martin Rohde from becoming a vigilante when he was confronted with the killer of his son.

These TV crime series make for uncomfortable 'family viewing'. While on the one hand espousing the family as a shared emotive horizon for the wellbeing of statist individualists, it is on the other a hotbed for violence and anti-statist vigilantes against whom the state's only hope is the personal sacrifices of necessarily 'deviant' detectives. This paradoxical position of the family in the Scandinavian welfare states, as presented in millennial crime narratives, was further explored in a Danish TV series, which explicitly framed 'family viewing' in the now ubiquitous serial-killer genre in order to explore 'family envy' as a new 'utopia' in the post-welfare state.

Serial killers and family envy in *Those who Kill*

Actual serial killers have been a rarity in Scandinavia. A former Danish chief of the mobile unit of the national police (known as 'Rejseholdet' in Danish, which was also the title and subject of the Emmy Award-winning TV drama series, *Unit One*, produced by DR, 2000–4), Bent Isager-Nielsen, explains the rarity of serial killers with the country's high success rate in solving murder crimes and the tight-knit, homogeneous welfare state, which registers its citizens and intervenes before murderers can kill again (Richter 2010). While *Those who Kill* may be the Scandinavian crime series with most serial killers, the fascination with this deviant figure was found already in Sjöwall and Wahlöö's first novel *Roseanna* (1965), even if it is not technically a serial-killer novel, as the police, also in this fictional case, intervened before the sexually deviant, yet stereo-typically everyman, rapist killer could strike again.

In the 1990s and 2000s the serial killer replaced the bank robbers and eco-socialist vigilantes of the 1960s and 1970s as the typical criminal in Scandinavian crime fiction, responding to a wider inter-national obsession with a figure, which was only named in the mid-1970s and subsequently popularized through horrific accounts of real killers such as Ted Bundy, 'The Killer Clown' and 'Son of Sam'. The serial killer became the 'movie monster' of the 1980s, adding to the discursive construction of the figure that blurred the border between fiction and reality, culminating in Jonathan Demme's *The Silence of the Lambs* (1991) (MacDonald 2013a: 2).

The popularization and cultural prominence of the serial-killer figure obviously has to do with the fact that serial-killer narratives lend themselves well to the effective thriller format across media, as it is the thrill of the chase rather than the whodunit that drives the plot. The serial killer taps into our ambivalent curiosity for and abhorrence of fictional spectacles of violent acts against, mostly, innocent bodies and our fascination with the killer's deviant psych-ology, which takes the serial killer beyond the borders of the human. According to Alzena MacDonald, the popularization of the serial-killer figure is symptomatic of late capitalism and at the same time 'the quintessential cultural figure utilized to critique this context of re-production' (6).

As a 'crime of our age', the repetitive killings of serial killers and their equally repetitive representations in crime fiction can be seen as symptoms 'of an economic milieu of rampant production and consumption' and ultimately a symptom of the objectification of human lives themselves. These are the social processes Chapters 1 to 3 in the present volume explored in a Scandinavian context with roots in critiques of the consumerist welfare state around 1970 and a central aspect of subsequent socio-critical crime novels such as in Mankell's critique of a post-welfare consumer society in which humans, in Wallander's allegory of lost virtues, are thrown away like old socks.

In this novel, Mankell's *The Fifth Woman* (1996), a sadistic female serial killer is targeting men who have a history of violating women. Wallander is at first unsure of her motivations, thinking that if they ever find her 'we'll be dealing with someone the likes of whom we've never encountered before', perhaps 'a female monster' (Mankell 2012b: 368). It turns out that the killer is seeking revenge for the murder of her unborn sister, violently taken from her mother by her stepfather, the 'terrifying experiences of her childhood' and the recent murder of her mother. She becomes a vigilante who takes her revenge on the 'threatening men lurking around every corner', and goes by a list of victims plotted into her train timetable.

Interrogating the killer, Wallander finds himself torn between her monstrosity and his reluctant admission that 'she had her own peculiar sort of truth' (430) – a truth connected to a wider systemic and social violence revealed by her testimony: 'criminal acts were always just the surface' (424). In Wallander's mind the question of her individual 'guilt' is a superfluous one. Instead he questions his own proximity to the vigilante killer and ponders how this singular case may point to a more systemic problem related to dysfunctional families and an impotent state: 'What are we actually doing to our children?' (430).

In Stieg Larsson's *The Girl with the Dragon Tattoo*, while investigating the case of Harriet Vanger's mysterious disappearance, Blomkvist and Salander discover in notes Harriet made in her bible (a similar premise to David Fincher's use of the seven deadly sins in the serial-killer film *Seven* from 1995) possible links between unsolved murders of women going back to the case of Rebecka in 1949. Eventually, Blomkvist and Salander realize that incestuous, serial-sex-murdering tendencies have been inherited from father to son in the Vanger family, and what to Blomkvist appears as 'an unbelievable idea' that 'an insanely sick sadistic serial killer was slaughtering women for at least seventeen years without anyone seeing a connection' is a reality (Larsson 2015a: 348). However, it might not be so preposterous a thought, as Salander suggests: 'We have several dozen unsolved murders of women in Sweden during the twentieth century. That professor of criminology [the crime writer Leif G. W.] Persson, said on T.V. that serial killers are very rare in Sweden, but that probably we have had some that were never caught' (348).

In the Danish TV crime series *Den som dræber* (TV2, 2011; *Those who Kill*, ITV3, 2012), written by the bestselling crime writer Elsebeth Egholm, the police detective Katrine Ries Jensen is part of a special unit investigating serial killings, a crime which has reached epidemic proportions in a near-future Danish welfare state. She is a recognizable Scandinavian detective with a dedication to her work bordering on monomania. Though lacking familial relationships of her own, she cares deeply for her friend and her child. In the police unit, she is under pressure to prove herself as a deputy chief inspector surrounded, as she is, mostly by male colleagues with a male chief inspector. Together with the obsessive forensic psychiatrist, Thomas Schaeffer, they investigate several brutal serial killings over ten episodes in recognizable contemporary Danish environments.

However, as the creators' description of the series intimate, the setting is to be understood as a near-future, dystopian vision of a wrecked Danish welfare state, where the hitherto almost nonexistent psychotic serial killers now roam the streets due to a breakdown of the welfare state:

> *Those who Kill* is a crime series about a violent criminal who is surrounded by fear and mystique – the serial killer. Up until now, we have been able to curtail their activities with early – and effective – interventions via the safety net of a comprehensive social welfare system in Scandinavia. But times have changed. Borders have opened up, social welfare is in decline, and slowly but surely the whole system has become imbued with a sense of resigned impotence and callous disregard for those it once sought to rescue. The rifts in the net have become so large that bigger fish are slipping through the mesh, and as a result, a new type of crime is starting to burgeon – killings not grounded in traditional motives and patterns of behaviour. You need a very particular kind of person to catch the serial killer; someone who knows and understands the killer's dark side, and the fantasies that plague him – someone like our two lead characters, Deputy Chief Inspector (DCI) Katrine Ries Jensen and forensic psychiatrist Thomas Schaeffer – a police detective and a "profiler", who in very different ways each possess a deep psychological

> understanding that connects them to the killer's victims and to
> the killer himself, driving them to pursue each case to the end of
> the line, again and again. (*Those who Kill*, Pressbook)

The description clearly outlines the imagined relationship between
the figure of the serial killer and the breakdown of the welfare state,
which was, albeit with a different emphasis, also suggested by the
former chief of the police mobile unit. At the same time, the description of the series suggests that the premise of *Those who Kill* is that
of a 'narrative of proximity', where the police team must be intimately 'connected' to the deviant, abnormal serial killer enabling
them, like the killer, to 'pursue each case to the end of the line' with
an ability to endure the compulsive repetition, 'again and again',
associated with this 'new type of [welfare] crime'.

One such new type of crime, 'not grounded in traditional motives
and patterns of behaviour', is found in the second episode entitled
'Utopia'. A mother and child are found brutally murdered in their
upper-class 'designer home'. When the father is found dead without
his wedding ring, the detectives realize that they are dealing with a
'raving mad' killer, whose modus operandi reveals that he has killed
before: First he abducts fathers of idyllic, affluent nuclear families in
order to take their place; he puts on their wedding rings and plays
happy families with the mothers (repeatedly profiled by Schaeffer
as 'beautiful' and 'motherly' looking) and their children until they
refuse to play along; when they break the fiction of his 'utopian'
family idyll, he kills them with a knife. The horror of the realization
is palpable in Schaeffer's expression: 'Damn, he executes families!'

While this is indeed an unusual plot in the tradition of
Scandinavian crime fiction, it is similar to Thomas Harris' *Red
Dragon* (1981). In this famous serial-killer narrative, the killer
Francis Dolarhyde, the uncanny 'tooth fairy', murders seemingly
random families in the American Deep South. Like Dolarhyde, the
serial killer in 'Utopia', Lars Werner, selects his victims from visual
records: he has access to a burglar's photographic record of affluent homes wherein the families also appear. Both narratives present
the 'act of watching', surveillance, as central to the killers' mode of
operation, which conforms to what MacDonald finds to be a defining characteristic of the serial killer genre (MacDonald 2013b: 35).
Yet, while, as MacDonald suggests, the serial killer may be read
as a synecdoche for the state, and these narratives as essentially

anti-statist and symptomatic of cultural anxieties associated with the 'Big-Brother' state's bureaucratic exercise of disciplinary power, it appears more appropriate to think of 'family viewing', as exercised in *Those who Kill*, as symptomatic of middle-class anxieties about the disintegration of family ties and idealized domesticity as represented by the visual culture of the consumerist, affluent welfare state. Considering the press release or preface to the series, its premise is overtly Scandinavian, which contrary to widespread American anti-statism, points out that it is exactly because of the absence of the state that the serial killers now slip through the mesh to prey, for instance, on innocent families and the very moral fabric of the state.

According to Leonard Cassuto, we should think of the serial killer as essentially an 'anti-family man. He is purely anti-sympathy, anti-domesticity, anti-sentimentality' (Cassuto 2009: 267). Through his monstrosity and uncanniness (un-homeliness), he confirms the ideal domesticity of the middle-class nuclear family at a time where such 'family values' have become little more than a myth more often encountered in fiction (or in visual advertisements) than in reality. Lars Werner's 'family envy', his brutal performance of 'idealized' domesticity, is gradually uncovered by detectives whose own homes or families are in the process of disintegration: Katrine Ries Jensen sleeps at the police station as she is afraid to return to her empty home where she was attacked in the previous episode; Thomas Schaeffer's relationship to his wife ends in separation due to the nature of his work, and symbolically, when he is signing the separation documents, she has taken off her wedding ring, effectually linking the familial situation of the profiler to the violated families and the profiled killer.

Compared to Dolarhyde, the anti-family man who can be seen to confirm society's conservative family values through his monstrous otherness, Lars Werner in *Those who Kill* might be an even more disturbing example of family viewing in contemporary crime fiction. He is, in fact, not an anti-family man; he is envious of families that conform to his and a widely diffused idealized image, particularly in advertisements, of not only affluent, aesthetically flawless families living in Scandinavian designer homes, but also families in which the wives, at least in the profiler's estimate, express an air of motherly care and old-fashioned homeliness (even if it is hard to see exactly how he reaches this conclusion by just looking at photos of them – photos prepared for a consumerist gaze – confirming, perhaps, the proximity of the profiler to the profiled, that also he and with him the wider consumer society desires outdated, nostalgic memories of female domesticity). It is clear that the idealized family is a fiction, and a dangerous one at that, even before the serial killer takes the place of the real fathers. It is the envy and idealization of the 'utopian', reactionary family image itself that is coded a monstrosity in *Those who Kill*. While the press release of the series suggests that the fall of the welfare state has resulted in a dystopian near future where serial killers cannot be contained by the diminished social services, the 'Utopia' episode suggests that it might be the other way round. It is the already present consumer society's nostalgic family utopias and rampant family envy, which poses the greatest threat to the welfare state and the wellbeing of individuals.

The triangulation of individual, family and welfare state, which in the Scandinavian welfare states emphasizes the close relationship between state and individual, is a central preoccupation in the millennial feminist crime novels, TV series and serial-killer narratives. They make for troubling 'family viewing'; not because they univocally symptomize anxieties about a lost utopia of traditional family values, or necessarily the denigration of the family in our liquid modernity, but instead because they remind 'statist individualists' of the dangers of sacrificing state-guaranteed independence for consumerist, idealized and reactionary family values. The triangulation of statist individualism and its place in contemporary discourses about the fate of the 'nation family' in an age of growing insecurities and terror is explored in a crime novel by Anne Holt written in the wake of the perhaps most traumatic attack on the progressive and humanitarian welfare state since the murder of Olof Palme.

The violent family in post-Utøya Norway: Anne Holt's *What Dark Clouds Hide*

In the opening scene of Anne Holt's crime novel, *Skyggedød* (2012; *What Dark Clouds Hide*, forthcoming), the fifth and final instalment in the series about forensic psychologist and ex-FBI profiler

Inger Johanne Vik and her husband detective Yngvar Stubø, Inger Johanne is faced with a 'macabre tableau' (Holt 2013: 13). She arrives at the home of her school friends Ellen and Jon in the affluent Oslo neighbourhood of Grefsen to help prepare for a class reunion, but instead of cheerful anticipation she finds Ellen grief-stricken on the sofa, screaming with agony and clutching her lifeless eight-year-old boy, Sander, in her arms. Distressed, the father Jon mutters frantically to himself: 'it's all my fault ... I should have taken better care' (5). It appears to Inger Johanne that a terrible, unforeseen accident has befallen this seemingly well-functioning, affluent and idyllic family. Sander, a child we learn has a history of erratic behaviour and an ADHD diagnosis, must simply have fallen from the stepladder, which appears strangely out of place in the living room festooned with wild flowers for the evening's party.

It is a scene of utter despair and confusion – a pastoral and social idyll disturbed. In her bewildered state, Inger Johanne senses trembling under her feet as if from a distant earth quake. She desperately tries to reach the police for help, but is cut off. Then she sees, out of the villa's panorama windows, a column of smoke rising above the city centre. It is 22 July 2011, and the family tragedy is from then on cast in the shadow of an unfolding Norwegian tragedy: the right-wing extremist Anders Behring Breivik's attacks on the government quarters in Oslo and his cold-blooded mass murder of sixty-nine young Social Democrats gathered on the island of Utøya for their yearly summer camp.

Throughout the crime novel the national tragedy remains a distant tremor; to the mother Ellen the world outside may well go off its hinges because of a mad terrorist for all she cares, 'she had enough in her own catastrophe' (Holt 2013: 115). Inger Johanne only senses the effects of the attacks through her mostly absent traumatized husband who cannot speak of his experiences and cries himself to sleep at night; and the policeman Henrik Holme, who eventually turns up at the bereaved family fresh out of the police academy, would rather have attended to the larger catastrophe than dealing with the accidental death of a child.

In *Skyggedød* the two catastrophes seem only connected by coincidence. However, the opening scene hints at the possibility that the family tragedy may be a small-scale fictional model of the larger national tragedy, which, in 2012 when the novel was first published in Norway, still demanded a great deal of collective soul searching.

As such we are led to suspect that the novel will investigate how an affluent and presumably idyllic family, and by extension a small wealthy welfare state, could have allowed such catastrophes to happen. If both incidents are not to be blamed on mental disorders or one monstrous individual alone, who should have taken better care to avoid the deaths of innocent children on that fatal day?

A Norwegian paradise lost

A few days after the attacks in Oslo and on Utøya, *The New York Times* and *The Guardian* published an article written by the bestselling Norwegian crime writer Jo Nesbø with the title 'In Norway, the past is a foreign country' (Nesbø 2011). Nesbø writes about his fear that Norway will be forever changed by the attacks: 'until Friday', he writes, 'we thought of our country as a virgin – unsullied by the ills of society'. This now 'foreign' country was the country of his (and by implication all Norwegian's) idyllic and carefree childhood, the country of the affluent, egalitarian, safe and trusting post-War welfare society. He recalls how in his youth the world outside was a dangerous yet titillating place full of 'coups d'état, assassinations, famines, massacres and tsunamis'. Returning home from his travels as a young man he would find a country where nothing much had changed, it was a country

> where everyone's material needs were provided for. Political consensus was overwhelming … Ideological disagreements arose only when the reality of the rest of the world began to encroach, when a nation that until the 1970s had consisted largely of people of the same ethnic and cultural background had to decide whether its new citizens should be allowed to wear the hijab and build mosques. (Nesbø 2011)

The trope is a familiar one to readers of Scandinavian crime fiction: an idealized harmonious welfare society in the process of succumbing to globalizing forces and moral decay. Think Henning Mankell's Kurt Wallander, whose body and mind gradually deteriorate throughout the 1990s in step with the corrosion of his Swedish welfare utopia. In *Faceless Killers* these 'ills of society' are associated with the victim's dying word 'foreigner', referencing the hitherto unseen violence that follows with the arrival of East European criminals, who cross the less visible borders of a new Europe and home-grown xenophobia exposed by the new presence of non-European asylum seekers.

However, in Mankell's novels as in Nesbø's account of Norway as a now 'sullied virgin', change did not arrive in Scandinavia with spectacular terrorist attacks such as the murder of Olof Palme or Brevik's mass murder in 2011; these were the symptoms of a grad-ual moral deterioration of the Scandinavian societies that reaches back to the golden age of the welfare state. Whether the threat has been seen to come from the outside in the shape of criminal gangs or from the inside in the shape of neo-Nazis or a right-wing terrorist, the fallen welfare state has since its heyday produced nostalgia for a simpler past to which there is no return. Such welfare nostalgia has become commonplace in Scandinavian crime fiction trading on anxieties shared by the political right and left alike (see Chapter 4).

As suggested by both Nesbø and Mankell, the political consensus that characterized the Scandinavian welfare societies was broken by polarization in the wake of mass immigration, which became a political issue with the rise of anti-immigration parties in the early 1970s and reached the political mainstream in the 1990s. On the left the inherent weaknesses of the fundamentally capitalist wel-fare society is seen as exposed in its inability to counter racism and foster solidarity with new disenfranchised groups; to the right the Social–Democratic welfare state has been held responsible for the erosion of social and cultural homogeneity by inviting immigrants and asylum seekers to share in the welfare.

In Norway, the mass murder was committed by a self-styled vigi-lante who directed his attacks at the centre–left government and the heart of the Social Democratic Party, which he blamed for the 'Islamic invasion' and the promotion of a permissive, multicultural society. The much-praised communal response led by the then prime minister Jens Stoltenberg was to counter fear and violence with togetherness and tolerance. However, even if the immediate after-math of communal mourning led to some consensus that extrem-ist hatred should be countered by a more tolerant public discourse about immigration and multiculturalism, the continuing portrayal of Breivik as a lone monstrous fanatic precluded any real examina-tion of more mainstream prejudices that may have taken part in shaping his distorted worldview (McDonald-Gibson 2013).

The resulting absolution from collective guilt through collective victimization is none the less surprising considering the fact that the terrorist did not, counter to the reports in the first hours of the events in Oslo, conform to the Western image of the 'outside threat', but was instead revealed to be 'one of us', a white Nordic male; not a Muslim, but a Muslim hater, demonstrating, in the words of Aslak Sire Myhre, that 'the heart of darkness lies buried deep within ourselves' (2011). To some, this unwillingness to turn a critical gaze inwards was finally confirmed in the loss of Stoltenberg's centre–left coalition to the anti-immigrant and neo-liberal Progress Party in the 2013 parliamentary elections. For the first time this party that once counted Breivik as one of its members entered government as part of a coalition led by the Conservatives on a bill that promised tax cuts and a smaller government.

However, apart from the 22 July Commission which suggested that the police could have prevented the attacks, several books have recently appeared in Norway that in different ways examine a society guilty if not of countering mainstream racism then at least of failing to intervene in the mass murderer's clearly dysfunctional childhood. To these we should count the father Jens Breivik's account in *Min skyld? En fars historie* (2014, My fault? A father's story) of his own sense of guilt of not having cared enough for his son, claiming partly that the authorities prevented him from doing so by denying him custody of his troubled son following the social services' intervention in the family.

In Aage Borchgrevink's astute analysis of Breivik and his notorious compendium in 'A Norwegian Tragedy', he is depicted as 'a child of his time': 'the consumer society's prodigal son, a loser in the capitalist battleground, a gamer who cannot distinguish reality from fantasies born online' (Borchgrevink 2013: 13). In his narrative, Borchgrevink highlights the fact that already as a child the authorities were involved in assessing Breivik's family, which showed signs of child neglect. To him the most important lesson to be drawn from the tragedy is not about immigration policies, the internet, ideology or the failures of the police but about child welfare and family services: 'Without knowledge of where the holes in the net of our society are to be found', he insists, 'it is difficult to mend them' (viii) – a statist logic similar in kind to the one prefacing *Those who Kill*.

The journalist Åsne Seierstad's *One of Us: The Story of Anders Breivik and the Massacre in Norway* (2015), as described by the author and as suggested by the Norwegian subtitle (*en berättelse om Norge*), is a book about Norway, posing the question 'what could go so wrong in such a peaceful and harmonious country?' (quoted in Flood 2014). In Seierstad's journalistic investigation, Breivik is also diagnosed as a product of his time, his society and family. His pathological relationship with his mother, his family's decent down the social ladder in the 1980s when also, according to Seierstad, the last Norwegian prime minister who believed in state governance of the economy was brought down by the 'wind from the Right that blew in over Norway from the US and Britain', and created a situation where a single mother with a difficult child who needed the welfare state were left to her own devices (Seierstad 2015: 18).

These accounts of the Norwegian tragedy suggest that it extends further back in time than 22 July. They also suggest that the mass murder could have been prevented if only the welfare state had lived up to its ideal of protecting a child against its own family. This may seem a wholly ludicrous assertion viewed from outside Scandinavia, but the argument conforms to the statist individualism explored by Berggren and Trägårdh. The Norwegian tragedy, then, reveals a range of failures incriminating an already fallen welfare state, and, it is suggested, we proceed at our peril with minimizing the role of the welfare state as the protector of neglected children.

In Anne Holt's crime novel, the distant tremor of 22 July functions as a disruption of normalcy that allows for and demands an investigation into a family and a nation's seemingly idyllic past that may not be as idyllic as we remember. What the family tragedy interrupted was a class reunion with its memories of the past innocence of youth suggested by the bucolic dressing of wild flowers. Now Inger Johanne is instead forced to confront, reluctantly, her dormant memories of Jon and Ellen and her sense that something was not quite as it should have been in the idyllic family.

The policeman in the ill-fitting uniform

It is also the state of emergency, the disruption of normalcy brought about by the mass murderer, who posed as a policeman to get close to his victims on Utøya, that allows the rooky policeman of the novel, Henrik Holme, repeatedly described as wearing an ill-fitting uniform (Holt 2013: 15, 42, 117, 267), to pursue a haphazard and amateurish investigation. He conducts the investigation against the will of his superiors with the conviction that however accidental Sander's death may seem – however unlikely it may be that a prosperous family could have committed foul play – a proper investigation, by the book, needs to be carried out. He is a policeman who makes up for what he might be lacking in experience with his conviction of proper unprejudiced and incorruptible police work, which makes him, according to a saying ascribed to Jon's late father of questionable moral character, the most dangerous animal on the planet (105).

The usual detectives in Anne Holt's series, Inger Johanne and Yngvar, are off the case for most of this novel. Inger Johanne will not allow herself to believe that her grieving friends could have anything to do with Sander's death even if she senses that something is not quite as it should be: all too soon any trace of Sander is erased from the family home and Jon has gone straight back to work leaving Ellen at home alone with her grief. However, Inger Johanne's thoughts return again and again to Ellen's dramatic change of character: from the successful, desirable and independent woman with her own dental practice she once knew, Ellen has become a stereotypical neurotic suburban housewife following her marriage to Jon.

Holme's investigation into Sander's case suggests a history of child abuse. His unorthodox interviews reveal that Sander was often bruised and had broken limbs without anyone suspecting foul play. His reading of other cases of violence against children leads him to suspect that the father should be his prime suspect. Jon is furthermore indirectly incriminated morally by being under investigation for insider trading as a partner in the public relations agency CommuniCare – a name it recently took (ironically) to demonstrate its modern corporate ethics and care for the community. The name is an apt metaphor for the neoliberal forces undermining the universalistic welfare state (the company mostly cares for former politicians and celebrities; 121). Additionally, the fact that Jon is revealed not to be Sander's biological father leads the grandmother to fear that he might be unjustly incriminated since recent media interest in cases of child abuse have focused on violent stepfathers. Ellen's discovery of pornographic images of children on Jon's laptop furthermore leads the reader to believe that Holme is on the right track with his suspicion. Jon is portrayed as a thoroughly immoral person and an uncaring father: the representative of dubious corporate care, a white-collar criminal and a child molester. The case seems perfectly clear, and Holt obviously relies on our preconception of masculine violence and illicit corporate care as detrimental to the wellbeing of the most vulnerable. Here the reader is wholly on the side of Holme.

Holme's interviews with Sander's teachers seal the case against Jon for him. Sander's regular teacher brushes away any suggestion of abuse; however, the case against Jon is strengthened by the assistant teacher who had been suspicious. She also claims that the regular teacher would never admit to any suspicion of wrongdoing on the part of the family as she is a strong believer in the Social–Democratic welfare system in which no such thing could possibly occur in a well-functioning family. She suggests that the regular teacher, as a typical permissive liberal, would also claim that the terrorist was a product of an unthinkable failure in the social system and the result of tolerated racism (217). Her view is that evil individuals do exist, and she suspects this is the case with Jon. Mary Evans has defined a similar opposition of views as signifying a crucial difference between crime-writing in Europe and the United States, 'the latter context being one where the thesis of the "bad" individual is more than likely to be offered as an explanation for criminal and indeed murderous behaviour' (Evans 2009: 146).

In the positions of the two school teachers, Holt, however, opposes two equally erroneous perceptions. The regular teacher, a state employee, appears blinded by the utopianism of the welfare state, which makes her unwilling to see and accept its possible flaws; Holme is angered by the fact that she does not seem to regret that Sander was abused, but rather that she might have revealed something incriminating the social system. Sander's assistant teacher, on the other hand, who we learn was paid for by Jon and Ellen (itself an expression of the caving of the universal welfare state to neoliberal forces), is unwilling to consider any extenuating circumstances and stands firm on a neoliberal belief in individual responsibility. In Holt's novel both positions prove misguided, as both fail to understand the real cause of Sander's death. It was not the father but the mother who abused and finally killed Sander. What Jon had meant by his rambling about his failure to care was that he failed to protect Sander against his own mother's fatal abuse.

While it is Inger Johanne who ultimately pieces together the puzzle, her gift as a profiler has also been largely disrupted throughout the novel partly due to her personal involvement with the family, her unwillingness to recognize oddities in their pattern of behaviour and obvious warning signals in the otherwise happy family. Her usually sharp vision is perhaps also blurred by the fact that she recognizes, unconsciously, much of herself in Ellen, who changed her personality after marrying Jon, giving up her career, and after going through three miscarriages before she finally opted for an assisted conception to get the child that she and Jon so desperately wanted. Now, Inger Johanne is herself an expecting mother, who keeps the pregnancy hidden from her traumatized husband, fearing that he would not want another child. Though Inger Johanne, in a final scene recalling a classic Agatha Christie novel, gathers the extended family and points out the guilty parties, Holt's novel is not a classic whodunit. While Ellen is guilty, Inger Johanne has herself, just like Jon, the family and social institutions, been a passive bystander to an enfolding family tragedy, blinded by the deceptive idyllic surface, and to some degree she too has been a reluctant detective and a failed profiler.

In recalling Ellen's behavioural changes following her marriage, giving up her career, and going through successive miscarriages, she succeeds in presenting the material for what could be read as an Ibsenesque doll's-house story for the late welfare society. It is, as in Ibsen's famous play, a classic bourgeois family story with its secrets and silences and an obsession with social respectability. It is also in other ways a depiction of an anachronistic family belonging more firmly to the 1950s than to a modern Nordic welfare state in which more than 80 per cent of Norwegian mothers with small children are employed (Johnsen 2012). Ellen gave up her career as a self-employed dentist when she married Jon, and Inger Johanne suspects that her retreat into a secluded life as a housewife played at least a part in her change of personality making her unable to care for a physically and socially demanding child.

Holt's presentation of Ellen as a 'bad mother' should be seen in the context of a recent trend in especially Norwegian literature as also in a wider range of Scandinavian feminist crime writing and TV drama in the new millennium. According to Melissa Gjellstad, Norway in the 1990s witnessed a growing trend for depicting the everyday lives of families and the rise of the mother as a central subject in particular (Gjellstad 2004). Globally known as one of the most progressive nations when it comes to gender equality and quality of life for families, Norway is, like the other Scandinavian nations, still struggling with de facto inequalities, particularly when it comes to more ingrained sociocultural expectations of motherhood. Toril Moi has written about 'moderskapsmaset' or 'the fuss about motherhood' in contemporary Norway, which reveals still-pervasive and deep-seated social norms and cultural pressures of 'idealized motherhood', which circulate widely as propaganda in the media and stigmatize women who decide not to have children (Moi 2004). Despite Norway's celebrated gender equality policies, there is still a widespread fear of being seen as a 'cold career woman', which was also a central conflict in Liza Marklund's *The Bomber*. The 'uncomfortable' representation in literature of broken families and 'bad mothers' has presented a counter-discourse and a critical interrogation of the idealization of the nuclear family and motherhood in society, which more than anything else keeps women in the patriarchal 'doll's houses' feminists have spent more than a century trying to dismantle (see Gjellstad 2004: 43).

Ellen's story as retold through Inger Johanne's memories and pseudo-psychologizing, or profiling, plays with these norms – simultaneously, and contradictory, the social norm of ideal motherhood and its 'feminist' critique. It is suggested, for instance, that her inability to conceive naturally has somehow contributed to her deviance and unsuitability as a mother and, consequently, as a woman; at the same time, Inger Johanne hints that when Ellen gave up her professional and economic independence she also made herself vulnerable and dangerously dependent on her dubious husband.

Ellen, more importantly, also shares with Nora a dark secret that she has kept from her husband. After several failed pregnancies, Ellen had taken it upon herself without Jon's knowledge to go through with an assisted conception in a Copenhagen clinic, where, unlike in Norway, such treatment was allowed without a husband's consent (this policy, which points to the more central position of the family in the Norwegian welfare state, is also criticized by Moi). Just as Nora could not obtain a loan without her husband's consent in Ibsen's day, forcing her to commit the crime of forgery, Ellen's 'crime' is that she chose assisted conception without her husband's consent, which would eventually give them Sander.

In the tradition of Nordic Gothic or naturalism the secret of the past has come to haunt the present, and it is in Holt's novel, as in Ibsen's play, that the unequal bonds of marriage in terms of gender sow the seeds of the family's destruction. However, there is a twenty-first-century twist. Ellen is no Nora. She has no door to slam but instead reacts violently and fatally towards her own child. Where Nora had to choose her own freedom from the encroaching walls of her doll's house at a time when the welfare state did not guarantee the individual's autonomy, Ellen's twenty-first-century pathology must be seen in the context of a failed system of care: Jon's neo-liberal care for the symptoms rather than their structural causes, his care for Sander rather than for Ellen and the state's reluctance to care for women's independence over the traditional patriarchal family.

Skyggedød is an example of Scandinavian crime writing exploring what Evans has described as what happens to social relationships in an age of prosperity, or what happens to care and responsibility in a Nordic welfare state turned neoliberal. While the connection between the family tragedy and the national catastrophe is, perhaps, kept in the shadows of the narrative, the societal vacuum left by the attacks, the broken social trust so monstrously figured in the fake policeman on Utøya, may still enable a new policeman to grow into his ill-fitting uniform and restore social trust for those who need it the most.

The death of the detective

Holt's crime novel expands on Jon's initial desperate reaction to the death of his son, 'it's all my fault ... I should have been more careful', to include a common 'we', at first through the reader's bystander surrogate Inger Johanne, and second through the novel's obvious (at least to Norwegian readers) reference to a second true crime story, which presumably has nothing to do with Utøya. In the postscript to the novel, Holt notes that it was a series of newspaper articles about the overlooked problem of violence against children in Norway and a true crime book about the death in 2005 of an eight-year-old boy, Christoffer Gjerstad Kihle, a death eventually revealed to be caused by his violent step-father, that encouraged her to treat the subject in a crime novel. Statistics on such crimes are made up of 'dark numbers' (mørketal), she writes, as they are rarely recorded and the perpetrators only occasionally prosecuted due to lack of evidence and witnesses.

As revealed in the case of Christoffer, and in Holt's fictional treatment, the shadow in which violence against children takes place is often the result of systemic and human failures in the near family, as also in the social system that should be in place to protect the most vulnerable in society. According to Holt, these documents 'point a finger at each and every one of us: Child molestation happens because we let it happen; because we cannot make ourselves believe; because it is easier to just look away' (Holt 2013: 334).

The story of Inger Johanne suggests a more symbolic and comprehensive incrimination of the wider society. Inger Johanne's fate is equally tragic. When she leaves the home of Ellen and Jon after having pointed out Ellen as the guilty party, she stumbles over a toy fire engine on her way down the stairs, her awkward landing ending her life. This is an effective way of ending a crime series, but also one that throws further shadows over the whole case. The name she has given Sander's fire engine is of particular relevance to understanding this final scene: Sulamit. The toy fire engine, which she had in the beginning of the novel herself pushed aside under the bushes on the staircase, reminds her of a similar toy her own daughter once had, which now lays buried in their garden. As such, the toy further intimates the connection between her own and the Ellen/Sander story. However, the word also has another meaning in the novel. When Jon's colleague Joachim rails against what he perceives as the superficial expression of togetherness in the Norwegian population after the terror attacks, he uses the Norwegian expression 'hele sulamitten', drawn from the Song of Songs, to denote the whole congregation, the population now gathered in communal mourning (144). What does this slide of metaphor suggest in terms of understanding the 'accidental' death of the detective?

Karl Ove Knausgård has written about the Norwegian tragedy that when it comes to the inhuman consequences of Brevik's actions, individual pathologies and the 'little' history becomes insufficient as explanation. We must see the bigger picture, Knausgård suggests:

> There must be a social safety net that makes actions such as Breivik's impossible. I'm not thinking of the social services or the

school system, nor the police either, I'm thinking of the bond that exists between people, I'm thinking of the presence of the other within ourselves, an openness towards a shared humanity around which all societies and cultures are build. (Knausgård 2012)

This bigger picture of a shared humanity and the necessity for developing and maintaining affective bonds in an age where the traditional 'social safety net' of the welfare state has weakened, has also been the running argument throughout this book's discussion of contemporary Scandinavian crime fiction. From Beck's renewed 'people's home' in the alternative community of his lover and landlord Rhea in Sjöwall and Wahlöö's *Novel of a Crime* to Stieg Larsson's dramatization of Lisbeth Salander's struggle to rebuild interpersonal trust in a world poor in trust capital; from the banker's missing relationships and artificial world in Bodelsen's *Think of a Number* to Smilla's confrontation with her own vulnerability, which will enable her to create social bonds with strangers; and from Mankell's play with his readers' trust in his detective, Wallander, in order to expose ingrained xenophobia to *The Killing*'s heroic Sarah Lund who sacrifices her own wellbeing to renew our trust in an incorruptible state, Scandinavian crime narratives have been popular reflectors for the anxieties and hopes of readers and viewers in Scandinavia and beyond.

We turn to genre fiction not only for entertainment and momentary escape from an increasingly complex and threatening world, but more importantly, we (over)indulge in crime stories because they allow us to diagnose and come to terms with our most abstract fears of dislocation and disintegrating social values in a rapidly changing world. At their best, Scandinavian crime novels not only present the symptoms, but they also let us work through the sacrifices, the introspective and affective work needed if we are to imagine more open, humane, equal and just individual bonds and societies.

When Inger Johanne stumbles on 'sulamitten', Sander's toy fire engine, it not only recalls her own motherhood, but also evokes the long tradition of socio-critical Scandinavian crime writing with its reference to Sjöwall and Wahlöö's clue in *The Fire Engine that Disappeared* – after four decades much has indeed changed in Scandinavian crime fiction, but the motivation to address social and collective issues, to use crime fiction as a mode of critique has not disappeared. As Inger Johanne falls, clumsily and tragically to her death with her unborn child, she brings the ultimate sacrifice, which symbolically calls for a collective response, involving the readers, to accept collective guilt for allowing the death of young children and the creation of a monstrous mass murderer in the shadows of our welfare societies. It is ultimately us, 'hele sulamitten', who like Holme have to grow into our ill-fitting uniforms and social responsibilities.

Conclusion

This book has primarily been concerned with how Scandinavian writers have used crime fiction as a generic form ready-made, so to speak, to capture and critically investigate the sociocultural symptoms of a 'shattered dream', which in these small nations in the northern periphery of Europe meant the self-assured utopian certainty of living in the most progressive, egalitarian and, not least, peaceful welfare societies. As the twenty-first century beckoned and unfolded on a backdrop of border-crossing crises and conflicts, environmental disasters, terrorism, forced migrations, financial meltdowns, rampant consumerism and individualism, prompting anxieties about national identities, state-guaranteed socioeconomic equality and justice, crime novels and TV series from Denmark, Norway and Sweden forged an idiosyncratic regional tradition within the by now globally shared super-genre of crime fiction, which this book has described as both exhibiting and working through the symptoms of shared anxieties about social and cultural change. Surprisingly, this region-specific and peripheral tradition became a global phenomenon at the end of the first decade of the new century, despite being originally written in less-widely spoken languages, depicting the lives and crimes of little-known small nations.

It would be fair to say that Scandinavian crime fiction only became a recognizable genre or subgenre as novels and TV series became widely translated, subtitled and adapted into foreign languages and markets. Scandinavian crime fiction or 'Nordic Noir', as it is often referred to in the English-speaking world, is arguably only understood as a distinct regional genre as a consequence of its international success – otherwise, Scandinavians would happily have continued to refer to their local specimens as simply 'krimi' (in Denmark), 'krim' (in Norway) and 'deckare' (in Sweden) without regional or national epithets. Scandinavian crime fiction, in other words, is perhaps only really 'Scandinavian' when viewed or read from abroad – when published, marketed and sold in bookshops, book fairs or at broadcasting trade fairs, where the branding of national peculiarities in a crowded and globalized field is essential for attracting the attention of potential funders, publishers and book buyers.

However, as Claire Squires has suggested by way of Tzvetan Todorov, genre is not merely a practical way of categorization, but 'an agency in the publishing field' through which 'art interacts with society' (Squires 2009: 72). Scandinavian crime fiction has undoubtedly become a desirable international brand, but it also suggests certain ways in which local Scandinavian societies and receiving cultures choose to codify particular fictions in correspondence with less explicated ideologies, needs and expectations.

This book has argued that Scandinavian crime fiction, as a particular 'use of genre', presents a formally and culturally diverse yet consistent ethos in relation to the historical and social realities of the Scandinavian welfare states and their crises since the late 1960s. I am, however, aware of the necessary dangers of such a broad perspective: the traits I have identified might not be particularly Scandinavian (as the obvious generic affiliation with American and British genre traditions may suggest) or may not even be shared in identical ways between the Scandinavian countries. Their historical, cultural and sociopolitical differences are indeed multiple, but they also share important similarities notably in the structural similarities of their universal welfare states, which have been the main context for my argument (Christiansen and Markkola 2006: 9; Nestingen and Arvas: 6, 8). When seen from Scandinavia, the national differences may seem more dominant, whereas when seen from abroad they seem very much alike and whatever differences there may be are miniscule. Both similarities and differences in the ways in which the crime genres have been employed are, perhaps, most visible in the three authorships treated in the first chapters of this book: the very vocal and explicit ideological critique of the modern welfare state in Sjöwall and Wahlöö points to a political culture and crime tradition particular to Sweden, whereas the existential treatment of the harried welfare man in Anders Bodelsen's *Think of a Number* conforms to literary and philosophical traditions, and perhaps a more individualistic ethos in Denmark, in comparison to the strong cooperative nature of the Swedish welfare state. Gunnar Staalesen's equally individualistic private eye with a well-developed social conscience is more of an American-style frontier man, who is a better fit for the northern periphery of Scandinavia and a Norway where more traditional family values shine through not only the sentimentalism of Veum but also Anne Holt's fictional response to the national tragedy of Utøya with a socio-critical crime novel centring on violence in the family.

Nevertheless, the social and cultural similarities are also tangible especially in the framework of the modern universal welfare state and its feared dissolution. As I have argued here, these particular sociopolitical, historical and culturally shared experiences and anxieties are reflected in the diverse, hyperlocalized fictional crime scenes that now dot the map of Scandinavia.

Arguably the most iconic fictional Scandinavian crime scene is the one that brings the monomaniac, socially inept Malmö detective Saga Norén and the recently vasectomized, convivial Copenhagen detective Martin Rohde together on a murder case in the widely distributed and the several-times-over adapted Danish–Swedish TV crime serial *Broen/Bron* or, as it is known in the UK, *The Bridge* (*Hans Rosenfeldt* 2011, 2013, 2015).

While writers such as Henning Mankell, Stieg Larsson, Liza Marklund, Jussi Adler-Olsen and Jo Nesbø have been central to the global popularization of a Scandinavian crime 'scene' over the recent decades with widely translated bestselling crime series around the world, the continuing global fascination with Nordic Noir today is perhaps mostly due to Scandinavian crime serials made for TV. Though audio-visual mediations such as TV, film and gaming may be the most promising present and future vehicles for Scandinavian crime fiction after decades of having saturated the markets with social-realistic crime novels, as I argued in the previous chapter, several of the most popular TV series continue and develop the tradition for welfare-crime fiction, which this book has traced back to the socially engaged and critical crime novels by Bodelsen, Sjöwall and Wahlöö and Staalesen in the late 1960s and 1970s. *The Bridge* is a case in point, and as a way of concluding my discussion of

Scandinavian crime fiction, I shall use this transnational series as a prism through which to review the main characteristics of the genre that I have traced; in particular, the ways in which Scandinavian crime fiction narrates experiences, values and conflicts associated with the welfare state in the form of highly localized responses to anxieties about wider social changes and crises prompted by the post-welfare state and global crises.

As the uncertain, shifting and slippery locations underneath the detectives of Peter Høeg, Kerstin Ekman and Mankell's crime novels from the early 1990s, the symbolic location of the crime scene in *The Bridge* suggests a similar motivation to deterritorialize, to make uncanny by way of a violent crime this monumental and carefully designed architectural expression (much like the urban renewal and social housing schemes in the seventies and nineties) of a well-functioning region invested in transnational mobility and progress. On the otherwise invisible border, half-way across the Øresund Bridge, a body has been placed; or, as it turns out, two bodies. Mirroring the transnational location of a near-borderless Øresund region in the wider Nordic Passport Union, where one Scandinavian nation merges into the other, the severed dead bodies of two women, a Malmö politician and a Copenhagen prostitute, have been joined to form an apparently intact body lying astride national and social boundaries. The location of the crime scene in the border zone between two nations on the iconic bridge demands a cross-national investigation, where the two detectives must collaborate, overcome personal, cultural and linguistic differences, and, importantly, constantly criss-cross the bridge in order to match a killer who respects no borders.

The symbolic gesture and spectacular arrangement of the crime scene is the modus operandi of an elusive serial killer, who sees himself as a vigilante 'protector of the truth'. Through websites and the press he proclaims that his killings are motivated by a desire to attract attention to the lack of care and social justice for the marginalized and dispossessed in society such as the mentally ill, the homeless and drug addicts. As such, the premise of *The Bridge* is a continuation of the tradition of Scandinavian welfare-crime fiction dating back to the 1970s, when crime writers in Denmark, Norway and Sweden began to 'scratch a collective itch'. The 'truth terrorist' in *The Bridge* is not unlike the 'truth terrorists' we find in Sjöwall and Wahlöö's *The Locked Room* (1972) and *The Terrorists*

(1975) – young mothers who became deadly avengers as a consequence of an oppressive sociopolitical system, in which they had become marginalized and isolated individuals.

Killers with a social conscience who take it upon themselves to right the wrongs of an unequal society, abandoned by the once socially progressive welfare state, are numerous in Scandinavian crime fiction. Harking back to the seminal case of the Norrmalms Square drama, as discussed in my introduction, where the hitherto clearly contrasting roles of the police and the criminal, good and evil blurred, the socially conscious vigilante has come to figure as a particularly Scandinavian welfare-crime villain who, at one and the same time, represents the welfare state's widely shared social ethos and its own undoing. In this sense, narratives about lone truth terrorists are always troubling symptoms or 'narratives of proximity', prompting the representatives of the law and the welfare state, readers and viewers by proxy, to confront their own collective responsibility for the corrosion of personal and societal bonds in the post-welfare state.

A similar social-critical villain was also employed in the Danish political thriller *Skytten* (1977, The shooter), which was co-written by Anders Bodelsen. In this film, an eco-terrorist shoots at symbolic and human targets (even the then internationally famed Danish football player Allan Simonsen) from the roof tops of Copenhagen to draw attention to the politicians' immoral plans to build a nuclear power plant in Denmark. The film was remade in 2013 by director Anette K. Olesen (with a cast that included Kim Bodnia who played Martin Rohde in *The Bridge*) now updated to feature an eco-terrorist who fights the government's plan to drill for oil in North-Eastern Greenland. In Scandinavian crime fiction, the truth terrorist is used not only to call attention to and dramatize local societal problems, but also to wider global challenges such as environmental change and transnational responsibilities. While the first season of *The Bridge* tackled social issues well known from decades of Scandinavian crime fiction, the second season featured vigilante eco-terrorists, whose main target was an EU summit on climate change in Copenhagen.

Narratives about vigilante criminals, who are driven to violence and murder by a welfare state that has abandoned its promise to protect marginalized individuals against the forces of capital and backed-down on its loftier moral values of social equality, also characterize novels from the 1990s by, for instance, Mankell (*The Fifth Woman*, 1996) and Unni Lindell (*The Snake Bearer*, 1996), as discussed in Chapter 7. These novels feature female avengers and serial killers who respond violently to male abuse by taking the place of an impotent, still patriarchal welfare state, which is found unable to deliver on its promise of social and gender equality. Most famously, an individualist vigilante, who seeks revenge in the ruins of the traditional welfare state, is central to the international success of Larsson's *Millennium* trilogy embodied in the hacker-investigator Lisbeth Salander. Where previously the vigilante criminal figured both as a threat to the stability of society and as a violated figure, with whom both the police and the readers could reluctantly empathize, Lisbeth Salander is a new heroine, whose recourse to criminal methods no longer appear disconcerting as it is now the state itself, the post-welfare state, which plays the role of the monstrous villain, a morally bankrupt and exceedingly violent state. The social critique levelled at the welfare state in the twenty-first century, then, appears to endorse vigilantism and employs the systemic structures which brought about the fall of the welfare state in the first place. Certainly, there is room for reading Larsson's trilogy along these lines – as part of the problem rather than part of the solution, a mere symptom. However, as I have suggested in Chapter 4, Larsson's crime fiction can also be seen to reinscribe (perhaps nostalgically) 'people's home' values of cooperation, inter-personal trust and decency – 'the bond that exist between people', as Knausgård formulated it – into a welfare state still in the grip of a financial and moral crisis.

As Larsson's *The Girl with the Dragon Tattoo* employs statistics about men's violence against women as attention-gripping 'authenticity effect', so does the truth terrorist in *The Bridge*, refer to actual reports about crime and social inequality to justify his actions. In a recorded message to the police, he takes responsibility for the murders of the two women with the statement: 'Our part of the world would be wonderful if we solved our problems. I would like to point out five in particular. The women on the bridge are just the beginning'. In the following episode, he calls attention to a series of 'facts' established in *The Swedish Crime Survey 2007* and in a survey among socially marginalized groups in Denmark (*SUSY-udsat*, 2008) conducted by the National Institute of Public Health and the Council for Socially Marginalized People. To the truth terrorist, these surveys demonstrate that not everyone is 'equal before the law': crime investigations target disproportionally marginalized groups, whose health and wellbeing continue to deteriorate in the Danish and Swedish welfare states.

These reports do indeed corroborate and lend an air of realism to the killer's social critique as they document actual continuing and deepening social inequalities. They do, however, also suggest, by their sheer existence, the social state's continuing determination to pursue and alleviate the negative consequences of social inequalities. As in several of the crime novels explored in this book – novels whose dystopian portrayals of crimes and anxieties in the neoliberal welfare state have popularized social critique as a particular generic trait – *The Bridge* is explicit about its welfarist egalitarianism, though it does not in the end endorse the vigilantism of the truth terrorist. He eventually turns out to have misled the detectives and the public with his social agenda in order to pursue a covert personal vendetta against the police detective Martin Rohde. Instead, it is Saga Norén's mental uniqueness, her naivety about social forms, her rationality, objectivity and her inability to speak nothing but the truth, which makes her an ideal protector of the law and the embodiment of the still thriving, disinterested yet egalitarian welfare state.

This role is humorously demonstrated when she questions the murdered politician's bereaved husband. Norén asks him whether his wife was in any way threatened or had upset anyone lately. The only thing he can think of is that she wanted to charge for library loans and that some disapproved. Norén's prompt reply is: 'That's foolish', and she elaborates: 'Reading becomes a money matter. Social differences will grow.' It is, however, as she says, unlikely that library fees was the cause of her death. From the very beginning of the series, the apparently socially dysfunctional representative of the state is the one who speaks up for the welfare state and its egalitarianism. Before we know that the crimes she and Rohde are investigating are motivated by social indignation, we have learnt that she, and with her the police, plays the role of an idealized, if not slightly out-of-touch or nostalgic, guardian of the incorruptible, rational and socially just state. When the truth terrorist in the end turns out to have used his militant social critique as a red herring, in order to manipulate Rohde into a position where he can carry out his personal revenge, Norén's disinterestedness, her unwavering dedication to the letter of the law and protocol, makes her, like Holme in Holt's *Skyggedød*, fit for the uniform, incorruptible and without personal interest beyond solving the case and catching the criminal. However, as in the case of Sarah Lund in *The Killing*, such disinterestedness and dedication demands personal sacrifices and the suppression of her own difficult past (Robbins 2015).

The Bridge is just one of the most recent examples of a shared Scandinavian preoccupation with how to narrate the welfare state in the form of crime fiction on paper and on screens. While these Nordic Noir fictions appear as made for representing an increasing and widely shared anxiety about dramatic social change, about a deteriorating social utopia and as popular vehicles for a social critique of the post-welfare state, they are also narratives that can be seen to shore up the values associated with the social welfare state in an age of austerity, neoliberalism and unequal globalization with their emphasis on collaboration, interpersonal trust, personal sacrifice, social responsibility and equality in their common exploration of the systemic structures that underpin the dramatic narratives of subjective violence, serial killings and mass murder. It is no surprise, I think, that such narratives have become the most widely consumed genre in the Scandinavian countries and have become unprecedented successful cultural exports in the uncertain and anxious first decades of a thoroughly globalized and unequal twenty-first century.

BIBLIOGRAPHY

Agger, G. (2011), 'Emotion, gender and genre: Investigating The Killing', *Northern Lights* 9: 111–125.

Agger, G. (2013), *Mord til tiden: Forbrydelse, historie og mediekultur*, Aalborg: Aalborg Universitetsforlag.

Aléx, P. (2003), *Konsumera rätt – ett svenskt ideal: Behov, hushållning och konsumtion*, Lund: Studentlitteratur.

Alnæs, K. (2000), *Historien om Norge: Femti rike år*, Oslo: Gyldendal.

Alter, A. (2010), 'Fiction's global crime wave', *The Wall Street Journal*, 1 July.

Andersdotter, A. S. (1999), 'Subjekt och landskap i Kerstin Ekmans författerskap', in I. Lærkesen, H. Bache-Wiig and A. G. Lombnæs (eds), *Naturhistorier: Naturoppfatning, menneskesyn og poetikk i skandinavisk litteratur*, Oslo: Cappelen, pp. 281–292.

Andersen, P. T. (2013), 'Norsk samtidslitteratur omkring årtusenskiftet: Uro i redet, antiindividualisme og den postmoderne psykologiseringen', in M. Bunch (ed.), *Millennium: Nye retninger i nordisk litteratur*, Hellerup: Spring, pp. 197–219.

Andersson, J. (2009a), 'Nordic nostalgia and Nordic light: The Swedish model as utopia 1930–2007', *Scandinavian Journal of History*, 34/3: 229–245.

Andersson, J. (2009b), *När framtiden redan hänt: Socialdemokratin och folkhemsnostalgin*, Stockholm: Ordfront.

Bauman, Z. (1997), *Postmodernity and Its Discontents*, Cambridge: Polity Press.

Bauman, Z. (2007), *Liquid Times: Living in an Age of Uncertainty*. Cambridge: Polity Press.

Bauman, Z. (2012), *Liquid Modernity*, Cambridge: Polity Press.

Berggren, H. and L. Trägårdh (2006), *Är svensken människa? Gemenskap och oberoende i det modera Sverige*, Stockholm: Nordstedts.

Berggren, H. and L. Trägårdh (2010), 'Pippi Longstocking: The autonomous child and the moral logic of the Swedish welfare state', in H. Matsson and S.-O. Wallenstein (eds), *Swedish Modernism: Architecture, Consumption and the Welfare State*, London: Black Dog, pp. 50–65.

Berglund, K. (2012), *Deckarboomen under lupp: Statistiska perspektiv på svensk kriminallitteratur 1977–2010*, Uppsala: Skrifter utgivna av Avdelingen för litteratursociologi vid Litteraturvetenskapliga institutionen i Uppsala.

Bergman, K. (2014), *Swedish Crime Fiction: The Making of Nordic Noir*, Milan: Mimesis.

Bodelsen, A. (1969), *Think of a Number*, trans. by D. Hohnen, New York: Harper and Row.

Bodelsen, A. (1970), 'Facts – dødvægt eller poesi?' in J. S. Thomsen (ed.), *Virkeligheden der voksede: Litterær kulturdebat i tresserne*, København: Gyldendal, pp. 164–169.

Bodelsen, A. (2007), *Tænk på et tal*, København: Gyldendal.

Booth, M. (2014), *The Almost Nearly Perfect People: The Truth About the Nordic Miracle*, London: Jonathan Cape.

Borchgrevink, A. (2013), *A Norwegian Tragedy: Anders Behring Breivik and the Massacre on Utøya*, trans. by G. Puzey, Cambridge: Polity.

Borevi, K. (2012), 'Sweden: The flagship of multiculturalism', in G. Brochmann and A. Hagelund (eds), *Immigration Policy and the Scandinavian Welfare State 1945–2010*, Houndmills: Palgrave, pp. 25–96.

Borg, A. (2012), *Brottsplats: Stockholm. Urban kriminallitteratur 1851–2011*, Stockholm: Stockholmia.

Boym, S. (2001), *The Future of Nostalgia*, New York: Basic Books.

Breivik, J. (2014), *Min skyld? En fars historie*, Oslo: Juritzen.

Brodén, D. (2008), *Folkhemmets skuggbilder: En kulturanalytisk genrestudie av svensk kriminalfiktion i film och tv*, Stockholm: Ekholm & Tegebjer.

Broen/Bron (2011, 2013, 2015, created by H. Rosenfeldt), television series, Nimbus Film/Filmlance International, København/Stockholm.

Bunch, M. (2013), 'Individualiseringens veje: Fra forbrugskritik og slægtsromaner til det private som det universelle i Kirsten Hammanns *Se på mig*', in M. Bunch (ed.), *Millennium: Nye retninger i nordisk litteratur*, Hellerup: Spring, pp. 23–43.

Burenstam Linder, S. (1969), *Den rastlösa välfärdsmänniskan. Tidsbrist i överflöd: en ekonomisk studie*, Stockholm: Bonnier.

Byström, M. and P. Frohnert (2013), 'Introduction IV', in M. Byström and P. Frohnert (eds), *Reaching a State of Hope: Refugees, Immigrants and the Swedish Welfare State, 1930–2000*, Lund: Nordic Academic Press, pp. 227–234.

Cassuto, L. (2009), *Hard-boiled Sentimentality: The Secret History of American Crime Stories*, NewYork: Columbia UP.

Chandler, R. (1988), *The Simple Art of Murder*, New York: Vintage.

Childs, M. W. (1936), *Sweden: The Middle Way*, London: Faber & Faber.

Christiansen, N. F. and P. Markkola (2006), 'Introduction', in N. F. Christiansen et al., *The Nordic Model of Welfare: A Historical Reappraisal*, Copenhagen: Museum Tusculanum Press, pp. 9–30.

Cronqvist, M., S. Kärrholm and L. Sturfelt (2008), 'Oro i lyckolandet: Mellan Sofiero och Norrmalmstorg', in M. Cronqvist, L. Sturfelt and M. Wiklund (eds), *1973: En träff med tidsanden*. Lund: Nordic Academic Press, pp. 37–55.

Dahl, A. (2012), *The Blinded Man*, trans. by T. Nunnally, London: Vintage.

Dahl, W. (1993), *Dødens fortellere: Den norske kriminal- og spenningslitteraturens historie*, Bergen: Anna.

Dahl, W. (1995), *Hjerte, smerte, blod og død: Artikler om trivialiteter og kriminaliteter*, Bergen: Anna.

Den som dræber (2011, created by E. Egholm), television series, Miso Film/TV2 Danmark, København.

Dussere, E. (2014), *America Is Elsewhere: The Noir Tradition in the Age of Consumer Culture*, Oxford: Oxford UP.

Egholm Andersen, F. (2010), *Den danske krimi: Nedslag i den danske krimi gennem de sidste 50 år*, Frederiksberg: Her&Nu.

Ekman, K. (1993), *Händelser vid vatten*, Stockholm: Albert Bonniers Förlag.

Ekman, K. (1995), 'Obsessed by society', *Swedish Book Review*, Supplement: Kerstin Ekman: 79–88.

Ekman, K. (1996), *Blackwater*, trans. by J. Tate, London: Vintage.

Ericsson, U., I. Molina and P.-M. Ristilammi (2000), 'Representationer av platser – en teoretisk genomgång', in U. Ericsson, I. Molina and P.-M. Ristilammi (eds), *Miljonprogram och media. Föreställningar om människor och förorter*, Stockholm: Rigsantikvarieämbetet, pp. 24–40.

Evans, M. (2009), *The Imagination of Evil: Detective Fiction and the Modern World*, London, New York: Continuum.

Fagerberg, J., Å. Cappelen, L. Mjøset and R. Skarstein (1990), 'The decline of Social-Democratic state capitalism in Norway', *New Left Review* 181: 60–94.

Fløgstad, K. (1979) [1976], 'Den dialektiske detektiv', in A. Tvinnereim (ed.), *Triviallitteratur, populærlitteratur, masselitteratur*, Bergen: Universitetsforlaget, pp. 251–271.

Flood, A. (2014), 'Anders Breivik is subject of Åsne Seierstad's new book', *The Guardian*, 7 February.

Forbrydelsen (2007, 2009, 2011), television series, Danmarks Radio, København, created by S. Sveistrup.

Forsås-Scott, H. (1995), 'Stories in a changing landscape: Kerstin Ekman's latest novel', *Swedish Book Review*, supplement: Kerstin Ekman: 74–78.

Forshaw, B. (2012), *Death in a Cold Climate: A Guide to Scandinavian Crime Fiction*, Houndmills: Palgrave.

Gazan, S. J. (2011), *The Dinosaur Feather*, trans. by C. Barslund, London: Quercus.

Giddens, A. (2002), *Runaway World: How Globalisation is Reshaping Our Lives*, London: Profile Books.

Gjellstad, M. (2004), *Mothering at Millennium's End: Family in 1990s Norwegian Literature*, Unpublished PhD thesis, University of Washington.

Graham, D. L. R., E. I. Rawlings and R. K. Rigsby (1994), 'Love thine enemy: Hostages and classic Stockholm syndrome', in *Loving to Survive: Sexual Terror, Men's Violence, and Women's Lives*, New York: New York UP, pp. 1–29.

Hägg, G. (2005), *Välfärdsåren: svensk historia 1945–1986*, Stockholm: Wahlström & Widstrand.

Handesten, L. (2014), *Bestsellere: En litteratur- og kulturhistorie om de mest solgte bøger i Danmark*, København: Spring.

Hansen, N. G. (2010), 'Forord', in N. G. Hansen (ed.), *Velfærdsfortællinger*, København: Gyldendal, pp. 7–15.

Harvey, D. (1989), *The Urban Experience*, Baltimore: Johns Hopkins UP.

Hauge, H. (2004), 'Det grønlandske spøgelse: Miss Smilla', *Spring* 22: 237–255.

Hausladen, G. (2000), *Places for Dead Bodies*, Austin: U of Texas P.

Hedegaard, F. and J. Støvring (1981), *Anders Bodelsen: Tænk på et tal*, København: Dansklærerforeningen.

Hedenborg, S. and L. Kvarnström (2004), *Det svenska samhället 1720–2000*, Lund: Studentlitteratur.

Henningsen, N. G. (2013), 'Demokratisk begær', *Kritik* 207: 29–38.

Hilson, M. (2008), *The Nordic Model: Scandinavia since 1945*, London: Reaktion Books.

Hobsbawm, E. (1995), *The Age of Extremes: The Short Twentieth Century, 1914–1991*, London: Abacus.

Høeg, P. (1992), *Frøken Smillas fornemmelse for sne*, København: Rosinante.

Høeg, P. (2005), *Miss Smilla's Feeling for Snow*, trans. by F. David, London: Vintage.

Holt, A. (2013), *Skyggedød*, Bergen: Vigmostad & Bjørke.

Huntford, R. (1971), *The New Totalitarians*, London: Allen Lane.

Hutcheon, L. (2002), *The Politics of Postmodernism*, London and New York: Routledge.

Huyssen, A. (2003), *Present Pasts: Urban Palimpsests and the Politics of Memory*, Stanford: Stanford UP.

Hylland Eriksen, T. (1993), *Typisk norsk: Essays om kulturen i Norge*, Oslo: C. Huitfeldt.

'Interview: Gunnar Staalesen, author' (2010), *The Scotsman*, 29 November 2010.

Johnsen, S. (2012), 'Women in work: The Norwegian experience', *OECD Observer* 293, November, web.

Jónsson, G. and K. Stefánsson (2013), 'Introduction', in G. Jónsson and K. Stefánsson (eds), *Retrenchment or renewal? Welfare States in times of economic crisis*. Helsinki: NordWel, pp. 13–25.

Kärrholm, S. (2005), *Konsten att lägga pussel: Deckaren och besvärjandet av ondskan i folkhemmet*, Stockholm: Brutus Östlings Bokförlag.

Keen, S. (2007), *Empathy and the Novel*, Oxford: Oxford UP.

Keetley, D. (2012), 'Unruly bodies: The politics of sex in Maj Sjöwall and Per Wahlöö's Martin Beck Series', *Clues* 30: 54–64.

Kirkegaard, P. (2010), 'Arne Dahl: Sjöwall og Wahlöö's sande arvtager', Arbejdspapir nr. 12, *Krimi og kriminaljournalistik i Skandinavien*, www.krimiforsk.aau.dk, web.

Kjældgaard, L. H. (2009), 'Fremtidens Danmark: Tre faser i dansk fiktionsprosa om velfærdsstaten, 1950–1980', *Kritik* 191: 31–43.

Knausgård, K. O. (2012), 'Breivik slaktade unga människor av samma rädsla för gränslöshet som drev fram fascismen', *Dagens Nyheter*, 22 July.

Kolbe, L. (2006), 'Urban destruction or preservation? Conservation movement and planning in twentieth-century Scandinavian capitals', in J. Monclús and M. Gùardia (eds), *Culture, Urbanism and Planning*, Aldershot: Ashgate, pp. 129–148.

Läckberg, C. (2011), *The Ice Princess*, trans. by S. T. Murray, London: HarperCollins.

Larsson, S. (2015a), *The Girl with the Dragon Tattoo*, trans. by R. Keeland, London: MacLehose.

Larsson, S. (2015b), *The Girl Who Played With Fire*, trans. by R. Keeland, London: MacLehose.

Leffler, Y. (2013), 'The devious landscape in contemporary Scandinavian horror', in P. M. Mehtonen and M. Savolainen (eds), *Gothic Topographies: Language, Nation Building, 'Race'*, Farnham: Ashgate, pp. 141–152.

Leffler, Y. (2015), 'Lisbeth Salander as Pippi Longstocking', in B. Robbins (ed.), *Nordic Noir*, Post45, *Contemporaries*, 6. July, web, 12 December 2015.

Lindqvist, J. A. (2009), *Let the Right One In*, trans. by E. Segerberg, London: Quercus.

Lingås, L. G. (ed.) (1970), *Myten om velferdsstaten: Søkelys på norsk sosialpolitikk*, Oslo: Pax.

Løchen, Y. (1970), 'Velferdsstatens krise', in L. G. Lingås (ed.), *Myten om velferdsstaten: Søkelys på norsk sosialpolitikk*, Oslo: Pax, pp. 204–215.

Lowenthal, D. (1985), *The Past is a Foreign Country*, Cambridge: Cambridge UP.

Lundin, B. (1981), *The Swedish Crime Story*, trans. by A.-L. Ringarp, Sunbyberg: Tidsskriften Jury.

MacDonald, A. (ed.) (2013a), *Murders and Acquisitions: Representations of the Serial Killer in Popular Culture*, New York: Bloomsbury.

MacDonald, A. (2013b), 'Serial killing, surveillance, and the state', in A. MacDonald (ed.), *Murders and Acquisitions: Representations of the Serial Killer in Popular Culture*, New York: Bloomsbury, pp. 33–48.

Macdougall, I. (2010), 'The man who blew up the welfare state', *n+1 Magazine*, 27 February, web, 12 December 2015.

Mai, A.-M. (2013), 'At holde samfundet levende og bevægeligt – Om forholdet mellem litteratur og velfærdsstat i Danmark', *European Journal of Scandinavian Studies* 43: 203–216.

Mai, A.-M. (2015), 'Eco-crime: Scandinavian literature takes on the environmental crisis', in B. Robbins (ed.), *Nordic Noir, Post45, Contemporaries*, 23 May, web, 19 December 2015.

Mandel, E. (1984), *Delightful Murder: A Social History of the Crime Story*, London: Pluto.

Mankell, H. (2004), *Before the Frost*, trans. by E. Segerberg, London: Harvill Press.

Mankell, H. (2009), *The Pyramid*, trans. by E. Segerberg with L. Thompson, London: Vintage.

Mankell, H. (2011a), *Faceless Killers*, trans. by S. T. Murray, London: Vintage.

Mankell, H. (2011b), *Mördare utan ansikte*, Stockholm: Leopard.

Mankell, H. (2012a), *The Fifth Woman*, trans. by S. T. Murray, London: Vintage.

Mankell, H. (2012b), *The White Lioness*, trans. by L. Thompson, London: Vintage.

Marcuse, H. (2002), *One-Dimensional Man: Studies in the Ideology of Advanced Industrial Society*, London and New York: Routledge.

Marklund, L. (2011), *The Bomber*, trans. by N. Smith, London: Corgi.

Mathiesen, A. (2000), 'Socialdemokratiet og nyliberalismen', in C. Clausen and H. Lærum (eds), *Velfærdsstaten i krise – en antologi*, København: Tiderne Skifter, pp. 236–261.

Mattsson, H. (2010), 'Designing the reasonable consumer: Standardisation and personalisation in Swedish functionalism', in H. Mattsson and S.-O. Wallenstein (eds), *Swedish Modernism: Architecture, Consumption and the Welfare State*, London: Black Dog, pp. 74–99.

McCorristine, S. (2011), 'The place of pessimism in Henning Mankell's Kurt Wallander Series', in Nestingen and Arvas (eds), *Scandinavian Crime Fiction*, Cardiff: U of Wales P, pp. 77–88.

McDonald-Gibson, C. (2013), 'Norway's far right may come to power despite memory of Anders Breivik's killing spree', *Time*, 19 August.

Messent, P. (2013), *The Crime Fiction Handbook*, Chichester: Wiley-Blackwell.

'Misterioso/The Blinded Man', *The Official Homepage of Arne Dahl*, n.d., web, 3 November 2015.

Moi, T. (2004), 'Moderskapsmaset', *Morgenbladet*, 2 January.

Moretti, F. (2000), 'Conjectures on world literature', *New Left Review* 1: 54–68.

Morton, T. (2010), *The Ecological Thought*, Cambridge, MA: Harvard UP.

Morton, T. (2012), 'Guilt, shame, sadness: Turning to coexistence', *Volume* 31:1, Guilty Landscapes: 16–18.

Munt, S. R. (1998), 'Grief, doubt and nostalgia in detective fiction or … "Death and the Detective Novel": A Return', *College Literature 25/* 3: 133–144.

Myhre, A. S. (2011), 'Norway attacks: Norway's tragedy must shake Europe into acting on extremism', *The Guardian*, 24 July.

Nesbø, J. (2009), *The Redbreast*, trans. by D. Bartlett, London: Vintage.

Nesbø, J. (2011), 'In Norway, the past is a foreign country', *New York Times*, 26 July.

Nestingen, A. (2008), *Crime and Fantasy in Scandinavia: Fiction, Film, and Social Change*, Seattle: U of Washington P.

Nestingen, A. (2011), 'Unnecessary officers: Realism, melodrama and Scandinavian crime fiction in transition', in Nestingen and Arvas (eds), *Scandinavian Crime Fiction*, Cardiff: U of Wales P, pp. 171–83.

Nestingen, A. and P. Arvas (2011), 'Introduction: Contemporary Scandinavian crime fiction', in A. Nestingen and P. Arvas (eds), *Scandinavian Crime Fiction*, Cardiff: U. of Wales P, pp. 1–20.

Newman, J. (2004), 'Postkoloniale parasitter: Peter Høegs *Frøken Smillas fornemmelse for sne*', *Spring* 22: 9–27.

Nicolajsen, K. (1977), 'Hvordan hverdagsmennesket lærte at sætte pris på sin hverdag: Om Anders Bodelsen: Tænk på et tal', in J. B. Jensen and K. Nicolajsen, *Romanen som offentlighedsform: Studier i moderne dansk prosa*, København: Gyldendal.

Norseng, M. K. (1997), 'A house of mourning: *Frøken Smillas fornemmelse for sne*', *Scandinavian Studies* 69/1: 52–84.

Pedersen, O. K. (2011), *Konkurrencestaten*, København: Hans Reitzels Forlag.

Petersen, J. H., K. Petersen and N. F. Christiansen (eds) (2012), *Dansk velfærdshistorie: Velfærdsstatens storhedstid*, vol.4, Odense: Syddansk Universitetsforlag.

Pittelkow, R. (1971), 'Det er (ikke) rart at være fremmedgjort', *Poetik* 4: 243–271.

Plain, G. (2001), *Twentieth Century Crime Fiction: Gender, Sexuality and the Body*, New York: Routledge.

Porter, D. (2003), 'The private eye', in M. Priestman (ed.), *The Cambridge Companion to Crime Fiction*, Cambridge: Cambridge UP, pp. 95–114.

Povlsen, K. K. (2010), 'Anna Pihl – Mor(d) på Bellahøj Politistation', in G. Agger and A. M. Waade (eds), *Den skandinaviske krimi. Bestseller og blockbuster*, Göteborg: Nordicom, pp. 37–47.

Pred, A. (2000), *Even in Sweden: Racisms, Racialized Spaces, and the Popular Geographical Imagination*, Berkeley: U of California P.

Reijnders, S. (2009), 'Watching the detectives: Inside the guilty landscapes of Inspector Morse, Baantjer and Wallander', *European Journal of Communication* 24: 165–181.

Richter, L. (2010), 'Serieforbrydere er sjældne – men har stor fascinationskraft', *Information*, 16 November.

Riget (1994), Directed by L.v. Trier, television series, Denmark: Danmarks Radio.

Robbins, B. (2015), 'The detective is suspended: Nordic noir and the welfare state', *Post45*, Nordic Noir: A series guest edited by Bruce Robbins, 18 May, web, 24 January 2016.

Rothstein, B. (2005), *Social Traps and the Problem of Trust*, Cambridge: Cambridge UP.

Rushdie, S. (1992), *Imaginary Homelands: Essays and Criticism 1981–1992*, London: Penguin.

Sagolandet (1988), Directed by J. Troell, film, Sweden: Bold Productions.

Salzani, C. (2007), 'The city as crime scene: Walter Benjamin and the traces of the detective', *New German Critique* 100: 165–187.

Scaggs, J. (2005), *Crime Fiction*, London: Routledge.

Scaggs, J. (2009), 'Double-identity: Hard-boiled detective fiction and the divided "I"', in M. Krajenbrink and K. M. Quinn (eds), *Investigating Identities: Questions of Identity in Contemporary International Crime Fiction*, Amsterdam: Rodopi, pp. 131–144.

Secher, C. (1984), 'Kriminalromanen som politisk våben: Om Sjöwall og Wahlöös Roman om en forbrydelse', in J. Holmgaard and B. Tao Michaëlis (eds), *Lystmord: Studier i kriminallitteraturen fra Poe til Sjöwall/Wahlöö*. Copenhagen: Medusa, pp. 371–420.

Seierstad, Å. (2015), *One of Us: The Story of Anders Breivik and the Massacre in Norway*, trans. by S. Death, London: Virago.

Seltzer, M. (1998), *Serial Killers: Death and Life in America's Wound Culture*, New York: Routledge.

Shaw, K. (2015), *Crunch Lit*, London: Bloomsbury

Simenon, G. (2006), *The Man Who Watched the Trains Go By*, trans. by S. Gilbert, London: Penguin.

Simonsen, P. and J. Stougaard-Nielsen (2011), 'Literature, welfare and well-being: Towards a poetics of the Scandinavian welfare state', *Scandinavica* 50/1: 9.

Sjöwall, M. and P. Wahlöö (2002), *The Laughing Policeman*, trans. by A. Blair, London: Orion.

Sjöwall, M. and P. Wahlöö (2007), *Murder at the Savoy*, trans. by J. Tate. London: Harper Perennial. Kindle.

Sjöwall, M. and P. Wahlöö (2011a), *The Locked Room*, trans. by P. Britten Austin, London: Fourth Estate.

Sjöwall, M. and P. Wahlöö (2011b), *The Terrorists*, trans. by J. Tate, London: Fourth Estate.

Sjöwall, M. and P. Wahlöö (2011c), *The Fire Engine that Disappeared*, trans. by J. Tate, London: Fourth Estate.

Sjöwall, M. and P. Wahlöö (2015), *Den skrattande polisen*, Stockholm: Pocketforlaget.

Skei, H. H. (2008), *Blodig alvor: Om kriminallitteraturen*, Oslo: Aschehoug.

Søholm, E. (1976), *'Roman om en forbrydelse': Sjöwall/Wahlöö's værk og virkelighed*, København: Spektrum.

Sørensen, V. (1959), 'Velfærdsstat og personlighed', in *Digtere og dæmoner: Fortolkninger og vurderinger*, København: Gyldendal, pp. 219–228.

Sørensen, V. (1991), 'The Grocer', in *Harmless Tales*, trans. by P. Hostrup-Jessen, Norwich: Norvik, pp. 48–82.

Squires, C. (2009), *Marketing Literature: The Making of Contemporary Writing in Britain*, Houndmills: Palgrave.

Staalesen, G. (1981), *Din, til døden*, Oslo: Gyldendal.

Staalesen, G. (1993), *Begravde hunder biter ikke*, Oslo: Gyldendal.

Staalesen, G. (1995), 'Kunsten å leve med en seriefigur', in A. Elgurén and A. Engelstad (eds), *Under lupen: Essays of kriminallitteratur*, Oslo: Gyldendal, pp. 172–184.

Staalesen, G. (2008a), *Tornerose sov i hundre år*, Oslo: Gyldendal.

Staalesen, G. (2008b), *Kvinnen i kjøleskapet*, Oslo: Gyldendal.

Staalesen, G. (2010), *Yours Until Death*, trans. by M. Amassian, London: Arcadia.

Staalesen, G. (2011), *I mørket er alle ulver grå*, Oslo: Gyldendal.

Starkman, D. (2014), *The Watchdog That Didn't Bark: The Financial Crisis and the Disappearance of Investigative Journalism*, New York: Columbia UP.

Stenius, Y. (2004), 'Ödesstund? Eller?' *Aftonbladet*, 2 August.

Stenport, A. W. (2007), 'Bodies under assault: Nation and immigration in Henning Mankell's *Faceless Killers*', *Scandinavian Studies* 79/1: 1–24.

Stenport, A. W. and C. O. Alm (2009), 'Corporations, crime, and gender construction in Stieg Larsson's *The Girl With the Dragon Tattoo*: exploring twenty-first century neoliberalism in Swedish culture', *Scandinavian Studies* 81/2: 157–178.

Stidsen, M. (2010), 'Konkurrencesamfundets bagside', in N. G. Hansen (ed.), *Velfærdsfortællinger*, København: Gyldendal, pp. 191–216.

Stigsdotter, I. (2010), 'Crime scene Skåne: Guilty landscapes and cracks in the functionalist façade in *Sidetracked, Firewall* and *One Step Behind*', in E. Hedling, O. Hedling and M. Jönsson (eds), *Regional Aesthetics: Locating Swedish Media*, Stockholm: Mediehistoriskt Arkiv 15, pp. 243–262.

Sutherland, J. (2007), 'US confidential', *NewStatesman*, 13 September.

Svendsen, G. T. (2012), *Tillid*, Århus: Aarhus Universitet.

Svensson, P. (1999), 'Syndafallet', in B. Eriksson (ed.), *I neonljusets skugga: Den moderna kriminalhistorien*, Lund: Boströms, pp. 167–183.

Svensson, P. (2003), *Dramat på Norrmalmstorg: 23 till 28 augusti 1973*, Stockholm: Bonnier.

Swenarton, M., T. Avermaete and D. van den Heuvel (2015), 'Introduction', in M. Swenarton, T. Avermaete and D. van den Heuvel (eds), *Architecture and the Welfare State*, Abingdon: Routledge, pp. 1–24.

Symons, J. (1974), *Bloody Murder. From the Detective Story to the Crime Novel: A History*, Harmondsworth: Penguin.

Tapper, M. (2010), 'Hans kropp – samhället självt: Manliga svenska mordspanare på ålderns höst. Kommissarie Jensen, Martin Beck, Kurt Wallander och Van Veeteren', in G. Agger and A. M. Waade (eds), *Den skandinaviske krimi: Bestseller og Blockbuster*, Göteborg: Nordicom.

Tapper, M. (2011), *Snuten i skymringslandet: Svenska polisberättelser i roman och film 1965–2010*, Lund: Nordic Academic Press.

Tapper, M. (2014), *Swedish Cops: From Sjöwall and Wahlöö to Stieg Larsson*, Bristol: Intellect.

Thisted, K. (2002), 'The power to represent: Intertextuality and discourse in *Smilla's sense of snow*', in M. Bravo and S. Sörlin (eds), *Narrating the Arctic: A Cultural History of Nordic Scientific Practices*, Canton, MA: Watson, pp. 311–342.

'Those Who Kill', Pressbook, Trustnordisk, Retrieved from http://files.trust-nordisk.com/files/ftpfiles/movies/TN31/public/docs/TWK_Pressbook_Final.pdf.

Toft Hansen, K. (2008), 'De sidste dages heldige: Om krimifiktion og Gunnar Staalesens forfatterskab', *Krimi og Kriminaljournalistik i Skandinavian*, Arbejdspapir nr. 7, www.krimiforsk.aau.dk, web.

Toft Hansen, K. (2012), *Mord og metafysik: Det absolute, det guddommelige og det overnaturlige i krimien*, Aalborg: Aalborg UP.

Trägårdh, L. (2012), 'Mellem liberalisme og socialisme: Om det særlige ved den nordiske model', *Kritik* 206: 40–50.

Trenter, S. (1945), *I dag röd …*, Stockholm: Bonnier.

Tuan, Y. f. (1979), *Landscapes of Fear*, New York: Pantheon. Kindle.

Urry, J. (2002), *The Tourist Gaze*, London: Sage.

Waade, A. M. (2013), *Wallanderland: Medieturisme og skandinavisk tv-krimi*, Aalborg: Aalborg Universitetsforlag.

Wæver, O. (1992), 'Nordic nostalgia: Northern Europe after the Cold War', *International Affairs*, 68/1: 77–102.

Walton, P. L. and M. Jones (1999), *Detective Agency: Women Rewriting the Hard-Boiled Tradition*, Berkeley: U of California P.

Wendelius, L. (1999a), *Rationalitet och kaos: nedslag i svensk kriminalfiktion efter 1965*, Hedemora: Gidlund.

Wendelius, L. (1999b), 'En mångtydig kriminalhistoria: en läsning av Kerstin Ekmans *Händelser vid vatten*', *Tidskrift för litteraturvetenskap* 28: 21–51.

Wilkinson, R. and K. Pickett (2010), *The Spirit Level: Why Equality is Better for Everyone*, London: Penguin.

Willett, R. (1992), *Hard-Boiled Detective Fiction*, Staffordshire: British Association for American Studies.

Worthington, H. (2011), *Key Concepts in Crime Fiction*, Houndmills: Palgrave.

Wright, R. (1996), 'Literature after 1950', in L. Warme (ed.), *A History of Swedish Literature*, vol. 3, Lincoln: U of Nebraska P.

Žižek, S. (2003), 'Parallax', *London Review of Books*, 25/22: 24.

Žižek, S. (2008), *Violence: Six Sideways Reflections*, New York: Picador.

INDEX